THE UNWRITTEN ALLIANCE

Institute of Latin American Studies
Columbia University

The Baron of Rio-Branco

THE UNWRITTEN ALLIANCE

RIO-BRANCO AND

BRAZILIAN-AMERICAN RELATIONS

E. BRADFORD BURNS

Columbia University Press   *New York and London 1966*

E. Bradford Burns is an assistant professor in the Department of History of the University of California at Los Angeles.

THE INSTITUTE OF LATIN AMERICAN STUDIES OF COLUMBIA UNIVERSITY

THE INSTITUTE of Latin American Studies was established by Columbia University in 1961 in response to a national, public, and educational need for a better understanding of the contemporary problems of the Latin American nations and a more knowledgeable basis for inter-American relations. The major objectives of the Institute are to prepare a limited number of North Americans for scholarly and professional careers in the field of Latin American studies and to advance our knowledge of Latin America and its problems through an active program of research by faculty, by graduate students, and by visiting scholars. Some of the results of the research program, as well as other research of direct interest to the program, are published in a series of the Institute of Latin American Studies. The faculty of the Institute believes that these publications will stimulate interest in and improve public and scholarly knowledge of Latin America and contribute to the advancement of inter-American relations.

The Institute of Latin American Studies is grateful to the Ford Foundation for financial assistance which has made this publication program possible.

Dedicated
with gratitude and love to
my parents

PREFACE

BRAZIL AND the United States mutually regard each other as close friends, a relationship each has considered to be "traditional." However, the history of their diplomatic relations in the nineteenth century fails to substantiate those claims to the existence of a "traditional" friendship. Only after the proclamation of the republic in Brazil in 1889 do their relations show a uniform harmony and intimacy. To accelerate that trend became one of the principal aims of the Baron of Rio-Branco, the Minister of Foreign Relations from 1902 to 1912. It is really from his ministry that the "traditional" friendship can be dated.

Rio-Branco decided to encourage growing Brazilian-American friendship as a means of better achieving his foreign policy goals. The moral support of Washington proved to be a great aid in the successful delineation of nine thousand miles of hitherto unmarked boundaries. Furthermore, the North American blessing helped Brazil to assert its diplomatic leadership over South America and to project itself onto the world diplomatic scene. For its own part, the United States, particularly during the administration of Secretary of State Elihu Root, found Brazil to be a great help in implementing some of its policies in Latin America. As a result of the intimate cooperation between the two nations during the Rio-Branco decade, Brazil shifted its diplomatic axis from London to Washington where it has since remained.

Few serious studies have been made in either Brazil or the United States of the diplomatic relations between the two countries. Even more neglected are their relations during the important Rio-Branco period, important because it was then that the two republics achieved their maximum rapprochement and because thereafter leaders of both countries would think in terms of "traditional" friendship. In an effort to make better known the events of that period, I analyze in this study the relations between Brazil and the United States at the turn of the century and explain why their contacts became most friendly at that particular time. In doing so, I emphasize the Brazilian viewpoint because the initiative for the approximation (used throughout this study in its primary meaning, a drawing together) came from Foreign Minister Rio-Branco.

To piece together and interpret the history of the approximation and the reasons for it, I used primary sources as much as possible. Of greatest importance were the rich diplomatic archives of the United States and Brazil. The National Archives in Washington, D.C., and the Historical Archives of Itamaraty, as the Ministry of Foreign Relations in Rio de Janeiro is called, gave a clear picture of the diplomatic relations between the two countries. In order to get a wider perspective as well as different points of view, I consulted the diplomatic dispatches sent from Rio de Janeiro by Argentine, Chilean, Mexican, and Panamanian diplomats of the period. Their dispatches were found in the respective foreign ministry archives of those four countries.

A less official view of the subject came from reading the private letters and memorandums available in Brazil of the principals involved. Many of the letters of Rio-Branco are found in his personal archive in Itamaraty. Likewise, the private archive of Joaquim Nabuco, the archive of the Casa Rui Barbosa, the National Library, and the private archive of David Carneiro contain letters written by Rio-Branco. The letters and diaries of Brazil's first ambassador to the United States, Joaquim Nabuco, were also valuable sources of information. They, too, are found in the private archives of

Rio-Branco, Joaquim Nabuco, and Rui Barbosa. The complete list of the archives consulted is located in the bibliography.

Another very useful source of information was the newspapers of the period. Especially rich in information were *La Prensa* and *La Nación* of Argentina, *O Paiz* and the *Jornal do Commercio* of Brazil, and the New York *Times* and New York *Herald* of the United States. Other newspapers were also helpful but of more limited value.

I want to make one brief comment concerning the hyphen in Rio-Branco's name. Common contemporary usage generally omits the hyphen. However, because Rio-Branco himself always hyphenated his name, I have followed his own practice rather than modern usage. Thus, Rio-Branco will be hyphenated in the text, whereas in citations, depending on their source, it might not always appear that way.

E. Bradford Burns

University of California, Los Angeles
May, 1965

ACKNOWLEDGMENTS

In the research for and preparation of this book I am indebted to a great many people and institutions that I wish to acknowledge briefly. Dr. Lewis U. Hanke of Columbia University, always ready with bibliographical information and suggestions, aided me in many ways during my research and writing. I deeply appreciate his help, without which neither this study nor its publication would have been possible. Dr. Manoel Cardozo expedited my research in the Oliveira Lima Library by his expert guidance. Minister Luiz Viana Filho helped me to locate sources and meet Brazilians. He read and commented on Chapter II. Ambassador Maurício Nabuco hospitably opened his home to me and allowed me to read his father's letters and diaries. He read and commented on parts of Chapter IV. Our many conversations and his reminiscence about his father and Rio-Branco were memorable hours in my stay in Brazil. I owe special thinks to Ambassadors Araujo Jorge and Moniz de Aragão, who recalled for me their memories of Rio-Branco, and to historian and Foreign Minister Afonso Arinos de Mello Franco, who discussed with me his ideas about Rio-Branco's role in Brazilian diplomacy. Professor Leandro Tocantins, the expert on Acre, answered my many questions about the history of Acre and read and commented on chapters II and IV. In our conversations, Professor Hélio Vianna of the University of Brazil contributed many ideas to my knowledge of Brazilian history and diplomacy. Constança Wright and her staff at the Historical Archives of Itamaraty tirelessly aided me in finding the documents

I needed. Most fondly I remember the pleasant days I spent in Curitiba, where Dr. David Carneiro spoke to me at length about Brazilian history and Rio-Branco. He opened his extensive private archives to me and kindly read and commented on the first five chapters. Dr. José Honório Rodrigues, Director of the National Archives, was at all times helpful. I want to give special thanks to Dr. Donald Warren Jr., who was in Brazil at the same time I was. He read the manuscript and commented at length on it. Our many conversations about Brazil will never be forgotten. I am also indebted to Professor Charles Wagley, Director of the Institute of Latin American Studies of Columbia University, for his encouragement and support. I regret that I must omit by name the many kind and generous people in New York, Washington, Mexico City, Panama City, Rio de Janeiro, Buenos Aires, and Santiago whose cooperation made this book possible. Finally, I am grateful to the Doherty Foundation for the fellowship which enabled me to spend one unforgettable year in Brazil. To all of these people and institutions I extend my sincerest thanks. Naturally I assume full responsibility for the statements, opinions, and any errors found herein.

CONTENTS

I. Peace, Progress, and Prosperity   1

II. A Man for the Times   21

III. Commerce as a Backdrop for Diplomacy   58

IV. From Suspicion to Friendship, 1902–1906   76

V. The Tribulations and Rewards of Friendship, 1907–1912   115

VI. The Monroe Doctrine and Pan Americanism Too   146

VII. The Reasons Why   160

VIII. Foreign Reactions to the Alliance   181

IX. Conclusions   199

Notes   213

A Bibliographical Essay on Rio-Branco   265

A Selected Bibliography with Annotations   275

Index   299

ILLUSTRATIONS

The Baron of Rio-Branco   *Frontispiece*

The Private Study of Rio-Branco at Itamaraty   34

Ambassador Joaquim Nabuco   66

The Baron of Rio-Branco, Secretary of State Elihu
   Root, and Ambassador Joaquim Nabuco at the
   Third Pan American Conference, Rio de Janeiro,
   1906   110

MAP

Territorial Settlements Made by Rio-Branco   41

THE UNWRITTEN ALLIANCE

CHAPTER I · PEACE, PROGRESS, AND PROSPERITY

AFTER THE fall of the empire in 1889, Brazil emerged as the world's largest republic. With three and a quarter million square miles, the new republic was larger than the United States, just slightly smaller than Europe. Geographically, it dominated South America and poked a strategic finger toward Africa. Covering half the land mass of South America, Brazil's multiracial population, descended from Europeans, Africans, and Indians,[1] jumped from seventeen million in 1900 to twenty-three million in 1910.[2] Compared with the other nations of the hemisphere, Brazil boasted not only one of the most varied racial compositions and amalgamations but also one of the largest populations. Its neighbors, Peru, Chile, and Argentina, for example, had only three, three and a half, and four millions respectively in 1902. As one of the giant republics of the world, Brazil found attention focused on itself to see what innovations might be instituted under the new form of government.

Of the many changes wrought by the overthrow of the empire, perhaps the most fundamental was the recognition of coffee as the principal crop in the Brazilian economy. After Pedro II's ascension to the throne in 1840, the expanding coffee industry began to challenge the predominance of the declining sugar industry, which had played a vital role throughout the colonial period and during the early years of independence. The sugar-plantation aristocrats, pledging to the monarch their firm support, exercised both economic and political control over the empire. In return for their support, the imperial government favored the moribund sugar economy and the sugar *fazendeiros*. An unobtrusive military coup d'état in 1889 broke the traditional alliance between sugar interests and the monarch and, in effect, destroyed both. Emperor Pedro II sailed to a European exile, and the sugar-plantation aristocrats yielded their economic and political control to the coffee interests which were to dominate the First Republic, 1889–1930.

Although coffee production had become steadily more important during the imperial period, its rapid increase after 1889 became the salient feature of the Brazilian economy during the First Republic. Cheap suitable land, high profits, large numbers of immigrant workers, and a rising world demand made coffee a popular and lucrative crop. By 1901, coffee accounted for approximately 46 percent of Brazil's exports, while at the same time sugar exports had declined to barely 5 percent of the total exports. The divergence continued. In 1908 coffee composed 53 percent of the exports, and in 1912 sugar accounted for only .007 percent of Brazil's exports. During this same period, coffee far out-distanced the second most important crop, rubber. In 1901 rubber provided 28 percent of Brazil's exports, whereas in 1912, although rubber was still an important export, the percentage had declined to 22.[3] These percentages prove the predominance coffee assumed in the national economy during the first decades of the new century when Brazilian coffee dominated the world market so completely that it amounted to 75 percent of the world's supply.[4]

Coffee's dominance over the Brazilian economy gave economic power to the area best suited to coffee production. The peculiar *terra roxa* soil in the states of São Paulo, Minas Gerais, and Rio de Janeiro, because it was deep, porous, and contained humus, was well suited for the healthy growth of coffee trees. Mild temperatures and adequate rainfall also contributed to coffee development in that area. Consequently, for topographic and climatic reasons, the production of coffee concentrated in the southeast of Brazil, giving the three coffee-producing states of that area a preponderant influence over the newly oriented economy of Brazil.

Within that tripartite control of the economy, the state of São Paulo played the most important role. Of the total exports of Brazil for the year 1916, São Paulo furnished 46 percent, whereas Minas Gerais supplied only 22 percent, and Rio de Janeiro 18 percent.[5] During certain years, São Paulo alone produced between 65 and 70 percent of all the coffee and furnished 30 to 40 percent of all the revenue to the national treasury.[6] The economic importance of São Paulo prompted one governmental official to write in 1912 that, "as is always the case," São Paulo held the first position as chief exporter of Brazilian states.[7] In that particular year São Paulo furnished 50 percent of Brazil's exports. In striking contrast, the formerly dominant sugar area of Pernambuco barely contributed 1 percent of Brazil's exports.[8]

A population boom accompanied the economic prosperity of São Paulo. The state population, owing to internal migration as well as an influx of immigrants, particularly Italians, more than tripled in three decades, increasing from 1,384,753 in 1890 to 4,592,-188 in 1920. Following this trend the two other states of the southeast, Minas Gerais and Rio de Janeiro, witnessed population growths commensurate with their expanding economic importance but somewhat less spectacular than the growth of São Paulo.[9] The capital of São Paulo state, also named São Paulo, became the dynamic financial and managerial center of the southeast. From a sleepy provincial capital of 35,000 in 1883, São Paulo grew to a thriving city of 340,000 in 1907; by 1920 it had passed the half million mark.[10]

The principal port of São Paulo, Santos, shipped most of Brazil's coffee to the burgeoning markets of the United States, England, Germany, and France. Between 1900 and 1914 the annual amount of coffee handled by Santos doubled from 5,742,362 sacks of 130 pounds each to 11,308,784.[11] Santos was eloquent testimony to the fact that São Paulo consistently harvested and exported more coffee than any other state. Emphatically, the economic center of Brazil had shifted from the northeast to the southeast, in particular from Pernambuco to São Paulo.

That shift of economic power was accompanied by a simultaneous shift of political power. As coffee became the principal national export and the primary source of federal income, the southeast gained political control of the nation. It has been observed that "Brazilian politics after 1900 revolved about the nearness, community, and affinity of Rio de Janeiro, Minas Gerais, and São Paulo," the primary coffee centers.[12] This statement is partially proven by noting the origin of the early presidents of Brazil during the First Republic. The first three civilian presidents, Prudente de Morais Barros, Manuel Ferraz de Campos Salles, and Francisco de Paula Rodrigues Alves, who governed from 1894 to 1906, were from São Paulo. The next two presidents, Afonso Augusto Moreira Pena and Nilo Peçanha, who governed from 1906 to 1910, were respectively from Minas Gerais and Rio de Janeiro. Coming from areas in which coffee dominated, these presidents carried out policies favorable to the coffee economy. In return the coffee interests supported, indeed arranged for, the election of those presidents. The First Secretary of the United States legation, G. L. Lorillard, ably described this reciprocity between coffee and politics:

All the Northern States are bitterly opposed to the hold the coffee planters have over the Government and complain that their legitimate needs are being sacrificed in favor of the planters. The Executive, however, clings to its purpose of doing everything to please the coffee interests. The President fully realizes that he was elected by the planters and that he must now return the favor.[13]

It was obvious, much to the displeasure of the rest of Brazil, that the coffee interests dictated at will the policies of the government. Commenting on that situation, Lorillard wrote:

At the present time, however, there exists a group of persons which is stronger than the Executive and Congress combined. As is universally admitted here, never before has the country and especially everyone connected with the Government been so much under the influence of the coffee planters as at present and any measure which is seriously desired by that element is sure of immediate passage by Congress.[14]

The alliance of the coffee planters and of the federal government came quickly after 1889 and superseded all previous political arrangements, so that political control by the coffee interests characterized the First Republic. Because São Paulo played a dominant role within that alliance, this period of Brazilian history has been characterized as one of *paulista* control.

The election of Rodrigues Alves to the presidency in 1902 confirmed the economic domination of coffee and the political ascendancy of São Paulo. Brazil was at peace. The years of confusion and tumult following the overthrow of the empire had given way to tranquillity, stability, and almost unprecedented prosperity. The first *paulista* president, Prudente de Morais, brought order and serenity back to Brazil, which had been agitated by the overthrow of the empire, the internal struggles for power, and the revolts in 1893 and 1894. The second *paulista* president, Campos Salles, with the assistance of his brilliant Minister of Finance, Joaquim Murtinho, financially rehabilitated the nation. Thanks to the successful efforts of his predecessors, President Rodrigues Alves inherited a nation at peace and in relatively good financial shape.

Throughout his career, Rodrigues Alves had associated with the conservative factions of São Paulo. His ideas reflected the economic interests of his state, and he was expected to carry forward those governmental policies favorable to coffee production. Politically, he had been active in the imperial government; he had received the title of Counselor of the Empire. Because he was an experienced statesman and moderate in his beliefs, the conservative groups supported him.[15] "A man of simplicity, sincerity, and great kindness of character and whose intellectual faculties have been well trained in his long public service," [16] President Rodrigues Alves appeared well suited for the tasks before him.

Shortly after his inauguration, President Alves focused his attention on the renovation of the underdeveloped and unhealthy national capital, Rio de Janeiro, initiating a program to beautify the city, build a first-rate port, and eliminate yellow fever. Pereira Passos, newly appointed prefect of the Federal District, received ample powers to rebuild Rio de Janeiro. Making full use of his authority, he broadened the main avenues, enlarged and redesigned the parks, constructed new public buildings, and cleaned up the most unpleasant parts of the capital. Meanwhile, engineers were rebuilding and expanding the capital's port facilities for which modern equipment was purchased and installed. Aided generously by a luxuriant and verdant Nature, Pereira Passos created the modern wonder of Rio de Janeiro, which has been a source of admiration and awe for tourists. After giving a lengthy description of the new Rio de Janeiro in its 1908 edition, the *Almanaque Brasileiro Garnier* rhapsodized, "The rapid transformation . . . turned this capital into one of the most beautiful cities and perhaps, without exaggeration, the most beautiful city in the world." [17]

The president entrusted the eminent Dr. Oswaldo Cruz with the task of eradicating yellow fever in the unhealthy lowlands upon which parts of the capital were built. For centuries yellow fever had been the scourge of Rio de Janeiro, making life there hazardous for residents and visitors alike. Fortunately, the years marking the turn of the century witnessed scientific advances which conquered that tropical disease. Taking his cue from the accomplishments of North American scientists and doctors in Cuba and Panama, Dr. Cruz vigorously undertook a four-point program to kill mosquitoes, destroy their breeding ground, isolate the sick, and vaccinate all the inhabitants of Rio de Janeiro. His energetic and effective campaign soon made the city as healthy as any contemporary European capital.

The metamorphosis of Rio de Janeiro did not take place without difficulties. The disruption and confusion caused by the rapid transformation of the city were the occasion for a military revolt which, although very limited in scope and consequence, was the most serious threat to President Rodrigues Alves during his tenure of office. The decree requiring obligatory vaccination against smallpox had seriously agitated the superstitious lower classes of the capital, which rioted in the streets. Opportunistic army officers, claiming to be disciples of positivism, took advantage of the popular indignation to hatch a plot "to save" the republic. On the evening of November 14, 1904, while the attention of the government centered on the barricaded mobs, the cadets, under the command of General Travassos, marched from the military school toward the presidential palace. The alarm sounded. Loyal troops rallied to oppose the cadets. When the opposing forces met, there was a furious exchange of shots, the most important casualty being the critically wounded General Travassos. Returning to Praia Vermelha, the leaderless cadets were surrounded by loyal army units on one side and naval vessels on the other. Resistance collapsed at once. The Travassos revolt received no support in the rest of Brazil except in Bahia where one army unit attempted to revolt but was quickly subdued.

The uprising was so limited and so quickly suppressed that it had no effect upon Brazil except to serve as a reminder to the civilian government that the victorious military coup of 1889 had established an undesirable precedent in Brazil. The military had successfully entered politics once; the military specter was now omnipresent to haunt the civilian governments. The Travassos revolt showed militarism to be a potential danger with which the coffee interests had to reckon.

Whatever else his activities or preoccupations, President Rodrigues Alves showed a deep interest in the affairs of the coffee industry during his term of office. Toward the end of his administration it became apparent that the coffee interests required considerable governmental help, particularly in the marketing of their crop.

The industry's difficulties originated with a rapid overexpansion of production. Beginning in 1840, and particularly after 1870, the amount of coffee exported rose so rapidly that by 1900 ten million sacks of coffee left Brazilian ports annually for overseas consumption. Profits were high and investments paid off handsomely. Consequently, even larger amounts were invested in coffee, and new plantations, which took only four to five years to begin producing, multiplied. By 1902, when the new speculative plantations were ready for harvest, the serious threat of overproduction became clear to everyone.

The threatened coffee interests presented their problems to the government, which undertook to help them. In 1902 the government prohibited any new coffee-tree plantings for five years. Nonetheless, because of considerable speculative planting before that date, coffee production began to rise at a much faster rate than world consumption. By 1905 Brazil had eleven million sacks of coffee in warehouse storage, and productivity was still rising as new trees matured. In 1906 Brazil produced a record coffee crop of twenty million sacks for a world market then capable of absorbing only twelve million sacks, and Brazil was not the only country with coffee to sell. Clearly Brazil was in economic trouble, and the coffee alliance expected the government to come to its rescue.

In order to avoid the financial debacle which such overproduction foretold, the government took steps to regulate coffee production. First, the government extended the prohibition of new coffee-tree plantings to 1912. Then, by means of the Convention of Taubaté, signed on February 26, 1906, the governors of São Paulo, Minas

Gerais, and Rio de Janeiro, with the approval and cooperation of the federal government, sought to control the production and marketing of coffee. The convention authorized a coffee valorization scheme whereby, if prices fell below a minimum level, the state and federal governments would remove coffee from the world market by purchasing and holding it in storage until the prices rose again. Valorization was popular with the three coffee states, and hence the government was obliged to support it. Other states complained bitterly, but ineffectively, about valorization.[18]

As the presidential elections of 1906 approached, opposition mounted against the efforts of President Rodrigues Alves to name his successor. Early in the republican era, because of the lack of national political parties, it had become customary for the outgoing president to select his successor. The favored candidate was assured of victory at the polls. Rodrigues Alves showed every indication of favoring another *paulista,* Bernardino de Campos, as the official candidate. At this point, however, political intrigue and maneuvering became extremely complex. The coffee interests felt that Rodrigues Alves had not given, and his chosen successor would not give, full and unqualified support to the Convention of Taubaté. Outside of the coffee alliance, opposition to the *paulista* dynasty and to official candidates centered in a group of politicians, who referred to themselves as the Bloque, led by the powerful gaucho-politician of Rio Grande do Sul, Pinheiro Machado. The original candidate of the Bloque was another well-known *riograndense,* Marshal Hermes da Fonseca. Hence, this campaign marked the first overt challenge of Rio Grande do Sul for the control of the federal government. At the same time, Minas Gerais supported one of its own distinguished citizens, Vice-President Afonso Pena, as the logical choice for the presidency. To avoid open dispute the various factions united to nominate Pena, who was a satisfactory compromise candidate for all. President Rodrigues Alves, seeing his hopes for Bernardino de Campos quickly dimming, could accept gracefully the elevation of his vice-president to the presidency. The Bloque could congratulate itself for having wrested the presidency away from São Paulo. Finally the powerful coffee alliance could rejoice in the election of a *mineiro* and a signer of the Convention of Taubaté who could be counted on to look after their economic interests. Therefore, in the election, a national majority supported Pena and his vice-presidential candidate, Nilo Peçanha.

Afonso Pena in many ways resembled his predecessor. As a Counselor of the Empire, he, too, had served Pedro II faithfully. Likewise, he shared many of the former president's conservative ideas and was linked closely to the coffee interests. While never acquiring any great popular following, Afonso Pena was highly respected and even admired. Two diplomatic representatives of the United States commented favorably on his "ability," "friendliness," "honesty," and his "simple and direct" methods.[19]

The coffee surplus problem, the valorization scheme, the world depression of 1907, and a consequent drop in coffee prices forced President Pena to devote considerable time and effort to the coffee situation. He proved his loyalty to the coffee interests by cooperating fully with the efforts of São Paulo to execute the provisions of the Convention of Taubaté.

During the Pena administration the principal objective of the coffee alliance was to limit the production of coffee and to withhold coffee from the market so that the enormous surplus could be sold at reasonable prices. With the aid of loans from foreign banks and the cooperation of the federal government, São Paulo alone held eight million sacks of coffee off the market in 1907. The following year São Paulo harvested one of the smallest coffee crops in a decade thanks to the policy of restricting planting as well as to adverse weather conditions. The federal government, when necessary, made loans to both São Paulo and Minas Gerais whereby those states continued buying excess coffee and removing it from the market. From 1908 through 1912 there were small harvests and the government gradually sold its stored coffee and liquidated its investment. During this particular period, the valorization scheme can be judged a success.

The world financial depression at the beginning of the Pena administration also affected adversely Brazil's second export crop, rubber.[20] The setback was only temporary. The lowest price paid for rubber in 1906 was $1.22 a pound; in 1907 the lowest price was 82 cents; in 1908, 67 cents. There was a rapid recovery in 1909 which sent the minimum price up to $1.20 a pound, and a year later the minimum was $1.50.[21] The increasingly important New York rubber market showed the same trends.[22]

For a short time the rubber of the distant Amazon appeared as if it might challenge the sovereignty of coffee. During the years of maximum rubber production, 1910–12, rubber earned $110,000,000, almost enough to equal the $125,000,000 earned by coffee during the same period.[23]

A fabulous boom in the rubber industry at the turn of the century reached its apogee in April of 1910. In that memorable year, rubber accounted for 39 percent of Brazil's exports.[24]

Manaus, the provincial river capital of Amazonas, 900 miles up the Amazon River, boasted of its large foreign colony, of its houses and public buildings as the equal of any on the South American continent, of its electric lighting, water system, and trolley lines.[25] A sumptuous opera house presented European theater and opera companies. Manaus "displayed more luxury for its size than Paris, and the best diamond market in the world was in this remote spot." [26] Alas, the golden days of Manaus were few. The highest prices paid for rubber were during the giddy days of April of 1910. Thereafter, the price began a slow but steady decline.

The cause of the decline was not a reduction in world demand. Rather, the well-organized, efficient, and cheaply-run rubber plantations of the Far East began to produce and could undersell the disorganized and expensive Brazilian producers. Asia first began to export rubber in 1900, but within a decade and a half replaced Brazil in the world market.[27] The rubber barons realized the seriousness of the challenge only after their prices began to decline. Their first reaction was to seek a valorization plan similar to the one which had aided the coffee industry during years of crisis.[28] But the Rubber Defense Law of 1912 and subsequent attempts at valorization proved to be too late and too impractical.[29]

In reality the exotic, isolated, and brief rubber boom had little apparent effect on politics in Rio de Janeiro. Naturally, the contributions from Amazonas to the national treasury in the form of taxes and to Brazil's international credit were important and appreciated. The fact that, in certain years, rubber provided one third of Brazil's exports did not go unnoticed. However, the rubber barons lived isolated unto themselves, and at no time did the political axis of the nation shift to the far north. Undoubtedly the most lasting effect of the rubber boom was the penetration of the rubber gatherers into the unexplored hinterlands of Amazonas. Their presence in remote, disputed areas allowed Brazil to claim those areas by right of possession. The rubber boom thereby contributed to the territorial aggrandizement of Brazil.

The rubber merchants, as well as the coffee planters, experienced economic hardships in the international markets because of Brazil's weak currency. Shortly after the establishment of the republic, the new government had resorted to the issue of paper money to meet its obligations. Once the printing presses were started, it was extremely difficult to shut them off. Unbacked paper money inundated Brazil with the customary consequences of financial instability, inflation, and foreign exchange fluctuations. To ameliorate the unfavorable situation, the business community sought government action to stabilize the currency. The coffee planters, oriented primarily toward the world market, urged the president to stabilize the national currency and to fix the rate of exchange.

Very early in his administration President Pena turned his attention to those pressing financial problems, and on December 6, 1906, he signed a law establishing the Conversion Office (Caixa de Conversão). Primarily concerned with external financial transactions, the Conversion Office received deposits of gold and issued against those deposits convertible paper bills with a fixed exchange value. The paper bills of the Conversion Office always equaled the amount of gold held by the office. The principal advantages of this plan were that a fixed exchange rate strengthened Brazil's links with the financial centers of the world, halted the constant rise in running expenses which weakened the planters' economic position, and improved Brazil's place in the world markets.

The Conversion Office was an immediate success, enthusiastically supported by the coffee interests. Other business groups quickly echoed the praise of the planters. The chairman of the São Paulo Railway at a meeting of the shareholders praised the Conversion Office after a year of operation with these unqualified words:

I will here get rid of the matter of exchange by telling you at once that the conversion scheme which was planned to keep a steady rate of exchange has worked with extraordinary success and is of the greatest benefit to all who are in business.[30]

Before the Pena administration ended, almost one quarter of the currency of Brazil was backed by gold.[31] This notable financial achievement highlighted the beneficial administration of Afonso Pena.

Prior to World War I there were few industries in Brazil and scant attention was paid to the establishment of factories. The majority of the population of twenty million was agrarian, and Brazil concentrated its energy on its many raw products. Transportation of these products to markets constituted one of the major problems of the era. Fleets of steam and sailing vessels plied along the extensive coastline and up and down the numerous rivers; fluvial commerce had been relatively well developed. Important as water commerce was, Brazil soon acknowledged the need for a complementary land transportation network. The railroad promised at least a partial answer to that need.

The 9,500 miles of railroad tracks laid before 1901 were insufficient in such a large country as Brazil. Realizing the desperate need for expanded transportation, the republican chiefs of state accelerated railroad construction. Of the approximately seven thousand miles of rails laid during the first decade and a half of the twentieth century, half was laid during the Pena administration. In a single year, 1910, the total trackage increased 10.8 percent with the addition of 1,200 miles of new rails.[32] Between 1906 and 1910, four important railway lines were built in diverse parts of the nation: Madeira-Mamoré, São Paulo–Caixas, São Paulo–Mato Grosso, and São Paulo–Rio Grande (uniting Rio de Janeiro with the Río de la Plata). By the outbreak of World War I, Brazil had increased her railroad network to sixteen thousand miles.

The enlightened administration of Afonso Pena ended abruptly with his sudden death in mid-June of 1909. The constitutional machinery functioned perfectly in the crisis. Vice-President Nilo Peçanha at once assumed the powers of the presidency. As a citizen of the coffee state of Rio de Janeiro and a signer of the Convention of Taubaté, he was expected to continue the policies of his predecessors. Only forty-one years old when he became chief of state, Nilo Peçanha was the first president who had not received his political education under the empire.

President Nilo Peçanha presided over a caretaker government. One of the most important acts passed during his administration was the creation in September, 1910, of the Indian Service, whose aim was to incorporate the diminishing Indian population of the hinterlands into the national family.[33] In reality, the remainder of the term of office devolving upon Peçanha was too brief for him to demonstrate his abilities or lack of them. The first closely disputed presidential campaign in the short history of the republic overshadowed his administration.

The presidential campaign of 1910 was well under way by mid-1909. In Brazil, the voters directly elected the president, and Congress declared the candidate receiving the most votes the winner. The campaign for popular support agitated political circles because two eminent public figures opposed each other. Statesman, jurist, writer, and diplomat, Senator Rui Barbosa of Bahia represented the liberal elements of Brazilian politics. Opposing him was Marshal Hermes da Fonseca of Rio Grande do Sul, a nephew of ex-President Marshal Deodoro da Fonseca, who had been instrumental in overthrowing the monarchy. Hermes da Fonseca had served as Minister of War in the cabinet of President Pena. As a representative of the conservative elements of Brazilian politics, he counted on the support of the government. Even so, the election was by no means a foregone conclusion. That campaign was notable because for the first time both candidates carried the issues to the people, especially Rui Barbosa, who indefatigably toured the provinces to gain popular support.

In the closely fought campaign, perhaps the mistake which cost Rui Barbosa the victory was his oversimplification of the issues. Opposing militarism and most specifically decrying a military man as president, Rui Barbosa characterized the election as one to select military or civilian control of the government. His sharp tongue bitterly attacked the military. Many military leaders formerly had opposed Hermes da Fonseca, but angered by the vehement anti-military tirades of Rui Barbosa and his followers, they gave their support to the Marshal as a means of self-protection.[34] One of the major effects of Rui Barbosa's campaign appears to have been the complete alienation of the military, a powerful and influential group since the coup of 1889.

This important presidential election was complicated further by state rivalries. São Paulo and Minas Gerais had controlled the presidency long enough to arouse the jealousy and distrust of the other states, which were eager to wrest that office from them. Although neither São Paulo nor Minas Gerais presented a presidential candidate in 1910, their large populations permitted them a strong voice in deciding the outcome of any election. Seemingly those two populous states did not look with favor on the presidential aspirant from neighboring Bahia. Their electoral philosophy seemed to indicate that it would be preferable to give the presidency to a man from the far south than to someone from their nearby rival state. Meanwhile, the feeling of growing importance on the part of the citizenry of Rio Grande do Sul excited them to exert every effort to capture the presidency.[35] The powerful political machine of Rio Grande do Sul, dominated by Pinheiro Machado, put all its influence behind Hermes da Fonseca. State rivalries, the issue of military versus civilian government, and, finally, personal ambitions and followings decided the election of 1910. The Brazilian Congress took a little less than three months to count the popular vote and then declared Marshal Hermes da Fonseca the winner. He assumed the presidency on November 15, 1910.

The election of a soldier to the presidency climaxed a period of growing militarism in Brazil. It would seem that militarism received an impetus from the successful quelling of the Travassos revolt. Although such an assertion needs further investigation, at least a tacit alliance seemed to form after the revolt between the coffee interests and the military, each showing a wide tolerance for the interests of the other. German violations of Brazilian sovereignty in the *Panther* case in late 1905 impressed upon the Brazilians their military inability to meet any foreign threats. Shortly thereafter the energetic military leaders, Admiral Júlio de Noronha and Marshal Hermes da Fonseca, reorganized the army and the navy. Arms purchases increased. Growing rivalry with Argentina prompted Brazil to buy new warships, and soon those two neighbors were competing in an arms race neither could afford. The Kaiser's invitation to Marshal Hermes da Fonseca to attend the annual

German army maneuvers in 1909 proved to be the capstone. The efficient German army fascinated the Marshal, and he returned to South America with some grandiose ideas. Overlying these specific causes for the rebirth of militarism in Brazil was the general military spirit abroad in a world which was arming itself noisily for the Grand Conflict. Brazil was simply following the trend of the times.

Ironically enough, one of the major consequences of Brazil's brief entrance into overt militarism was a series of naval revolts in late 1910 whose potential seriousness startled the nation. President Hermes da Fonseca hardly had settled down in the Palace of Catete when the sailors of the renovated navy mutinied. On November 23, 1910, the enlisted men of three battleships and one scout mutinied and killed several officers. The crews of seven other warships in the Rio harbor abandoned ship. The capital waited nervously as the mutineers turned landward the powerful guns of the new battleships. The ships fired only sporadically at a helpless city whose "defenses were not prepared to meet dreadnaughts." [36] The revolt proved to have no political significance. The sailors, exhausted and overworked, had decided to take dramatic steps to air their grievances. They complained of harsh corporal punishment, excessive hours of work, insufficient pay, and the bad quality of the rations. A later congressional investigation substantiated the complaints of overwork and frequent flogging. It was found that the crews were considerably below complement. The *Minas Gerais*, for example, had a crew of only three hundred when it should have had one thousand. After an amnesty and a promise of improved conditions, the sailors surrendered meekly and allowed their officers back on board on the twenty-fifth. At once the government landed all the munitions and the breechblocks of the principal guns, rendering the expensive warships as "harmless as steamboats." [37]

But more was in store. Hardly had the battleships been disarmed when the five hundred marines stationed on the Isle of Cobras, situated just off the waterfront of Rio de Janeiro, revolted against the government. About 10:00 p.m. on December 9, 1910, they began firing at the Marine Arsenal. The sailors aboard one warship mutinied and adhered to the cause of the marines. The critical situation required the government to use force as well as to grant another amnesty before the marines would surrender. After the victory of the loyal forces, the government announced that the marine revolt was "devoid of political significance," but declined to give any further explanations.[38]

These naval revolts sounded a discordant overture to the Hermes da Fonseca administration; unfortunately, they were not the only armed clashes to sully the Marshal's term of office. At the same time the rubber bubble burst, and the Amazon faced an unmitigated economic decline. Generally speaking, inaction characterized the four-year term of President Hermes da Fonseca, and Brazilians became increasingly restive about their choice for president. Lest the history of the Hermes da Fonseca administration appear too gloomy, it should be stated that coffee continued to sell well and managed to keep the economy buoyant. Also, President da Fonseca continued the expansion of the railroad network. Little else was accomplished.

The most powerful figure in the administration was probably not the president but the *riograndense* politician, Pinheiro Machado, who directed many of the actions of his compatriot, Hermes da Fonseca. Pinheiro Machado attempted to force a premature shift of the political axis of the nation from the southeast to the far south.[39] In addition to the president and his political mentor, Dr. Barbosa Gonçalves, the second Minister of Public Works, Rivadávia Correia, the Minister of the Interior, Justice, and Education, and General Mena Barreto, the Minister of War, were from Rio Grande do Sul. None of them had either the ability or the strength to effect such a shift, not while coffee ruled unchallenged. Clearly it was still several decades too soon for such a shift of political power.

Internal maneuvering for power did not adversely affect the growing feeling of nationalism in Brazil. Once the republic was on solid ground, an intense feeling of patriotism burst across the land. It manifested itself in diverse ways: the beautification of the capital, the new warships for the navy, the presence of Brazil at its first world conference, and the flowering of Brazilian literature. Dozens of Brazilians like poet João Evangelista Braga cried out, "Brazilians, let us aggrandize the Fatherland!" [40] Others, like the talented novelist Graça Aranha in his *Canaan,* stirred national feeling with more intelligent and probing, but nonetheless patriotic, thoughts. The same can be said for Euclides da Cunha's classic *Rebellion in the Backlands.* Novelists like Lima Barreto and Machado de Assis, poets like Olavo Bilac and Raymundo Correia made it a golden age of Brazilian letters which animated a feeling of national pride. They helped to make Brazil conscious of itself and known abroad, and by so doing they contributed at the turn of the century to the wave of nationalism inundating Brazil, then confident for the first time of its new republican institutions.

In retrospect the era from the turn of the century to World War I emerges as one of the most fruitful periods in Brazilian history. The few revolts which mar the period were minor, localized, and swiftly quelled. They were exceptions to a general tranquillity and to the economic, social, and political stability which characterized the period. Many historians pause to pay tribute to the good order and material progress during the *paulista* domination.[41] The Mexican diplomatic representative in Rio de Janeiro informed his government that Brazil was enjoying peace, progress, and prosperity "greater than even the most optimistic had hoped for." [42]

Prosperous and peaceful at home, Brazil could turn its full attention to international relations and could concentrate its energy on the formation and execution of a constructive foreign policy for the first time in several decades. It was a happy selection which President Rodrigues Alves made when, in 1902, he entrusted the Ministry of Foreign Relations to José Maria da Silva Paranhos Jr., the Baron of Rio-Branco, who, during the succeeding decade, would successfully direct Brazil's foreign policy.

CHAPTER II · A MAN
FOR THE TIMES

Appointed minister of Foreign Relations in November of 1902, the Baron of Rio-Branco did not arrive in Rio de Janeiro from his diplomatic post in Berlin until December 1, 1902.[1] His arrival was a hero's return to Brazil. The Brazilian people knew him as the diplomatic victor at Washington and Bern where, in the settlement of disputed territories by arbitration, Brazil had received awards which, in addition to settling potentially dangerous border conflicts, increased the size of Brazil by one hundred and fifteen thousand square miles, nearly four times the size of Portugal. By the able presentation of Brazil's claims, the Baron won for his country through two arbitration awards far more territory than Brazil had obtained in battle. For that reason, his return to his homeland after an absence of fifteen years was a triumphant entry. A witness to the reception described it in these words:

It was a warm and bright December day. Merchant ships dressed with pennants and crowded with people filled the harbor. In the midst of them, Rio-Branco descended from the transatlantic liner into the royal barge of João VI, which, to the slow and majestic rhythm of the sixty oars manned by sailors from the Brazilian navy, transported him to shore. Rockets and shouts resounded; multicolored flags waved in the breeze. For a moment the barge stopped and the powerful figure of Rio-Branco appeared waving a large, grey top hat. The acclamations redoubled. A military band, approaching in another vessel, played a brisk air bearing his name, a song soon to become famous. On shore the manifestation assumed frightening proportions.[2]

What a distinct change this welcoming scene was from his lonely departure a quarter of a century earlier. Nearly unknown, overshadowed by the renown of his father, the younger José Maria da Silva Paranhos had left Brazil for England in 1876 as sort of an exiled Bohemian of whom little was expected in the future. However, behind that deceiving veneer of free living (and loving) had been laid the solid foundations upon which he would build his future career.

The ancestors of the young Paranhos were humble people from Bahia. In 1836, at the age of seventeen, José Maria da Silva Paranhos moved to the imperial capital, Rio de Janeiro, to pursue a military career. After marrying the attractive and modest Teresa de Figueiredo Faria, he energetically began to improve the family's fortunes. In 1845 Teresa gave birth to their first child, promptly baptized José Maria da Silva Paranhos Jr., more intimately called Juca.

Changing politics to support the Conservative Party, Paranhos continued gradually to improve his family's status when, in 1850, the Viscount of Paraná, recently appointed Minister Plenipotentiary in the Plata area, invited him to become the secretary of the diplomatic mission. Paranhos traveled to the restless Plata region with the Viscount, whose instructions were to protect Brazil's interest in the lingering disputes with Argentina and Uruguay.

The mighty Río de la Plata and its numerous navigable tributaries drained large portions of southern and western Brazil and were the highway of commerce and travel to otherwise almost inaccessible areas of Brazil. A river of such tremendous strategic and commercial importance played a principal role in Brazilian diplomacy. Demanding that the mouth and channel of the Plata remain open to their traffic at all times, Brazilian interests in the Plata frequently clashed with those of the other riparian nations, Argentina, Paraguay, and Uruguay. A special diplomatic mission to the strategic Plata always assumed primary importance in Brazil's in-

ternational affairs. Certainly with rebellious forces in the Plata on
the verge of overthrowing the truculent Argentine dictator, Juan
Manuel Rosas, after a twenty-one-year rule, this mission had important tasks to accomplish.

Secretary Paranhos worked diligently and displayed an understanding of the complex diplomatic situation, which prompted Emperor Pedro II to appoint him minister to Uruguay in 1853. He
exercised this new responsibility only a few months because later
in the same year the emperor summoned him back to Rio de
Janeiro to assume the Ministry of the Navy.

Paranhos did not leave the Plata for long. In the course of the
following decade and a half, he had frequent opportunities to aid
in the shaping of the history of that region. Dom Pedro II dispatched
him to the Plata area during four more crises: 1857, 1864, 1869,
and 1870.

In 1863, as a reward for faithful service to the throne, Paranhos
received the lifetime appointment to the prestigious position of
Senator of the Empire. Between 1868 and 1870, during the difficult
years of the War of the Triple Alliance, he served as Minister of
Foreign Relations. As a further reward for his devoted service to
the nation, Dom Pedro II conferred the title of Viscount of Rio-
Branco on him in 1870. Brazilian nobility was appointive, not
hereditary. The peerage was regarded as a recognition for merito-
rious service to the crown.

In 1871 the emperor once again summoned the Viscount of Rio-
Branco to the capital from diplomatic duties in Montevideo to
assume the highest appointive position in the empire: Prime Minister. As the chief minister, he enacted one of the most notable
laws of the empire, the popular Rio-Branco law of 1871, which declared all children born of slaves automatically free. The law
doomed the institution of slavery in Brazil. His ministry lasted until 1875, when the collapse of the Mauá Bank and the financial in-

stability which followed that disaster required the formation of a new government. For the remaining five years of his life the Viscount was politically inactive.

Meantime, Juca received an education proper for the son of a minister and senator. After returning from his childhood visit to Uruguay in 1853, he enrolled in Pedro II College, considered to be the outstanding preparatory school of the empire. He chose the Law Faculty at São Paulo to continue his studies. He studied there from 1862 to 1865, and following the custom of young aristocrats of the period who wanted to know two of Brazil's principal regions, he transferred that year to the Law Faculty in Recife from which he was graduated in 1866 with high marks. Law was a means to an end. It was the door through which he planned to enter his future career, but his inclinations did not favor the practical application of his legal knowledge.

History, particularly Brazilian history, attracted him much more than law. In 1860, when only fifteen, Juca began his research on the military history of Brazil in the Plata, a project which fascinated and occupied him for the rest of his life. Undoubtedly his father's active role in the history of the Plata, as well as his childhood visit there, helped to create his preference for that area of Brazilian history. His research was not without its reward. Early in 1862 he published a brief biography of a forgotten Brazilian hero of the war of 1825–28 with Argentina, Luiz Barroso Pereira.[3]

Throughout his university days, Juca seemed to devote more time to the study of national history than to his prescribed law courses. In 1864 he published two more articles concerning the War of the Plata.[4] His fellow students later recalled that Juca lost himself in the study of Brazilian history and often in his small student room was surrounded, if not buried, in history texts and documents.[5]

When the War of the Triple Alliance began in the Plata in 1864, Juca combined his interests in the war and in writing through his reporting to the Parisian periodical *L'Illustration*. A war correspondent who did not see the distant battlegrounds, he solicited news from Caxias, Andrade Neves, Osório, and others who participated actively in the war. Photographs and maps illustrated his news reports, which were published regularly in Paris.[6]

Serious dedication to Brazilian history was one side of the complex personality of Juca. The opposite side revealed a convivial Bohemian, a not uncommon collegiate type of the period. His thin frame and ascetic face appeared at raucous university parties; nocturnal serenades and amorous adventures formed part of the customary schedule. Such diversity of activities almost seemed to indicate a dual personality: the serious law student devoted to the history of his country and the happy-go-lucky *bon vivant*.

Uncertain of his future career after graduation, Juca decided to tour Europe to complete his formal education, a procedure frequently followed by the sons of aristocratic Brazilian families. Departing in March of 1867, he visited most of the western European countries and enjoyed life on the continent. He divided his time between museums and libraries and the intoxicating night life of imperial Paris.

Back in Brazil in 1868, young Paranhos taught history for a short time at his alma mater, Pedro II College, before accepting a legal position with the government in Nova Friburgo. At the same time, still displaying a preference for history, he became a member of the Brazilian Geographical and Historical Institute and published in the institute's journal another biographical study of a hero of the Cisplatine War.[7]

An unexpected opportunity to visit the scene of his historical interests came in 1869 when his father returned to the Plata to prepare for the peace to follow the War of the Triple Alliance. Juca accompanied him as he did again in 1870. On the second trip, he served in the official capacity as secretary. Thus, the young Paranhos initiated his diplomatic career precisely as his distinguished father had done two decades before. Furthermore, Juca had the valuable experience of beginning his diplomatic career under the watchful eye of the empire's ablest diplomat.[8] He always showed a strong filial devotion and admiration for his father. Undoubtedly the experience, example, and success of the Viscount of Rio-Branco exerted a decisive influence on him. On these missions, Juca observed the skillful and successful conduct of Brazilian diplomacy during one of its most glorious epochs. At the same time, he supplemented his theoretical knowledge of the history, politics, diplomacy, and geography of the controversial Plata region with practical experience and firsthand observation.

Before following his diplomatic proclivities, young Paranhos had a brief and undistinguished political career. In 1869 it was arranged for the voters of Mato Grosso to elect him as their deputy to the imperial parliament. He returned to Rio de Janeiro from the Plata to assume his legislative duties. Although he served in the Chamber of Deputies for six years as a representative of Mato Grosso, he was never very happy in that political atmosphere. Frequently he did not bother to attend the sessions.[9]

The uncertain political life of a Brazilian deputy offered little security and was not conducive to historical research. In 1875, after serving as a minor official of the Chamber of Deputies, the young historian resigned from politics. He confessed, "I left politics because I understood that the only man who could be a politician was one who had plenty of money and did not need a government job." [10] Paranhos had little money, and he was interested in a secure government position which would allow him time for his avocation, Brazilian history. He preferred the tranquillity of a study to the agitation of a legislature.[11] Decades later, when offered the candidacy for president of Brazil, he unhesitatingly and emphatically rejected it. Politics proved to Paranhos that he was not an orator. Nor did he enjoy public speaking. His forte was to be writing.[12]

Soon after Paranhos abandoned politics an excellent position in the consular service opened: the post of consul at Liverpool. That position was desirable because the work was minimal and it was one of the highest paid consulates, ideal for one who wanted time to pursue historical studies and the opportunity to explore European archives and libraries. Unfortunately he was not the only Brazilian to appreciate the advantages of good pay and free time. Some highly recommended and qualified men sought the post too, and the emperor had a difficult decision to make. Paranhos was pessimistic about the outcome. His open relationship with the beautiful actress, Marie Philomène Stevens, whom he married years later, and his notorious reputation as a Bohemian did not please thte rigidly moral Pedro II. There was a rebellious spirit within Paranhos[13] and such lack of discipline must have disquieted the emperor. The applicants impatiently awaited the royal decision. Apparently the valuable services of the Viscount of Rio-Branco weighed heavily in favor of the son. After a period of anxious waiting, Paranhos received the appointment as Brazilian consul in Liverpool and left for Europe in 1876.

His formal entrance into the foreign service changed his life. At thirty-one he was ready to begin a career, and the foreign service, so well served by his father, was his preference. He wanted to end once and for all his reputation as a "gay young blade." From Liverpool, he announced to his confidant, Guido Bezzi: "You tell me that it is necessary to end my Bohemian existence. I know that well, my dear friend, and it has ended for me." [14]

The following fifteen years as consul gave Paranhos abundant time to travel in Europe. The bibliophile visited the archives, libraries, and museums and expanded his collection of notes, documents, and books. It was an historian's paradise. The notes preserved in the Arquivo do Barão do Rio-Branco and his many annotated maps found in the Map Library, both located in Itamaraty, testify to his historical activities. He was engrossed in a project to criticize, correct, and annotate the *History of the War of the Triple Alliance* written by the Prussian L. Schneider. He continued that project as well as work on his own book, *Military History of Brazil,* for which he was to conduct research and investigation for the rest of his life.[15] He contributed a lengthy article on Brazil to the 1889 edition of the French *Grande Encyclopédie.* His own words reflect his pride in that article: "I was able to get for our country more space than it has ever had in a publication of this nature, and in it I inserted much new information which I have found during my many years of research." [16] As an official representative of the Brazilian Geographical and Historical Institute, he traveled to Luxembourg in 1878 to attend the Congress of Americanists. His varied historical activities were preparing him thoroughly to understand the contemporary problems of Brazil.

Not all of the trips of Paranhos from England to the continent were for research and pleasure. The Brazilian government accredited him as their official delegate to the Exposition of St. Petersburg in 1884. His mission, an important one for a country becoming increasingly dependent on coffee exportation, was to encourage the consumption of coffee in Russia. There he had the pleasure of serving the Brazilian beverage to Czar Alexander III, who visited the Brazilian display at the exposition.

The same year Pedro II named him a Counselor of the Empire in recognition of his service to Brazil abroad. His consular reports were full of information, statistics, and practical suggestions helpful for Brazilian commerce.[17] To reward his loyal services the aging Pedro II in 1888 conferred upon Paranhos the title of Baron of Rio-Branco. Henceforth he would be known by the same name as his beloved father, who had died in 1880.

The newly elevated Baron of Rio-Branco had only a short time to serve his emperor. When a military coup on November 15, 1889, deposed Pedro II and established a republic, the future of the consul was in doubt. A known monarchist, Rio-Branco feared that the republicans would terminate his appointment. With a wife and five children to support and educate and with scant other income except his salary (the Viscount had lived genteelly but modestly and left little inheritance to his son), he passed several apprehensive and uneasy months. Although he spoke occasionally of becoming a coffee planter, he was trained and suited for only one occupation, the diplomatic service. However, the new government of Marshal da Fonseca did not disturb the Brazilian consul in Liverpool until 1891, when he was appointed director of the Immigration Service of Brazil in Paris. He could then live permanently in his favorite European city.

To add to the pleasures of the environment, Rio-Branco indulged again in journalism. The new *Jornal do Brasil* invited him to write the historical section of the paper, the ephemerides. Such an assignment provided ample opportunity to display his knowledge of Brazilian history. Later, when these ephemerides were collected into a single volume, *Efemerides Brasileiras,* they totaled 625 pages.[18]

Those were the apprentice years of the diplomat when his skills, interests, knowledge, and ability were organized and intensified.[19] Those years in Europe gave Rio-Branco practical experience in diplomacy, introduced him to the sources of Western culture, required him to perfect his knowledge of foreign languages, expanded his personal acquaintanceships in diplomatic and social circles, permitted him to visit European libraries and archives, and provided the historian with leisure hours which he could devote to the study of history. As one Brazilian observed, "Here was the desert for meditation, the laboratory for research."[20] Rio-Branco obtained a new perspective of his own country. From a foreign vantage point, the young diplomat had ample opportunity to study Brazil's position in the world.

The stimulating atmosphere of Paris, the frequent calls of Brazilian friends passing through France, the regular visits to the Bibliothèque Nationale, the strolls on the Champs-Elysées, the epicurean meals in quaint restaurants, all these delights of Rio-Branco were short lived. Across the Atlantic in the much quieter

and more provincial Washington, D.C., the Brazilian government
was preparing its claims to the Missions territory for submission to
the arbiter, President Grover Cleveland. Argentina, the other party
to the dispute, also was preparing its claims. At the beginning of
the preparation of the Brazilian case, the chief of the special mission
to Washington, Baron Aguiar de Andrade, died. The Brazilian
government was in a quandary as to whom they should appoint
to lead the important mission. It was then that official circles began
to remember Brazil's historian of the Plata, Rio-Branco, son of the
Viscount of Rio-Branco, who had done so much to consolidate
Brazil's position in the troublesome Plata. Who else knew the region better than Rio-Branco? Years of study, firsthand experience,
and a reputation among Brazil's intellectuals for his studies of the
Plata qualified him to head the Brazilian mission to Washington.

After receiving the appointment in March of 1893 and before departing from Europe in May, Rio-Branco energetically undertook
some last-minute research on the question. His knowledge of the
area made him confident that Brazil's claim was valid. Many years
of research and study began to pay dividends. He knew the geography of the Missions area well; its history he had mastered years
before. He was aware of the old maps, charts, and documents he
would need to prove Brazil's claims. They demonstrated that history and geography would validate Brazil's case.[21] The genius of
Rio-Branco in this particular case was the skillful combination of
history and diplomacy into one victorious force.[22] The apprentice
years had ended. The master began to work.

In the United States, Rio-Branco had an excellent opportunity to
display his linguistic abilities. Years of residence in England had
enabled him to master English. Dealing with the Argentines, he
called upon his more limited knowledge of Spanish which he had
obtained during his trips to the Plata.[23]

Selected to lead the Argentine mission to Washington was a
rising scholar, intellect, and lawyer named Estanislau Zeballos.

These two able diplomats, later to become the ministers of foreign relations in their respective countries, had their first encounter in Washington, where the seeds of discord between them were sown. Concerning his opponent in the Missions dispute, Rio-Branco remarked in his diary, "I received a note from Zeballos today, a note in which he lies with the greatest imprudence." [24]

While in the United States, Rio-Branco secluded himself much of the time in his study in a rooming house in New York. He chose to live away from the social life of the legation and Washington. On one of his few trips outside that city he visited the World's Columbian Exposition in Chicago and stopped at Niagara Falls on his return to New York. On his occasional trips to Washington, Brazilian Minister Salvador de Mendonça introduced him to various Americans.[25] He became acquainted with Secretary of State Walter Gresham, Secretary of War Daniel Lamont, General Benjamin Tracey, a friend of the President, and E. Hopkins, the editor of the Detroit *Free Press*. He became more closely associated with Under Secretary of State Edwin F. Uhl, with whom he corresponded later. The most important and closest friend Rio-Branco made in the United States undoubtedly was Professor John Bassett Moore, a renowned authority on international law. Their correspondence and friendly relationship, as well as mutual admiration, were to last until Rio-Branco's death. Social activities, however, formed a very small part of the Baron's mission in the United States.

Rio-Branco's first important diplomatic assignment absorbed his interest and energy. When Graciano de Azambuja passed through New York and stopped to visit Rio-Branco he left this verbal description of what he saw:

Rio-Branco had begun to write his memorandum working in a spacious room of a modest house on 32d Street. There he was surrounded by maps, documents and old books. There they brought him his lunch and dinner. He seemed feverish to me and his concentration on the subject which preoccupied him was intense enough to produce a fever.[26]

In the preparation of that memorandum, the Baron based his arguments on eighteenth-century documents and maps as well as on Brazilian settlement of the area. So skillfully had he mastered the material that he used Argentine arguments to strengthen the Brazilian claim.

When President Cleveland delivered the arbitral award on February 6, 1895, Rio-Branco won an overwhelming victory over Zeballos. The Missions territory, 13,680 square miles, was given to Brazil. The diplomatic victory overjoyed Brazil. The newspapers chanted a triumphal hymn and praised Rio-Branco.[27] From the unknown director of the Immigration Service in Paris he became overnight a Brazilian hero. "You are truly the man of the day," wrote Constâncio Alves in a letter congratulating him.[28] Perhaps the greatest triumph for Rio-Branco was his role in the definitive and successful settlement of the perplexing questions upon which his father had worked for many years.

Instead of visiting Rio de Janeiro to collect the tribute due him, Rio-Branco quietly returned to the banks of the Seine. Then the Brazilian government, impressed with his success, requested him to begin a study of the troublesome boundary between Brazil and French Guiana. France for some time had made exaggerated claims which extended down to the mouth of the Amazon. A showdown between France and Brazil over the disputed lands, known as Amapá, was approaching rapidly. Being less acquainted with the geography and history of northern Brazil, Rio-Branco found the question somewhat more involved than the Missions. Consequently he returned to the libraries and archives of Spain, Portugal, England, and France, and the meticulous research began anew.

When France and Brazil agreed to submit the boundary dispute to arbitration, they selected the president of Switzerland to decide the claims. Envoy Extraordinary and Minister Plenipotentiary Rio-Branco presented to the Swiss Council on April 5, 1899, his credentials as chief of the special Brazilian mission. Once again there were the detailed memorials to write in which history and geography became the handmaidens of diplomacy.[29] Writing to encourage him, the abolitionist and statesman Joaquim Nabuco predicted, "If this comes out in our favor, your position will be higher than that of any government. Having given us the Missions territory and Oiapoque [Amapá], you will be an undeniable national hero." [30]

On December 1, 1900, the Swiss president awarded the disputed territory to Brazil. Amapá, approximately 101,000 square miles, was another complete victory for Rio-Branco, who now had triumphed in both the north and the south, permitting Brazil to expand peacefully in both directions and to mark the frontiers which had vexed it for four hundred years. At home, the crowds cheered the welcome news and with the press extolled their diplomatic giant.[31]

After more than two decades, during which time the once brilliant imperial diplomacy had declined to banal routine, Rio-Branco successfully projected national interests into the international sphere. Brazil returned from two international tribunals vindicated, first with a victory over its archrival, Argentina, and then with an award over a major European nation, France.

Although declared a hero in his homeland, Rio-Branco chose to remain in Europe, far from the popular acclamations. Undoubtedly his aloofness from the celebrations and his continued absence from Rio de Janeiro served to strengthen and to encourage the prestige and respectful awe which rapidly were enveloping his name. The Brazilian government then permitted him to select his own diplomatic post, and he asked for the newly vacant ministry to Germany. He presented his credentials to Kaiser Wilhelm II on May 28, 1901. His duty in Berlin was brief.

On July 6, 1902, Rodrigues Alves, the newly elected president, asked the Baron to accept the Ministry of Foreign Relations. Such a promotion was logical for the successful diplomat, but after living twenty-six years in Europe, he was uncertain about returning to Brazil and to the political intrigues which infested Rio de Janeiro.

He confided to Joaquim Nabuco, "I hesitate; I think it would be best not to jump into that fire." [32] He frankly expressed his reservations to the newly elected president and suggested that Nabuco would make a better Minister of Foreign Relations. Although personally unacquainted with Rio-Branco, Rodrigues Alves was determined to include him in the new cabinet. Appealing to his patriotism and assuring him that the Ministry of Foreign Relations would never be subjected to politics, the president-elect finally persuaded him to accept the portfolio.

Thus, after a quarter of a century of living abroad and after an absence from Brazil of fifteen years, the Baron of Rio-Branco returned to Rio de Janeiro aboard the steamer *Atlantique* on that "warm and bright" first of December of 1902. The obscure consul who sailed for a lonely post in Liverpool in 1876 returned as the Minister of Foreign Relations and as a wildly cheered national hero.

Rio de Janeiro had changed and so had Rio-Branco. His tall frame had filled out, his hair was gone, and a heavy, white moustache graced his upper lip. Clear, forceful eyes, a classic nose, and well-shaped lips combined to form a patriarchal face. Indeed, he resembled what he had been meant to be, a noble of the imperial period. Meticulously attired in the latest European fashions, he evinced nothing of his former Bohemianism. In short, a distinguished gentleman, he looked the part he was to play so well.[33]

He undertook his new duties with enthusiasm and dedication. A widower now with most of his children in Europe, he devoted all of his time and energy to the task before him, centering his life on the Ministry of Foreign Relations, its archives and library.[34] Equipped with a small bed, his book- and map-strewn office served frequently as home as well. Once involved in some complex problem he concentrated all his force and thoughts in his efforts to find a solution.[35] Often, priding himself on his limited requirement for sleep, he remained at his desk for days at a stretch working through-

The Private Study of Rio-Branco at Itamaraty

out the night and sleeping a few hours in the morning.[36] His capacity for work, his attention to detail, and his vision of the task before him impressed those who were acquainted with his work.

Rio-Branco brought to the Ministry of Foreign Relations qualities which ensured the success of Brazil's foreign policy. His knowledge of South American history and geography made him intimately familiar with Brazil's neighbors and the interrelationship of the countries of South America. As a savant in public office, a rarity in any country, he possessed an historical perspective of Brazil's position in South American politics. Twenty-six years spent in a variety of diplomatic posts made him knowledgeable in the practice of diplomacy as well as its theory. Finally, he possessed and developed the characteristics of a statesman.[37]

From his father as well as from his own experience, he was acquainted with the traditional diplomacy of Brazil, that is, the successful diplomacy of the Second Empire prior to 1880. He prided himself on carrying forward the policies of his father. To this task he naturally brought his own preferences and prejudices. He believed that a strong central government and internal stability were requisite for an effective foreign policy. In a candid letter expressing many of his political beliefs, he wrote to Nabuco:

I was never in favor of the federation as it was established among us with governors elected by each state. I always though that by developing the Additional Act we would be able to have the best federations, similar to the English type existing in Canada and Australia. Without speaking of the bankruptcy of the various states nor of the many abuses which have taken root in them, the inconveniences of a federation in the American style reveal themselves right now in what is said about our foreign policy. Some incidents of the Acre question are showing that. As to the so-called presidential regime which you don't like, I understand that it is what we have needed for some time. In the midst of the general anarchy which still reigns, without two large parties, strong and disciplined, it would be imprudent to attempt to reestablish the parliamentary regime. The ministers only represent the transitory alliances of state groups, that is, a league of small interests and parish intrigues. They only last two or three months, thereby increasing the political instability which is always an evil.[38]

Furthermore, he believed that only a well-armed nation capable of self-defense could negotiate for peace. In his opinion, peaceful coexistence within South America, as well as within the world community of nations, required a strong and self-reliant Brazil. He felt that his country could not hope for a full enjoyment of its sovereignty if it were militarily weak.[39] These beliefs did not mean that he was either militaristic or belligerent, although his critics abroad accused him of being both. A study of his diplomacy, speeches, and private statements reveals him to be devoted to international peace, but he felt that only the strong could truly enjoy an honorable peace.[40]

As subsequent chapters will discuss more fully, Rio-Branco turned the full attention of Brazil to the New World despite the fact that his education, travel, and diplomatic experience had created in him a very favorable attitude toward Europe. The pleasant years spent in Paris endeared France especially to him. In short, his orientation prior to 1902 encouraged respect and admiration for the Old World.[41] Regardless of those inclinations, he was realistic and understood that Brazil's future was in the New World, not in Europe. The United States was Brazil's principal market and the Spanish-speaking countries were its neighbors. Under the empire, Brazil, partly because of its unique governmental system in a continent of republics or would-be republics, had isolated itself from the other nations of the hemisphere and emphasized its relationship with the monarchies of the Old World.[42] Joining the ranks of the new world republics in 1889, Brazil then had a closer political kinship with its neighbors than with distant, monarchial Europe. Hence, there were cogent reasons for the new emphasis.[43]

To execute his foreign policy, Rio-Branco received carte blanche from the Brazilian government. He held the portfolio of foreign relations from December 3, 1902, until his death on February 10, 1912, a Latin American record of nine years and two months. During that long span, he neither entered politics nor advised any government leader on internal policies. Each of the four presidents under whom he served considered his foreign policy to be in the best interest of the nation. A study of the period reveals not a single example of any lack of confidence or enthusiasm on the part of the government in the policies of Itamaraty. The four presidents respected and encouraged the Baron's diplomacy by isolating it as much as possible from partisan struggles. The unique combination of long tenure and of general approval gave the Brazilian foreign policy a continuity which permitted the advantageous settlement of pressing international problems.

In addition to continuity and governmental support and cooperation, a great deal of the success of Rio-Branco's foreign policy was due to the relative peace, progress, and prosperity within Brazil. Without those three internal conditions, it is doubtful if even so talented a foreign minister as the Baron could have directed a successful foreign policy. Brazilians always have felt that their external policy depended directly upon internal conditions. In the words of a recent high official of Itamaraty, "There exists . . . an intimate connection between national action and international action, between domestic policy and foreign policy, both being two distinct aspects of a same fundamental thought and ultimate desire." [44] That interrelationship of internal conditions and external policy seldom has been better illustrated than during the first decade and a half of the twentieth century. Peaceful elections, increased production, a favorable treasury balance, material progress, the flowering of Brazilian literature, financial rehabilitation, all internal, were reflected in Brazil's external policy.

Those favorable conditions permitted Rio-Branco to formulate a positive foreign policy. The multiple aspects of that policy can be summarized in three goals which he strove to reach: the restoration of Brazil's prestige abroad, the leadership of Brazil in South America, and the settlement of all Brazil's frontiers. The Baron had an ambitious program and the times were propitious for its execution.

Rio-Branco began by strengthening Itamaraty, the principal instrument he would use to carry out his new plans. For many years he had been aware of its antiquated organization and the need for its reform before a dynamic foreign policy could be implemented. For that reason, as one of the conditions of his acceptance of the portfolio, he received the approval of the president to modernize it.

One major obstacle, the old-fashioned Director General, blocked the path of modernization. Since his appointment in 1865, the Viscount of Cabo Frio had assumed increasing responsibility and authority. Indeed, during the tenure of a weak minister, Cabo Frio effectively ran Itamaraty. His tenure of office over the decades guaranteed a certain continuity. In fact, he was such a stabilizing force that in 1889 the new republican officials declined to replace him. If, on the one hand, Cabo Frio provided a desirable continuity to Brazil's foreign policy, on the other hand, he resisted all change—good or bad. He presented a dilemma to Rio-Branco, who did not want to offend an old family friend and childhood adviser but who did want to make fundamental changes. Tactfully, the Baron began to limit the Director General's duties and responsibilities to routine administration, thereby opening the way to reform.

Rio-Branco introduced Itamaraty to the twentieth century. In 1902 the ministry employed a staff of only twenty-seven, whereas in 1859 its employees had numbered thirty-eight. Brazil's increasing role in international affairs meant that the trend should have been reversed. The new foreign minister steadily augmented his staff to handle the increasing work load. Finding the ministry too small for its expanding activities, he ordered new additions to Itamaraty. The original building had been a private residence, a fine example of the aristocratic homes of the empire, with high ceilings, large rooms, and sweeping staircases. It was a perfect setting of grandeur for his policies, but the chancellor did not hesitate to modernize it when necessary. A myriad of anecdotes testified to this. When he discovered that Itamaraty had no suitable bathroom, for example, he ordered a commodious one installed at once. Later, when the bill reached the proper minister, David Campista, for payment, he was heard to exclaim, "Never in my life have I heard of such an expensive bathroom." [45] The Baron was not one to economize when he felt money should be spent for a sound reason. He refurbished the ministry to make it a splendid "reception room" for the Brazilian nation so that foreign visitors and diplomats would be favorably impressed on their initial contact with Brazil. Luxurious furniture, works of art, rich curtains, and carpets added a brilliance hitherto unknown to the Ministry of Foreign Relations. Finding Itamaraty without a library, the bibliophile minister created one and then proceeded to organize the archives. Displaying his understandable respect for maps, he inaugurated an extensive map division and library. Cartographers appeared on the salary rolls of Itamaraty for the first time. By 1905 the former cramped and disorganized Itamaraty had been transformed into an up-to-date, efficient, and tightly run ministry. The metamorphosis made it capable of successfully implementing the new foreign policy.

These reforms and innovations, as well as salary and allowance increases, instilled a high *esprit de corps* among foreign service officials both at home and abroad. The foreign service officials, rejuvenated by the infusion of new and young blood, displayed a marked enthusiasm and dedication in executing Rio-Branco's policies.

Under his direction, the foreign ministry personnel, both in Rio and abroad, took on more youthful, attractive, and intellectual features. Rio-Branco made it a point to attract literary figures into the foreign service. Soon after *Rebellion in the Backlands* appeared, for example, the Baron invited Euclides da Cunha to accept a position at Itamaraty. Concerned with Brazil's image abroad and influenced by contemporary racist doctrines, the foreign minister sent tall, handsome Brazilians of European appearance to foreign posts. The pleasing figure which the handsome, intelligent, and charming Nabuco cut in foreign capitals became the ideal diplomatic type the Baron wanted to send abroad. At his dinners, balls, and receptions at Itamaraty, he customarily surrounded himself with attractive and vivacious (and white) Brazilian youth, doubtless as a symbol of the Brazil he was trying to project abroad.

The principal international problem facing Brazil in 1902 was the demarcation of its boundaries. Latin American history shows that unmarked or ill-defined boundaries serve as excellent tinder to start wars. In fact, the origins of nearly all of South America's wars can be traced to territorial disputes. Faced with nine thousand miles of frontiers touching every South American country except Chile (at the turn of the century Ecuador still fronted on Brazil), Rio-Branco wanted to define Brazil's boundaries.

Since the Treaty of Tordesillas in 1494, when Spain and Portugal divided the New World between themselves, the frontiers of Portuguese America, Brazil, had been vague. The union of the Portuguese and Spanish crowns from 1580 to 1640 and the internal expansion of the Luso-Brazilians in search of gold and Indian slaves served as the means whereby Brazil had grown from a thin coastal band hugging the Atlantic Ocean to a gigantic subcontinent reaching to the foothills of the Andes. Apprehensive of continued Portuguese expansion, Spain sought to define the boundaries of Spanish and Portuguese America. By the treaties of Madrid in 1750 and San Ildefonso in 1777, the two European powers came to a new agreement dividing South America in general terms—vague because much of the interior of the continent was unknown. In these treaties Spain recognized the expansion of Portugal. The settlement of the frontiers in the eighteenth century resembled a twentieth-century map of South America.[46] However, it was necessary to fill

Territorial Settlements Made by Rio-Branco

1. French Guiana, Territory of Amapá
   Arbitral Award of the Swiss Federal Council, December 1, 1900
2. British Guiana
   Arbitral Award of King Victor Emmanuel III of Italy, June 6, 1904
3. Colombia
   Treaty of Limits and Navigation, April 24, 1907
   Clarified by the Treaty of Limits and Navigation, November 15, 1928
4. Peru
   Treaty of Demarcation of Frontiers, September 8, 1909
5. Bolivia, Territory of Acre
   Treaty of Petrópolis, November 17, 1903
6. Argentina, Treaty of Missões
   Arbitral Award of President Grover Cleveland of the United States, February 5, 1895

in the details, and, of course, it was in those details that the danger of border conflicts existed.

The statesmen and diplomats of the Second Empire made various efforts to settle the frontier questions, and they laid the groundwork for future settlements. The treaties with Peru in 1851, Uruguay in 1851 and 1852, Venezuela in 1859, and Bolivia in 1867 were preliminary agreements on the long road to a definitive solution.[47]

At the end of the imperial period, only two of eleven frontiers had been marked. The War of the Triple Alliance and a treaty signed in 1872 established the frontier with Paraguay. The boundary with Uruguay was marked, but the Uruguayans resented the settlement and clamored for modifications. It was apparent that some alterations had to be made on that southern frontier.

Prior to becoming foreign minister, Rio-Branco successfully marked two more of Brazil's disputed frontiers. In 1895 he settled the frontier with Argentina and in 1900 with French Guiana. Remaining to be defined were the enormous Amazon tracts.

Brazil, concentrating its attention on its neighbors as the new century opened, sought to eliminate the potential causes for conflict omnipresent in ill-defined boundaries. Rio-Branco recognized the primary task before him: he must complete the boundary demarcations he had begun auspiciously in 1895. In fact, there was no time to lose because the hinterlands of the Amazon, an area known as Acre, were erupting in armed conflict over disputed territory. Only rapid action could avert open warfare between Brazil and Bolivia, with the possible involvement of Peru.

That unexplored portion of South America had evoked claims and counterclaims throughout the nineteenth century. Brazil, faced with a war in Paraguay in 1864, desired to placate the Bolivians unsympathetic to the cause of the Triple Alliance and, in effect, to neutralize them in the conflict. A special Brazilian mission visited Bolivia and negotiated the Treaty of La Paz de Ayacucho, a treaty of amity, limits, navigation, commerce, and extradition, signed on

March 27, 1867. That important treaty recognized the principle of ownership by settlement at the time of independence. Among its provisions, the treaty of 1867 defined a boundary which, as far as the geographical knowledge at the time revealed, seemed to confirm Bolivia's claims to Acre. However, no boundary commission was ever able to come to an agreement on the implementation of the terms. For three decades thereafter, Bolivia demonstrated scant interest in the distant and isolated Acre and did not exert any effort to enforce its titular sovereignty to the vaguely defined area until the end of the nineteenth century. Then it discovered that the accelerating Amazon rubber boom had filled Acre with adventurous Brazilian rubber gatherers who had no intention of submitting to the "foreign" authority of Bolivia. When Bolivia attempted to exert its theoretical authority, the Brazilians revolted. In 1899, under the leadership of Luís Gálvez, the rubber adventurers of Acre declared the independence of that territory and sought annexation by Brazil. For those who like to study parallel events in the histories of several countries, the situation of Acre of this epoch bore a resemblance to that of Texas some seventy-five years earlier.

The succeeding years witnessed turmoil, intrigue, and frequent bloodshed. At the beginning of 1902, the newly arrived Bolivian governor imposed harsh laws on the inhabitants of Acre, including new taxes and threats to their land claims. The inevitable result was a new revolution by the Brazilian rubber gatherers. Led by Plácido de Castro, they once again declared the independence of Acre. The Brazilians, as was natural, sympathized with their compatriots-in-arms. Rio-Branco became foreign minister just as President Juan Manuel Pando of Bolivia began to lead troops into Acre to repress the Brazilians.

It was necessary for Minister Rio-Branco to turn his initial attention to the Acre imbroglio, fortunately not a new subject for him. He had an intimate knowledge of the negotiations over Acre during the empire. Furthermore, while he was in Europe, the Brazilian minister to Washington, Assis Brasil, in a series of private letters, had kept him abreast of the worsening Acre situation.[48] Hence, when the new foreign minister decided to take action in Acre, he was cognizant not only of the historical and geographical facts of the conflict but of the state of current affairs as well. He reversed the policy of his predecessor, Olynto de Magalhães, who believed that Acre belonged unquestionably to Bolivia and therefore had paid a minimum of attention to the area.

Facing his first test as foreign minister, Rio-Branco resolved to base his action on the traditional principles which Brazil invoked during border disputes. These principles, as the Baron codified them in the Acre disputes and used them thereafter, were three. First, he refused to recognize the treaties of Madrid and San Ildefonso between Spain and Portugal as anything more than a preliminary settlement of borders. By their very nature vague and ill-defined, the treaties could not provide a definite settlement of the frontiers. In other words, the two treaties might serve as a guide to the independent nations of South America but they were in no way a mandate. As Rio-Branco himself stated, "We always maintained the nullity of the preliminary or provisional treaty of limits of 1777." [49] Second, the Brazilian rule for the establishment of ownership of disputed territory was the doctrine of *uti possidetis,* that is, real and effective possession of territory. The criterion for ownership would be whose citizens inhabited the disputed area, a concept inherited from the Portuguese.[50] As an independent nation, Brazil first referred to the rule of *uti possidetis* in 1841.[51] The Viscount of Rio-Branco used that principle in his negotiations as early as 1856. His son employed it successfully and consistently in the settlement of all the frontiers. Third, Brazil followed the policy of never conducting multinational boundary conferences. The Baron preferred direct negotiations between the two disputing nations. Although he had achieved his fame in courts of arbitration, he regarded arbitration as a last resort. In the Acre case, he energetically avoided arbitration in favor of negotiations. With these three traditional policies as a guide, Minister Rio-Branco closed Brazil's extensive frontiers.

Before Brazil and Bolivia could sit down calmly at the conference table, it was necessary to end the sporadic fighting in Acre. To complicate the situation, Bolivian President Pando, accompanied by Minister of War Ismael Montez and numerous troops, set out for Acre on January 26, 1903. His presence there would be a threat both to peaceful settlement and to Brazil's claim. Rio-Branco requested the president to dispatch Brazilian troops to occupy the area in order to defend the Brazilian population, which was "in revolt because Bolivian authorities shot various Brazilians and punished those who requested their salaries." [52] Brazil occupied the area before the Bolivians, under President Pando, could reach the distant scene of dispute. In effect, Bolivia thereby proved its sovereignty to be ineffective.

With the area relatively at peace, the chancellor began negotiating. The geographical errors and vagueness in the treaty of 1867, as well as the fact that Acre was inhabited by approximately sixty thousand Brazilians and almost no Bolivians, gave strong substance to Brazil's claims to the area. [53] Because of the rubber boom, which increased activity in the Amazon in the last decades of the nineteenth century, Brazilian rubber gatherers, in the tradition of the seventeenth-century *bandeirantes* of São Paulo, had fanned out into the unexplored hinterlands searching for the lucrative white milk of the rubber tree. The new explorers rapidly established themselves in the rubber-rich Acre region, and by their presence they substantiated the claims to the ownership by *uti possidetis*. [54]

Acre was so distantly removed in terms of realistic geography from the Bolivian heartland that it was extremely difficult, indeed nearly impossible, to communicate with La Paz. The Bolivian governor of Acre in early 1903, Lino Romero, complained to his government that too much distance and too many obstacles separated his political charge from the Bolivian capital. He summed up a variety of reasons (distance, lack of communication, foreign population, and bad climate) why Bolivia should not press its claims to Acre and concluded, "The Bolivians feel like strangers here just as much as they would in the most remote colonies of Asia. Men and nature are both wholly adverse to us." [55] His statements were pathetic but realistic. Bolivia was not destined to hold Acre.

Shortly after the Brazilian occupation of Acre, Brazil and Bolivia reached a *modus vivendi*. By the terms of a preliminary agreement signed on March 21, 1903, Brazil occupied militarily and administratively the disputed territory. Negotiations continued for several more months while Brazil emphasized the principle of *uti possidetis* as the basis for a final settlement. Finally, on November 17, 1903, both nations signed the Treaty of Petrópolis, from which Brazil received Acre, approximately 73,000 square miles, more than twice the size of Portugal, Belgium, and Holland combined. In return, Bolivia received a small strip of territory which gave her access to the Madeira River and thus to the Atlantic, a perpetual pledge of freedom of river navigation, ten million dollars, and Brazil's promise to construct a railroad on the right bank of the Madeira which would bypass the rapids and give Bolivia access to the lower Madeira. The soaring rubber market soon reimbursed Brazil for any expenses incurred in the fulfillment of the obligations of the treaty.[56] According to Rio-Branco's reasoning, Brazil did not buy Acre from Bolivia; rather, "We thus recuperated by means of an indemnity our ancient Luso-Brazilian title." [57] Be that as it may, the Treaty of Petrópolis completed the demarcation of the frontier from the Atlantic Ocean in the south to Peru in the west.

Peru, claiming Acre for itself, as well as a large part of Brazil's Amazon basin, vociferously protested the settlement wrought by the Treaty of Petrópolis. After the successful settlement of Brazil's frontier with Bolivia, Rio-Branco focused his attention on the Peruvian claims in order to define Brazil's boundary in the far west. Determined to use negotiation rather than arbitration, he began discussions with the Peruvian minister in Rio de Janeiro, Hernán Velarde. Once again, as in the case of Bolivia, there were irritating border clashes and reprisals accompanied by vitriolic accusations. The Baron continued to negotiate with Minister Velarde in Rio de Janeiro throughout all the annoying disturbances along the distant frontier. On July 12, 1904, the two nations signed a *modus vivendi*. However, Peru persisted in using delaying tactics in the hope that somehow time would favor its case; but if time favored anyone, it was Brazil. In Peru, the change of foreign ministers and diplomatic representatives to Brazil weakened the presentation of the Peruvian case, whereas the five years of negotiations of Brazil under one minister provided a continuity which strengthened Brazil's position. Finally, on September 8, 1909, Lima consented to sign a treaty defining the boundaries. Once again, the principle of *uti possidetis* was used to determine ownership.[58] The extensive area claimed by Peru proved to be inhabited mainly by Brazilians. Approximately 63,000 square miles were awarded to Brazil as well as the newly acquired Acre which Peru had claimed; Peru received less than ten thousand square miles. In addition, Rio-Branco defined the 972-mile frontier with Peru, thereby closing Brazil's far western boundaries.

While the protracted negotiations with Peru ran their course between 1904 and 1909, Rio-Branco attended to other frontier problems. The frontier between Brazil and British Guiana had been the subject of numerous negotiations, claims, and counterclaims between Rio de Janeiro and London. Since direct negotiations had been unsuccessful, Brazil and Britain agreed in November of 1901 to submit the disputed boundary to arbitration. The Brazilian government named its minister to England, Joaquim Nabuco, as counsel; and the two governments selected the king of Italy as arbitrator. Nabuco presented Brazil's first memorial to the Italian king in August of 1902. Shortly thereafter, Rio-Branco became Minister of

Foreign Relations. The Baron, his success in arbitration now a legend, cooperated fully with Nabuco, supported him in every respect, and offered suggestions from time to time. Brazil seemed to have a strong case. Thus, it was a shock to Brazil and a disappointment to Nabuco when, on June 6, 1904, King Victor Emmanuel III rendered a decision unfavorable to Brazil. Of the 8,500 square miles submitted to arbitration, he awarded 5,000 to Great Britain and 3,500 to Brazil. Brazil resented the decision, which seemed unfair because the arbitrator gave Brazil "fewer rights than those hitherto recognized by England." [59] Some foreign jurists also questioned the wisdom of the decision. [60] Regardless of a feeling of injustice, Brazil remained true to its agreement and accepted the award. Perhaps this award persuaded Rio-Branco not to entrust Brazil's dispute with Peru to arbitration. At any rate, he never once used arbitration as a means of defining frontiers during his tenure of office. Whatever the merits of Victor Emmanuel's decision, it did settle once and for all the disputed frontier with British Guiana.

The boundaries with Bolivia, Peru, and British Guiana were the most troublesome, and by comparison the demarcation of the other frontiers was simple. In 1904 Brazil and Ecuador signed a treaty resolving their boundary problems. A treaty with Venezuela in 1905 settled that northern frontier. Brazil and the Netherlands negotiated an agreement in 1906 which determined the limits of Surinam; in 1907 Colombia and Brazil reached an understanding which later would permit them to mark their frontiers.

The foreign minister capped the final demarcation of Brazil's frontiers with the magnanimous treaty of 1909 with Uruguay. A treaty in 1851 had marked the Brazilian-Uruguayan frontier. Uruguay recognized this treaty but lamented the fact that it prohibited use of the Jaguarão River and Lake Mirim upon which it bordered. Rio-Branco heard the complaint sympathetically, and in an act of friendship he suggested that a new treaty be signed giving Uruguay the right of navigation on those two bodies of water.

Uruguay quickly agreed, and the new treaty signed on October 30, 1909, readjusted slightly that boundary.

In fifteen years the Baron had marked Brazil's boundaries, the cause of debate and conflict for four centuries. He carried to a conclusion the work which the statesmen of the empire, among them his father, had begun.[61] The most obvious result of his boundary settlements was the addition of approximately 342,000 square miles of territory to Brazil.[62] More graphically stated, he gained for Brazil an area greater than France. Somewhat more difficult to measure, and likewise of greater importance, were the potential causes for war, misunderstanding, and dispute which he eliminated.

His advantageous settlement of the boundaries was doubtless his greatest contribution to Brazil. A newspaper account of the period summed up opinion and judgment on his demarcation of the frontiers in these words, "No greater service could be given to a nation." [63] Passage of time in no way refuted that judgment. Contemporary historians who have specialized in the study of the period concur that the settlement of the extensive frontiers was the major achievement of the Baron.[64]

Another part of his foreign policy envisaged a close approximation of the United States and Brazil. The success of this policy will be treated in detail in Chapter III and thereafter.

Rio-Branco's patriotism guided his policy to increase Brazil's prestige in the world and to raise it to a position of dominance in South America. Nearly every diplomatic act he performed reflected the desire to achieve those dual objectives.

The Baron foresaw the prestige which would accrue to Brazil if it were the first Latin American nation to receive a cardinalate. As late as 1904, there was not one Latin American cardinal, a curious fact when one realizes that the area was a bastion of Roman Catholicism. Pressure was mounting on Rome to elevate a Latin American to that eminent body. The first Latin American nation to receive the honor would enjoy a singular distinction.

The foreign minister requested the Brazilian diplomat at the Vatican, Bruno Gonçalvez Chavez, to suggest to the Pope that Brazilian Catholics would be pleased to have a cardinal. Minister Chavez had a strong case. The Vatican had dispatched a Nuncio of the First Class to Rio de Janeiro in 1823, an event which traditionally gave the recipient nation the right to petition for a cardinal. Also by comparison with the rest of Latin America, Brazil had maintained good relations with Rome. The Brazilian minister was not reticent about pointing out to the Vatican that Brazil had displayed more loyalty and consideration than other Latin American countries, such as Argentina. He also used the effective arguments of size and population. The reasoning was sound, and the decision of Rome was not long in coming. In the consistory of December 11, 1905, Pope Pius X created as cardinal the distinguished archbishop of Rio de Janeiro, Joaquim Arcoverde de Albuquerque. The announcement was a diplomatic victory for Brazil. For thirty years thereafter, Brazil was the only Latin American nation with a cardinal.

In pursuit of his policy to increase Brazil's prestige and leadership in the Western Hemisphere, Rio-Branco strengthened his nation's diplomatic ties throughout Latin America. He discovered that Brazil had had no diplomatic representative in either Quito or Bogotá since 1898 and that for three years prior to that date those two neighboring capitals had shared the same Brazilian diplomat. In 1904 he corrected that error and dispatched resident ministers to both Colombia and Ecuador. In 1906 Brazil accredited a diplomatic representative to Costa Rica, Cuba, Guatemala, Honduras, El Salvador, Nicaragua, and Panama for the first time. The only Latin American capitals to which he did not accredit a diplomat were Port-au-Prince, Haiti, and Santo Domingo, Dominican Republic. When necessary, the Baron conducted his diplomatic relations with those insular republics in Washington. Buenos Aires, Santiago, and

Lima became the most important posts in Latin America, and he assigned to those three capitals his ablest diplomats and closest associates. Assis Brasil, Domício da Gama, and Gomes Ferreira, for example, served in those posts. Recognizing the importance of Mexico in the Pan American community, he established a legation there in 1906, thereby separating the previously joint Washington–Mexico City diplomatic post.

Outside of this hemisphere, the Baron accredited a diplomatic representative to Norway in 1908, Egypt in 1910, and Greece in 1911. By 1912, Brazil maintained diplomatic representation in thirty-nine countries in the Americas, Europe, Asia, and Africa. Twenty-eight nations reciprocated by sending diplomatic representatives to Rio de Janeiro. Thirteen of these were Latin American representatives. Six small Middle American countries accredited no diplomats. Two other nations, China and Persia, sent special missions to visit Brazil during the Rio-Branco ministry.[65]

Expanding the Brazilian foreign service was not the Baron's only effort to make Brazil better known in the world. He also increased Brazilian participation in international conferences. In 1904 Brazil took part in the Montevideo Sanitary Congress; in 1906, in the Geneva Conference on the Red Cross, the Brussels Sugar Conference, the International Institute of Agriculture in Rome, and the International Conference of Radiotelegraphy in Berlin; in 1907, the Hague Peace Conference; in 1910, the Fourth Pan American Conference in Buenos Aires. The year 1908, while perhaps not being a strictly typical year, shows the determination of Rio-Branco to have Brazil represented in a variety of world conclaves. In that busy year, Brazil sent delegates to the International Geographical Congress, Geneva; the Pan American Medical Congress, Guatemala City; the International Congress of Americanists, Vienna; the Fourth International Congress of Fisheries, Washington; the International Congress of Irrigation, Albuquerque; the International Congress of

Refrigerator Industries, Paris; the first Congress of Electrical Units and Standards, London; the Pan American Scientific Congress, Santiago; and the International Telegraphic Conference, Lisbon.[66]

Not only were the Brazilians busy attending conferences abroad but they were the hosts to several important ones at home. In October of 1905, the Third Latin American Scientific Congress convened in Rio de Janeiro. The following July, the Third Pan American Congress met there. Both meetings were successful, and the hosts, under Rio-Branco's direction, made every effort to impress their sister nations. Thanks to the great natural beauty of Rio de Janeiro and to the renovation of the city, that task was not difficult.

Rio-Branco's projects to make his country known abroad extended into other fields. The newly equipped navy visited a larger number of foreign ports to show the flag. Brazil had an elaborate display at the St. Louis Exhibition in 1904, and a smaller pavilion as well as a large naval representation at the Jamestown Exhibition in 1908. Official delegations paid tribute to Argentina, Chile, Mexico, and Venezuela at their elaborate centennial celebrations of independence.

During his ministry, more distinguished foreigners visited Brazil than during any previous decade. The foreign minister greeted and entertained all of them. Among others, he welcomed Sarah Bernhardt, William Jennings Bryan, Georges Clemenceau, Paul Doumier, Guglielmo Ferrero, Anatole France, Roque Saenz Peña, Julio Roca, and Elihu Root. From their statements to the press and from their own writings, it is apparent that these visitors carried away with them a favorable impression of the country.

Another of his favorite projects was to negotiate general treaties of arbitration. Although the chancellor seemed to have looked with disfavor on arbitration after the king of Italy's award in 1904, he later encouraged Brazil to sign such treaties in an apparent effort to distinguish his country as an outstanding world leader in peaceful solutions to international problems and to counteract complaints against its rearmament program. When he assumed the foreign ministry, not one such treaty had been ratified by Brazil. During his administration, Rio-Branco signed thirty-one conventions with nations in the Americas, Asia, and Europe.[67] Nineteen of these treaties bear the date 1909. At that period only the United States and Spain had signed more treaties of arbitration than Brazil.

The diplomacy of Rio-Branco did not neglect the commercial interests of Brazil, particularly the coffee upon which prosperity depended. Internally, commerce and politics were closely intertwined; externally, too, commerce and diplomacy frequently went hand in hand. As will be pointed out in greater detail in Chapter III, the foreign minister jealously guarded Brazil's market in the United States. In Europe as well, he strove to maintain as favorable a coffee market as possible. In 1904 he persuaded the French government not to carry out its intentions to raise its coffee tariff. By a series of treaty extensions, he also prevented the Italians from raising their duty on coffee.

Rio-Branco did not formulate and execute his foreign policy alone. A group of distinguished and intelligent men surrounded and supported him. Some of these, such as Joaquim Nabuco, Francisco Veiga, João Pandiá Calógeras, Gastão da Cunha, J. F. Assis Brasil, Euclides da Cunha, and Dunshee de Abranches, were already men of importance who had proved their ability in either politics, literature, diplomacy, history, philosophy, or journalism before Rio-Branco brought them into association with the ministry. Others, such as Domício da Gama, Enéas Martins, Alfredo Gomes Ferreira, Moniz de Aragão, and Araujo Jorge, were to be "discovered" by the Baron and to contribute significantly to Brazil's international life. The talents of all these men facilitated the task of the foreign minister and ensured victory for his policies.

The powerful personality of Rio-Branco ruled Itamaraty. He outlined the foreign policy and planned the methods to achieve its goals. His critics have accused him of treating his aides as mere

clerks, but it seems unlikely that he domineered over such a diverse
and able group of independent men as those which surrounded him.
Had the Baron wanted obedient puppets, he would never have selected men with reputations for independent thought and action.
For two of his most important missions, the ambassador to Washington and the chief delegate to the Second Hague Peace Conference,
he selected Nabuco and Rui Barbosa. It would be difficult to think
of those two brilliant minds as messenger boys of anyone.[68] As
these two examples illustrate, there seems to have been some room
for maneuvering within the limits of his foreign policy so that his
subordinates were not reduced to complete subserviency. One of his
closest associates, João Pandiá Calógeras, revealed that anyone who
worked with him would have to subject himself to true and intimate collaboration.[69] There is a vast difference between "intimate
collaboration" and "domineering." The charges that he domineered
over his subordinates seem to be exaggerated and probably originated in the ranks of his enemies.

The Baron was not without critics. At home a small number of
unsympathetic Brazilians objected to the foreign minister and his
policies. Barbosa Lima, a federal deputy, was one of the most outspoken of these critics. He delighted in attacking Rio-Branco in the
Chamber of Deputies. He disapproved of the chancellor's heavy ex-
penditures and failure to account for the funds or actions of Itamaraty. Indeed, the Baron tended to run the foreign ministry in ac-
cordance with his own desires and felt himself responsible only to
the president and to public opinion. After his first year in office, he
never again submitted the required annual report to Congress. Such
independence, if not arrogance, angered Barbosa Lima and others.
Gabriel de Piza, minister to France for many years, was the most
unreasonable and vitriolic critic whose remarks passed the limits of
both good taste and common sense. After Rio-Branco removed him
from his Parisian post, de Piza assailed the chancellor in speech
and print. The foreign minister was a megalomaniac, he cried, who

sought to orient Brazil's foreign policy to suit his own whims and to flatter his own exalted egoism. Other charges of egoism were also made against the foreign minister. Manoel de Oliveira Lima and Salvador de Mendonça, both diplomats who coveted the post of Minister of Foreign Relations, seldom missed an opportunity to try to undermine the Baron's prestige. They both believed that he appointed only his favorites to positions of importance and responsibility. Oliveira Lima led a faction opposed to the shift of Brazil's diplomatic axis from the Old World to the New. They continued to look to Europe for their inspiration and distrusted the United States and disliked Spanish America. Among themselves, intimates of these two diplomats referred sardonically to Rio-Branco as the "All Powerful of Itamaraty" when they did not use less printable nomenclature.[70]

Newspaper criticism of Rio-Branco within Brazil was isolated and mild. In truth, he enjoyed a special status. His diplomatic victories had raised him to the rank of a national hero and thereby "untouchable" by journalistic critics. Consequently public, printed criticism was minimal. It appears to have increased slightly during the last half of his ministry. One of the harshest attacks, published in the last year of his ministry, berated him for his vanity and attributed his success to good luck.[71]

Abroad Rio-Branco encountered his severest critic in the Argentine foreign minister and journalist, Estanislau Zeballos, who showed himself to be an implacable foe. The Argentine accused the Brazilian of plotting to isolate Argentina in the New World. The growth of Brazil through advantageous boundary settlements also irritated him. In opposing Brazil's expansion, Zeballos found kindred souls in other nations neighboring on Brazil. Together they set up a cry of imperialism. Those detractors, both at home and abroad, formed a small minority.

Throughout his long term of office, the chancellor was extremely popular with the Brazilian people. In 1903 one observer wrote, "The prestige of the Baron is, as you know, simply enormous, everyone admires him." [72] In 1906 Euclides da Cunha confided in a private letter, "I have a slight knowledge of the frontier questions which occupy us in the extreme north, but that little knowledge of affairs is enough to convince me that the substitution for Rio-Branco of anyone else will be a calamity." [73] And in 1909 another commentator noted, "There is no doubt that Rio-Branco is the most popular man in Brazil today." [74] Those three personal opinions were representative of the attitude of the entire nation. A perusal of the newspapers of the period, not only those of the capital but those of other major Brazilian cities, demonstrates dramatically the high degree of popularity and prestige he enjoyed in his own country.

The name of Rio-Branco and respect for his abilities spread beyond the confines of Brazil. Foreigners also spoke well of the "Chancellor of Peace." The press of the United States, Secretary of State Elihu Root, Professor John Bassett Moore, and American diplomatic officials esteemed Rio-Branco. [75] A large group of Latin American diplomats and statesmen admired him. [76] After a tour of Brazil and an interview with the "Golden Chancellor," the Uruguayan journalist Manuel Bernárdez wrote of the Baron's talent and the popular admiration for him. [77] Two observant Englishmen who were in Brazil around the same time, Charles W. Domville-Fife, traveler and writer, [78] and the English diplomat James Bryce, [79] echoed those observations. The French statesman Georges Clemenceau, returning from an extended visit to Brazil, affirmed that the Baron possessed "remarkable talents" as a diplomat and enjoyed the confidence and praise of all his fellow citizens. [80] These opinions were shared by the majority of the foreigners who came into contact with him.

Doubtless one of the reasons for his popularity at home was his effort to represent in the nation's foreign policy the aspirations of the majority of Brazilians. Studiously avoiding politics, Rio-Branco raised foreign policy above partisan polemics, so that instead of representing one or another party it reflected the desires of the entire nation. Brazilian foreign policy became identified with the idea of unified nationality.[81]

The decade as foreign minister was, personally, a difficult one for Rio-Branco. His wife and parents dead, his children preferring to stay in or go to Europe, he remained alone in Rio de Janeiro. Concentrating his energy and time on his job, he began to neglect his health. Although he often claimed he was built "to last a hundred years," he failed to realize that no man could work at full speed for an extended period without harming himself. There were warnings that his health was failing, but no one realized the end was near. A shocked nation read of his uremic attack on February 5, 1912. His condition rapidly grew more serious until, five days later, he was dead. The nation paused. Perhaps in its large, black headline of that day, the Rio newspaper *A Noite* summed up Brazil's feeling: "The Death of Rio-Branco Is a National Catastrophe." [82] An era closed. But it had not closed without the successful achievement of the foreign minister's goals, one of which was to strengthen the relations between Brazil and its republican model, the United States.

CHAPTER III · COMMERCE AS
A BACKDROP FOR DIPLOMACY

THE RELATIONS between Brazil and the United States began in the late eighteenth century, when North American political thought and independence exerted an influence on Brazil's first separatist movement, the Inconfidência. Admiration for the American Revolution prompted a young Brazilian student in France, José Joaquim da Maia, to ask Thomas Jefferson, in 1786, for the support of the United States for the independence movement then being planned in Minas Gerais. The enlightened class was acquainted with the United States Constitution, which had been translated into Portuguese by 1789, and the *Federalist Papers*. Failure of the plot in Minas Gerais did not end Brazilian interest in American political ideas.

When the court of João VI hastily fled to Rio de Janeiro in 1807, the United States accredited a diplomatic representative there. Brazil thus became the first Latin American country to have a resident North American diplomat. In 1824 the United States was the first country to recognize Brazilian independence, declared two years earlier. Brazil, in its turn, was the first nation officially to acknowledge the Monroe Doctrine; it even suggested a treaty of alliance. In 1828 the two governments signed a Treaty of Friendship, Navigation, and Commerce.

The friendly relationship begun so propitiously soon deteriorated. The United States sent to Rio de Janeiro an unfortunate selection of diplomats, whose ineptitude and, at times, cantankerousness put a strain upon the friendly relations. Condy Raguet, 1825–28; Henry A. Wise, 1844–47; and General James Watson Webb, 1861–69, arrogantly made trouble in Brazil and behaved in a boorish manner which could only reflect poorly upon the United States government. Minor incidents, which ordinarily are the daily duty of diplomats to solve, became major crises under their handling.

During this same period, Brazil revealed little skill in dealing with the United States. The diplomats representing the imperial government in Washington behaved themselves, to be sure, but seldom were of the highest caliber. The small and isolated capital of the United States did not attract the outstanding Brazilian diplomats as did the capitals of Europe. Furthermore, the government of the United States resented the Brazilian position during the American Civil War. Tolerant of the Confederacy, Brazil precipitated a series of bitter disputes with Washington by granting the South a belligerent status and the use of Brazilian ports. After the Civil War, the migration of some Confederate families to Brazil had the double effect of confusing relations between the two countries in some respects and of improving them in others. There is no reason to reminisce fondly about friendly relations between the United States and Brazil during the years 1825–75.[1]

In a visit to the United States in 1876, Emperor Pedro II discovered Brazil's northern neighbor and vice versa. Curious Americans welcomed the philosopher-emperor from the tropics. An equally curious emperor examined the booming North American colossus. Both liked what they saw and Dom Pedro's visit was a great success.[2] That imperial visit set the stage for the beginning of the "traditional" friendly relations some years later.

Although relations after the visit were cordial, it was impossible to classify them as extraordinarily so. Becoming more aware of one another, the two countries forgot past difficulties. The United

States had become the principal market for Brazil's coffee and rubber, and the trend accelerated. However, both nations were otherwise involved. Great Britain still monopolized the primary role in Brazil's economy and diplomacy. The United States, pre-occupied with the settlement of the West and with industrialization, felt little need to pursue an active policy of friendship toward the South American empire.

The period of friendly neglect ended in 1889. With the proclamation of the Republic of Brazil on November 15, the United States, pleased to welcome another nation into the republican fraternity, especially one that openly took the Constitution of 1787 as its model, quickly recognized the new government. The provisional government was grateful to the United States for being the first international power to do so. Belonging to the same republican brotherhood, Brazil and the United States shared more in common than ever before, and as a consequence a period of closer friendship began.

The republican government accredited to the United States a new minister, Salvador de Mendonça, who was enthusiastically pro-American. As Brazilian consul in New York since 1875, he had dedicated himself to the improvement of relations between the two countries.[3] Understanding the importance of the North American market for Brazilian products, he tried to solidify commercial relations with a formal treaty.[4] His efforts resulted in a reciprocity agreement which became effective in 1891, barely a year after his promotion to the post of minister. Under that agreement, Brazil's principal exports, rubber, coffee, sugar, and hides, entered the expanding American market either duty-free or nearly so. American exports received similar concessions from Brazil. Mendonça hailed the agreement as

the beginning of a new era, whether in their international relations or in the internal economy of our States, because it not only places us at the right hand of the powerful North American Union as a partner

of its policy for the maintenance of the republican institutions of peace
and of prosperity on this continent, but it also guarantees us the virtual
monopoly of this great market for our principal products.[5]

The Brazilian Congress failed to share the minister's enthusiasm
and terminated the agreement in 1894. Momentarily disappointed,
he received new encouragement from the Dingley Tariff of 1897,
which placed nearly all of Brazil's principal exports on the free
list. As an impetus to trade, it would draw Brazil closer to the
United States. He firmly believed that commerce could interlace
the two nations into a tight diplomatic community.

During the years in which Mendonça was minister in Washington, 1890–98, relations between the two countries did grow more
cordial. The United States manifested its solidarity with republican Brazil during the naval revolt in the harbor of Rio de Janeiro
in 1893. The rebels threatened to overthrow the republic, but the
opportune maneuvering of the United States navy in favor of the
established government helped to thwart the attempt. The Brazilian government expressed its gratitude. So anxious was the
Brazilian government to encourage amiable relations that it suppressed and confiscated Eduardo Prado's book, *The American Illusion,* criticizing the United States, when it appeared in 1893. The
following year Brazil dedicated a monument to James Monroe,
whose doctrine found an echo of approval in Rio de Janeiro. The
award of President Cleveland to Brazil in the Missions dispute
was another positive contribution to the strengthening of friendly
feelings of Brazil toward the United States. The increasingly amiable relations between the two nations help to explain why Brazil
was the only Latin American nation sympathetic to the United
States during the Spanish-American War. Those events of the
final decade of the nineteenth century created bonds of good will
which, thereafter, were referred to as the "traditional friendship"
of the two nations.

When Mendonça left Washington in 1898 for a new post in

Lisbon, he did not abandon his project to strengthen Brazilian-American relations. In Lisbon, Mendonça had a new perspective from which he could reflect on Brazil's foreign policy. In a remarkable letter written in 1902 to President Campos Salles, Mendonça expounded his thoughts on United States–Brazilian approximation. He urged that the president adopt a policy of frank friendship with the United States based on understanding and cooperation. Pointing out that Brazil had nothing to fear from the United States, he suggested that Brazil become the link between the United States and Latin America. The Monroe Doctrine, he believed, really benefited Latin America. Finally, he confided his thoughts that a friendly United States would be an advantage to Brazil in solving her numerous frontier problems.[6] In a surprising number of respects, that advice coincided with Rio-Branco's ideas about Brazilian-American relations. Years later Mendonça laconically remarked, "When the Baron of Rio-Branco sent Mr. Joaquim Nabuco to discover North America, it was already discovered, measured, and marked."[7] There is no reason to believe that Rio-Branco's policies had their source in Mendonça's ideas, but Mendonça does deserve more credit than he has received as the precursor of friendly United States–Brazilian relations. Furthermore, by encouraging trade between the two nations, he laid a firm foundation for a close political friendship which would follow.

The pragmatic Rio-Branco understood that relationship between commerce and diplomacy. Long experience as a consul had made him aware of the importance of foreign commerce to Brazil,[8] and he seemed to have developed an academic interest in agriculture.[9] As early as 1882, Rio-Branco wrote a twenty-four-page report on the consumption of coffee in Great Britain, and his last letter to Ambassador Domício da Gama in Washington thirty years later discussed commercial matters at length.[10] The sale of several natural products, particularly coffee, in the world market ensured Brazilian prosperity. Prosperity brought progress and together they strengthened the Baron's chances of successfully carrying out his foreign policy. For that reason, he concerned himself with commerce, especially with the United States, which annually bought up to 40 percent of Brazil's exports.[11]

For many years North Americans had been the principal purchasers of Brazil's three major exports: coffee, rubber, and cocoa. Since 1865, the United States had taken the single largest share of Brazil's coffee; and after 1870, with the abolition of import duties on coffee, the United States bought more than half of the Brazilian coffee beans sold abroad.[12] By 1912, New York had become the world's largest rubber market and nearly 60 percent of the rubber traded there was Brazilian.[13] Likewise, the United States consumed more Brazilian cocoa than any other country.[14] The result was that in 1912 the United States bought 36 percent of Brazil's exports, while the second most important market, Great Britain, purchased only 15 percent.[15]

The free list of the Dingley Tariff of 1897 encouraged Brazilian imports to the United States. Coffee, rubber, cocoa, crude cotton, nuts, precious stones and metals, medicinal plants, and other products entered free of duty. In fact, by 1902, the United States admitted duty-free 94.5 percent of the Brazilian imports and collected an average duty on total Brazilian imports of 4.8 percent. On the other hand, Brazil admitted no imports from the United States duty-free, the average duty amounting to 45 percent.[16]

The Brazilian tariff policy was unfavorable to North American imports and in no way reciprocated North American generosity. A cursory glance at the trade statistics during the period graphically shows the trade imbalance in favor of Brazil, which sold in the American market and purchased in the English market. In 1902 the United States sold imports to Brazil amounting to fourteen million dollars and bought Brazilian exports totaling sixty-five million dollars. Eight years later the figures had increased to thirty and one hundred and twelve millions respectively.[17] The trade discrepancy during the Rio-Branco period remained constant: Brazil sold four times as much to the United States as it bought. Those statistics indicate the nature of the commercial policy each nation followed toward the other. The United States sought to increase its exports to Brazil by receiving preferential tariffs. Since Brazil's principal exports already entered the United States duty-free, Itamaraty's chief concern was to maintain that favorable treatment.

The American developed the coffee-drinking habit in the last half of the nineteenth century and Brazil happily—and profitably —catered to his new taste. Free from import duties, Brazilian coffee became a common item in American kitchens. But as coffee exports multiplied so did Brazilian anxieties lest the United States tax coffee. As early as 1880, Salvador de Mendonça fretted over the possibility of a tax on Brazilian "slave-grown" coffee in favor of Mexican "free-labor" coffee.[18] His worries were infectious. During the Rio-Branco ministry more than one governmental official feared he saw the specter of a coffee duty hovering nearby.[19] Those officials tried to frighten off that ghost with rationalization and specious arguments. To tax coffee, so their reasoning went, would be to raise the price of an item of necessity of the working man, his cup of coffee, and "there is one thing Americans won't stand and that is taxing coffee."[20] The argument sounded good but, alas, never really convinced the Brazilians who maintained a close vigil over tariff legislation in Washington.

Because the early years of the century had witnessed a sharp rise in production and a decline in prices, the Brazilians were sensitive to any threat, real or imagined, to their coffee market in the United States. The price per pound had dropped from a pleasing seventeen cents in 1890 to a discouraging five cents at the turn of the century. The Convention of Taubaté promised to reverse the trend, and, indeed, coffee prices were on the rise again by 1909.

In that year, Brazil's worst fears materialized: the United States Congress began to discuss a new tariff which included duties on coffee. The threat of a tariff caused Brazilians to realize, as they might not have before, the vital importance of the free American market, which they had come to take for granted. Feelings of anxiety spread throughout Brazilian business circles.[21] Adversaries of the policy of approximation with the United States took advantage of the pending crisis to point out that Brazilian efforts and sacrifices in the name of friendship were to be betrayed for selfish interests as they had predicted.[22] Both Foreign Minister Rio-Branco and his ambassador in Washington, Joaquim Nabuco, understood the danger which the tariff threatened to the policy of friendship between Brazil and the United States. The Baron lamented, "If the duties are voted, the blow would be terrible for our plantation owners and our commerce and would have the gravest political consequences."[23] Foreseeing those consequences all too clearly, Nabuco believed that "it would for our Coffee industry be the end of the world."[24]

Consideration of a duty on coffee resulted from the general discussions of a new tariff in the United States Congress early in 1909. There was some sentiment in the United States favoring a coffee duty because the Brazilian states imposed an export tax on coffee, which, according to the proponents of the tariff, was one way of getting the North American consumer to pay Brazilian taxes. The coffee duty would be a retaliatory measure against the indirect taxation of the coffee drinker. Representative Sereno E. Payne, the principal congressman advocating the duty, used that argument. Furthermore, lobbyists from Puerto Rico and the Philippines were urging the taxation of "foreign" coffee in favor of their own.

Nabuco energetically defended Brazil's commercial interests in Washington during the tariff debates. He argued that Brazilian friendship was more valuable to the United States than any revenue which could be obtained from a coffee tax. Fortunately, by 1909, the personable ambassador had made many influential friends in Washington, and he was ready to enlist their aid to thwart the

menace to Brazil's economy and to Brazilian–United States relations. Nabuco discussed the coffee question with Senators Aldrich,
du Pont, Elkins, and Root and with Congressman Douglas.[25] The
ambassador did not stop there. He went directly to Secretary of
State Philander C. Knox and asked him to intervene in Brazil's
behalf so "that [my words] may have some weight, through you,
with the Tariff Committees in both Houses of Congress, not to
revive a tax that has been dead for nearly forty years to the great
benefit of our growing friendship." [26] Nabuco received help from
an even higher source. President William H. Taft, sensitive to the
excellent relations his predecessor maintained with Brazil, supported Nabuco's efforts by announcing he favored the "free break-
fast table." [27]

Throughout most of March and April, both houses of Congress
debated the possibility of including coffee in the new tariff. During those months Nabuco kept the cables busy between Washington and Rio de Janeiro, informing an anxious Rio-Branco of the
details of the debates.[28] By the end of April, Nabuco learned, much
to his relief, that coffee would not be included in the new tariff.
Indeed, when the President promulgated the tariff on August 6,
1909, it gave free entry not only to coffee but also to cocoa, rubber,
and hides. To a great extent, Brazil owed her victory to the inde-
fatigable efforts of Nabuco to protect his country's interests. His
task was made considerably easier thanks to the influence, understanding, and good offices of Root, Knox, and Taft, who favored
a generous tariff policy toward Brazil in the name of friendship.[29]

A couple of years later Brazilian coffee faced a second threat in
the United States. In September, 1911, the office of the Attorney-
General, after a lengthy investigation, issued a report stating that
coffee held in the United States under the valorization scheme
was in restraint of trade. The purpose of storing the valorized
coffee was to keep it off the market until the price rose. Since the

Ambassador Joaquim Nabuco

United States consumed about 950 million pounds of coffee every year, each penny increase per pound would cost the American consumer about ten million dollars, and the valorization plan already had raised the price of coffee more than six cents a pound.[30]

Because of those transactions, the Attorney-General filed a suit against the "coffee trust" in the United States. The Brazilian ambassador protested, and the American ambassador in Rio de Janeiro pointed out that the suit would have unfavorable consequences for American business in Brazil. The two governments came to a mutually satisfactory compromise in which the United States agreed to drop the suit if Brazil would sell on the open market before April 1, 1913, the valorized coffee stored in New York.[31] The satisfactory solution of the second crisis for Brazilian coffee did not occur until after the death of Rio-Branco.

Rubber did not fare as well as coffee either in the North American market or under Rio-Branco's commercial policy. When the price of rubber began to decline, after reaching its maximum in April, 1910, the Amazonians blamed the United States, the largest importer of rubber, for their economic reverses.[32] The First Commercial, Industrial, and Agricultural Congress of the Amazon, which met in Manaus in 1910, urged, with unheeded pleas, that the federal government take the same interest in rubber it took in coffee. The federal government, closely allied with the coffee interests, had no commitments to or interests in the rubber merchants of the north. Rio-Branco, because of the rubber gatherers, successfully based Brazil's territorial claims in the Amazon on *uti possidetis*,[33] but he never showed any inclination to reward the rubber *bandeirantes* by supporting their commercial interests abroad. Perhaps he had sufficient commercial insight to see that coffee could be helped but that rubber was doomed on the world market because of the efficient and economical plantation system in Asia. Events proved that when the government halfheartedly came to the aid of the rubber barons, shortly following the Rio-Branco ministry, there was nothing that could be done in the face of that Asian competition.

While Brazil's commercial goal was to maintain its favored position in the North American market, the aim of the United States commercial policy toward Brazil during the Rio-Branco ministry was to obtain tariff benefits for American products. That aim was not new. For many years the State Department had kept up a campaign in Rio de Janeiro to persuade the Brazilian government to modify its restrictive tariff policy.[34] The importance of the United States as a market for nearly half of its products failed to convince the Brazilian government that it should change its tariff policies in favor of Yankee merchants. However, after Rio-Branco took charge of the Ministry of Foreign Relations, Brazil showed indications of modifying its tariff policy toward its best customer.

Rio-Branco appeared to be sympathetic to the commercial importunities of the North American diplomats.[35] At least he listened attentively and nodded appreciatively to their arguments. What is important, he promised to take some action. It was due principally to his pressure that the Tariff Committee in 1903 did not discuss a proposed 60 percent increase of duty on flour, an item the United States long had sought to have on a free list.[36] The Brazilian presidents and ministers of finance of that period also tended to be sympathetic to American requests.[37] Congress, on the other hand, was a fortress of protectionism, hostile to any suggestions to create a breach in the high tariff wall.[38] Not only did the tariff protect national industries but it provided a sizable share of the federal revenue, too, both cogent reasons with the Brazilian Congress for not tampering with the high tariff.

Shortly after the Senate defeated, on December 27, 1903, the government-proposed tariff concessions to the United States, President Alves decided to act on his own. As had been customary in the annual budget law, Congress routinely authorized the president to make tariff concessions, a power unused until then. Giving as his reason that the United States "is the greatest importer of coffee, which enters its markets free of duties,"[39] the president, by decree on April 16, 1904, granted a 20 percent tariff reduction on wheat flour, condensed milk, rubber manufactures, clocks, watches, varnishes, and paints from the United States. Rio-Branco hailed the decree as proof of the government's "good will in maintaining, improving, and continually developing the commercial relations between Brazil and the United States of America,"[40] but confided later that any "new concessions would produce a violent revolt of opinion."[41] In other words, Brazil had done as much as possible at the time to reciprocate the liberality of American tariff laws.

Within Brazil, the reaction to the president's decree was unfavorable. Not only was Congress hostile to the concessions, but the newspapers and public opinion opposed them also.[42] The principal argument against the concessions was that Brazil had granted the United States an economic advantage without receiving one in return. Brazilians did not consider the free entry of coffee into the United States as a favor.[43] Editorial comment in the *Gazeta de Notícias* summarized opinion as follows:

We have constantly maintained . . . equality of treatment to all countries. We should only depart from that line of conduct in view of positive and undisputed compensations. And it is advisable not to forget that . . . our system of revenues is based on customs receipts.

In the concession to the United States . . . we have reduced our duties 20 percent and have received no compensation. Perhaps it will be said that the United States might decree a duty on coffee, which now enters duty free. Such an action would be met by the resistance of the commercial groups in the United States before we would have time to protest. . . .

As a business transaction we must confess that this concession does not represent the ideal for Brazil and for the interest of Brazilians.[44]

No editorials appeared in Rio de Janeiro favoring the tariff concessions.[45] Minister Thompson blamed the poor newspaper reception on subsidies paid by the English flour mills to the editors.[46] The diplomatic corps did not remain silent in the face of those concessions to the United States.[47] Seven governments sent their official protests to Itamaraty.[48]

The pleasure of the United States government with the concessions was short-lived. They expired on December 15, less than nine months after their promulgation, and Congress withdrew the privilege previously given the president to grant tariff preferentials. Commercial relations returned to the *status quo ante* April, 1904, and the Department of State doubled its efforts to persuade the Brazilian government to make some tariff concessions.[49] Rio-Branco told the American minister that he and the Minister of Finance had done everything possible to maintain the concessions but that the protectionist sentiment, particularly in the Chamber of Deputies, "obliged of the Government the relinquishing of the concessions much to its painful surprise." [50] In keeping with the spirit of better and closer relations, the Brazilian administration continued to exert pressure on Congress to enact a bill reducing the import duties on certain articles of American manufacture.[51] Within the Chamber of Deputies, Dr. Ignácio Tosta, an influential member of the Finance Committee, lent his support to those efforts.[52]

The turning point in Brazil's attitude toward a tariff policy in favor of the United States came after Secretary of State Elihu Root announced his intention to visit Brazil in 1906. Those days marked the apogee of Brazilian-American friendship, and the Brazilian Congress played its role well. In early July, 1906, a new Brazilian tariff preferential granted 20 percent reduction on flour, rubber manufactures, dyes, varnishes, watches, clocks, condensed milk, typewriters, pianos, scales, windmills, inks, and ice boxes from the United States. Rio-Branco welcomed the concessions as the solidi-

fication of commercial bonds between the two nations appropri-
ately made on the eve of Root's visit.[53]

During his visit and immediately thereafter, Root showed a lively
concern for the trade relations between the two nations. In the
world's busiest coffee port, Santos, he reminded his audience that
the United States bought most of Brazil's coffee but sold only a
small amount of its products to Brazil. He stated the American
case frankly and diplomatically:

I should like to see the trade more even; I should like to see the
prosperity of Brazil so increased that the purchasing power of Brazil
shall grow; and I should like to see the activity of the purchasing power
turned towards the markets of the North American Republic.[54]

Shortly after returning to the United States, the Secretary of State
made another foreign trade speech, addressed to businessmen gathered in Kansas City, in which he called for closer commercial relations between the United States and Latin America and an improvement in transportation and communication between the two
areas. His optimistic statements and hopes, reported in the Latin
American press, made a favorable impression upon the Brazilian
administration.[55]

Once the precedent of tariff concessions had been established, it
became easier to renew them annually. They were maintained
throughout the remainder of the Rio-Branco ministry.[56] In 1910,
apparently as a grateful response to the free entrance of coffee
under the Payne-Aldrich Tariff of 1909, the Brazilian Congress
further authorized a 20 percent tariff reduction on cement, dried
fruit, furniture for schools, corsets, and desks. In the following
year duties on flour were reduced by 30 percent owing to the
efforts of the Baron's protégé and confidant in Itamaraty, Enéas
Martins.[57] Public opinion had become much more tolerant of the
tariff concessions by then so that the often antigovernment *Correio
da Manhã* could editorialize in favor of the concessions:

The United States is an excellent customer of Brazil. It is not only buys our coffee but our cocoa, sugar, and tobacco. . . . Statistics show that each year it becomes a better customer. . . . It is clear that we have the task of guaranteeing our consumer markets in the United States.[58]

The best way of guaranteeing those markets was to make some tariff concessions to North American businessmen, and that is what Brazil did.

Contrary to American hopes, the tariff concessions did not measurably increase exports to Brazil.[59] Increased freight rates canceled any advantages of the tariff preferential for flour.[60] American flour had difficulty competing with cheap Argentine flour in southern Brazil and found competition very stiff in northern Brazil.[61] No appreciable increase in United States imports into Brazil was noted until 1911 when Vice-Consul J. J. Slechta reported:

With reference to other preferential favored products, special attention is called to the considerable increases in imports of clocks and watches, prepared paints, rubber manufactures, scales, pianos, and typewriters. The increases in these articles aggregated about $250,000, which, together with the phenomenal increase in flour imports, makes a net gain of $1,250,000 in the imports of goods on which a preferential is granted.[62]

It took several years, then, before the tariff preferentials began to show any effects; even so, the increase was modest. Nonetheless, the United States jealously guarded her favored position in the Brazilian market,[63] and throughout the Rio-Branco period maintained its monopoly as the only nation receiving tariff reductions.[64]

One of the principal reasons for the lack of firm commercial ties was the fact that North American businesses were not prepared to export in quantity to Brazil, nor, for that matter, to any part of South America. One North American, amazed at the potential of the Brazilian market as well as at America's failure to take advantage of it, believed that exports of the United States to Brazil could not hope to equal those of Great Britain or Germany as long as the Americans had no steamship transportation, linguists, agents, agencies, or banks in Brazil.[65] Indeed, there appeared to be a surprising commercial indifference on the part of North American business toward Brazil[66]—despite the enthusiastic preaching of a handful of North Americans who saw a commercial El Dorado in the sprawling republic.[67] During the period of Rio-Branco's ministry, no American, despite the persistent efforts of the State Department to get tariff concessions, acted on the advice of those business prophets.

Steamship service between Brazil and the United States remained in the hands of Europeans. Almost all freight and passengers between the ports of the two republics were carried by British and German ships which made the triangular trade between South America, North America, and Europe. Brazil opened a direct steamship service with New York in 1906 and deplored the fact that no American steamship company existed to take advantage of and encourage the trade.[68] As late as 1911, not one steamship and only five sailing ships flying the Stars and Stripes entered a Brazilian port. The following year eleven American steamships and seven sailing ships called at Brazilian ports.[69] Dependent on foreign vessels to carry his products, the American exporter was also subject to the whims and rates of their European owners. In more than one case, the foreign steamship lines, by charging higher rates, nullified the tariff reduction the Brazilian government gave American products.[70] What was true of transportation between the United States and Brazil also was valid for communications. There was no direct telegraphic communication, and messages had to be routed either via Europe or Argentina.[71]

Other factors compounded the commercial stagnation. The American colony in Brazil was small,[72] and had no American bank to serve its needs until 1915, when the National City Bank of New

York City established two branches in Brazil.[73] That was a slow start considering that in 1904 there were three English and two Italian banks in Rio de Janeiro, plus one German, one French, and one Portuguese bank.[74] In the same year the American bank branches opened, an American Chamber of Commerce for Brazil was established in the Brazilian capital.[75] Until World War I, American investments in Brazil were practically nil.[76]

Throughout the Rio-Branco period, United States–Brazilian reciprocal trade was extremely limited. The United States bought large amounts of Brazilian coffee, rubber, and cocoa, but the transactions were handled through European banks and by European transportation companies. The United States had few facilities to market its products in Brazil despite the limited trade preference which the Brazilian government conceded. The Brazilians favored closer commercial exchange with the United States,[77] but only a handful of American governmental officials and businessmen saw the potential of that South American market. Possibly Ambassador da Gama, in a conversation with Senator Isidor Rayner of Maryland, correctly analyzed the situation when he stated:

Without American business houses, without American steamship companies, without American banks, without American enterprises, without American capital entering into competition with the capital of other nations, long established and patiently employed among us, American industry and commerce cannot hope to open markets in Brazil with the intervention of the State Department alone.[78]

That commentary accurately summed up the situation of American business in Brazil during the Rio-Branco ministry. It would take a world war and the consequent dislocation of trade with Europe to awaken the American business community to the Brazilian market.[79]

But from the Brazilian point of view, commercial relations were nearly perfect. Brazil's chief exports entered the lucrative American market at ever increasing volume, and a dollar surplus building up in Rio de Janeiro permitted the purchase of a wide variety of European goods. Dependence on the American importer, however, pulled Brazil closer to its giant neighbor in the north. Brazil's new diplomatic policies reflected that situation.

CHAPTER IV · FROM SUSPICION
TO FRIENDSHIP, 1902–1906

To STRENGTHEN the friendship between Brazil and the United States was one of the basic objectives of Rio-Branco's foreign policy. Building upon existent foundations, the foreign minister succeeded in diplomatically aligning the two nations. His ministry marks the apogee in their friendly relations.

THE ACRE DISPUTE

Before Rio-Branco could pursue a policy of approximation with the United States, it was necessary to clear the air of any suspicion or potential strife which the Bolivian Syndicate might cause. Only after diminishing those tensions could Brazil implement a positive policy of friendship.

Investments of American citizens complicated the imbroglio between Bolivia and Brazil over Acre. In a last desperate effort to save Acre, Bolivia's minister to Great Britain, Félix Aramayo, devised a plan to lease the territory to a foreign company. Bolivia hoped that a prosperous foreign company would be able to settle and to hold in its name the Amazonian territory it claimed. To achieve that goal, Minister Aramayo signed a contract in London on July 11, 1902, with Frederick Willingford Whitridge of Wall Street, New York City, the representative of the newly formed Bolivian Syndicate. Similar in many ways to the contracts under which foreign companies worked in Asia and Africa, the Bolivian Syndicate's contract gave the entrepreneurs power to administer, police, and exploit Acre. In effect, Bolivia surrendered to the syndicate all but the most nominal and theoretical authority over the heartland of South America. Given control for thirty years, with the option of another thirty years, the syndicate could exercise almost total sovereignty over Acre.[1]

The contract between Bolivia and the syndicate surprised the Brazilian government. The first word Brazil received of the impending negotiations was a telegram from Minister Assis Brasil in Washington dated March 7, 1901.[2] When questioned about the reports of the contract the Bolivian government denied them. Brazil confronted a *fait accompli* when the contract was made public. Later, a newspaper confessed that the "Yankees" had "surprised" the government when the generous contract was signed.[3]

Brazil reacted unfavorably to the Bolivian Syndicate. Anti-American editorials and cartoons filled the newspapers[4] and caused North American periodicals to comment on the hostile attitude which the syndicate had aroused in Brazil.[5] A diplomatic dispatch informed the Secretary of State of the "symptoms of great alarm and ill feeling toward the United States" which the Brazilian government, press, and people manifested.[6] A highly respected Latin Americanist and diplomat, William I. Buchanan, summed up the causes for Brazil's reaction when he commented:

Brazilians generally . . . are disposed to feel resentful toward the American syndicate which seeks to establish a dominion with extraordinary commercial powers on the borders of Brazil and in the heart of South America. It is hard to convince them that the so-called Bolivian Syndicate, organized under a concession granted by the Bolivian government to F. W. Whitridge of New York, is a purely commercial enterprise and that the United States government has no part or interest in it.[7]

Brazilians feared the Stars and Stripes would soon follow business interests into the heart of South America. Extremists declared that the Bolivian Syndicate was "only a harmless name for a military outpost of the Yankee expansionists."[8] Latin America would not easily forget the lessons of Texas and Puerto Rico. Indeed, the entrance of North American capitalists into the Acre question added a new complication, and an unpleasant one, for the Brazilians whose boundaries in that area were still undefined. Brazil was confident it could deal successfully alone with its neighbor. However, Bolivia allied to American capital protected by the United States government presented a threat.

Both the Bolivian government and the syndicate sought the support of the United States government in Acre. Bolivia, as early as 1900, evidenced a desire to receive the moral if not physical support of the United States for its claims.[9] Since the American government was becoming increasingly involved in the protection of its citizens' investments abroad, Bolivia reasoned that the syndicate would serve as a guarantee of North American intervention in favor of the contract and in support of American investors, especially since one of them was W. E. Roosevelt, the President's cousin. The Brazilian minister in La Paz reported repeatedly and at length to Itamaraty that the Bolivian government counted on the intervention, direct or indirect, of Washington in Acre, and he pointed out the dangers to Brazil of such an occurrence.[10] Secretary of State John M. Hay mentioned to Minister Assis Brasil that Bolivia had requested the good offices of the United States as a means of protection against the aggressions of a stronger Brazil.[11] Hay also mentioned that American interests were involved in Acre.[12] The syndicate, counting among its shareholders many politically influential men, also entertained similar hopes of support by the Department of State.[13]

Toward the syndicate the State Department took the position that American citizens who had invested their money in good faith in the enterprise ought to have their investments protected. Prior to receiving any instruction from Washington, Minister Charles Page Bryan informed the Brazilian government in early May of

1902 that his government had no interest in the controversies between other nations of the Western Hemisphere but that the rights and interests of American citizens "wherever" and "whatever" had to be "protected." [14] Shortly thereafter, the Secretary of State telegraphed to Bryan instructions which expressed neutrality in the disputed question between Bolivia and Brazil but called for "proper consideration for the interest of American citizens whose rights may be affected." [15] In reply, Bryan assured Hay that he had used "firm language" with the Brazilian Minister of Foreign Relations and had notified him that American interests in Acre would be "vigilantly watched and resolutely protected by us." [16] That undefined commitment to protect American capital in Acre was exactly what Bolivia and the syndicate desired.

From Washington, Minister Assis Brasil confirmed the words of the American minister in Rio de Janeiro. His reports repeated Hay's insistence on neutrality in the boundary dispute.[17] At the same time, he reported that the State Department was following with interest the treatment of "innocent" American capital which had been legally invested.[18] In statements somewhat milder and more explicit than those of Bryan, Hay told him that the American government would intervene to protect the interests and investments of is citizens only if justice were denied to them.[19] Assis Brasil thought Hay appeared reluctant to condemn chartered companies, because the Americans had an interest in obtaining from Colombia broad privileges similar to those of a chartered company to build a canal.[20] The conclusions Itamaraty could draw from its minister's dispatches from Washington were consistent with statements made in Rio de Janeiro by the American minister: the United States would not intervene in the boundary dispute between two South American nations but would maintain a lively interest in the treatment of the investments of its citizens. Left undefined were the measures the United States was willing to take to protect the "innocent" investments of its citizens in Acre. That unknown factor disquieted the Brazilian government and called for a prudent diplomatic policy.

For some time, the Baron had understood the threat posed by the alliance of Bolivia with foreign capital. While minister to Germany, he received reports from Assis Brasil detailing the syndicate's activities in the United States.[21] In Germany, he was successful in halting the syndicate's efforts to recruit capitalists.[22] He also kept track of its activities in England, France, and Belgium. His first task as foreign minister was to define and execute a policy which would eliminate the syndicate from the Amazon without alienating the United States. To achieve that goal, he evolved a three-step plan.

First, he determined to continue the prohibition of free navigation of the Amazon to the Acre territory proclaimed by the Minister of Finance in a circular dated August 8, 1902. Brazil's nineteenth-century declaration of free navigation did not include the rivers penetrating Acre, which had been opened to international navigation only on the tolerance of Brazil.[23] The United States delayed its only protest, extremely mild in tone, until mid-January of 1903. The note of protest invited the attention of Rio-Branco to the hardship the prohibition caused North American business interests in eastern Bolivia and expressed the hope that the decree soon would be rescinded.[24] Great Britain, France, and Germany protested the closing of the upper Amazon more loudly.[25] Rio-Branco sustained the policy despite foreign protests. The prohibition was Brazil's strongest weapon against the syndicate because without access to Acre—and the Amazon was the only practical entrance—the concession was worthless. The Bolivian Syndicate possessed vast powers in Acre but they proved useless if it had no means of communicating with its domain.

The second part of the policy was to enlist American sympathy for the Brazilian cause. Rio-Branco pointed out to the American government the illegality of Bolivia's concessions. It had leased territory whose boundaries were undefined and whose ownership was questionable and in litigation among Bolivia, Peru, and Brazil.[26] Furthermore, Bolivia ceded part of her sovereign powers to a foreign company, at very best a dubious practice in international law. Such a concession introduced into South America charter companies, "monstrosities of law" found in Africa and Asia but "unworthy" of the American continent.[27] To buttress those arguments, the foreign minister sought the advice of an old friend, the eminent international lawyer, John Bassett Moore, of Columbia University. As a paid consultant, Moore supported Brazil's position in Acre and contributed legal arguments to its case.[28]

Rio-Branco evoked the Monroe Doctrine in a further effort to obtain American sympathy for Brazil's position. He pointed out to the American minister in Rio that the syndicate violated the Monroe Doctrine.[29] Composed of foreigners, Europeans as well as Americans, the syndicate posed a threat to continental security because there was always the possibility that it might come under German or British control. Assis Brasil conversed with Hay on the same subject.[30] The Brazilian diplomat noted that in later conversations the Monroe Doctrine argument seemed to impress the Department of State. Under Secretary of State Francis B. Loomis "leaked" to the press statements from their conversations concerning the danger that "the admission of chartered companies in South America would lead to a partition of that continent among European countries." [31] Thereafter, the Monroe Doctrine became one of the principal and most cogent arguments against the Bolivian Syndicate. Salvador de Mendonça perhaps was a little harsh in his judgment, but not incorrect, when he observed that Rio-Branco was willing to use the "prestige of Washington" to obtain Acre for Brazil.[32]

The third step in Rio-Branco's policy was to buy out the Bolivian Syndicate in order to rid South America of its potential menace.

The idea was not a sudden or a new one. The former Minister of Foreign Relations, Olynto de Magalhães, had spoken to the Bolivian minister in Rio de Janeiro about such a project.[33] When Assis Brasil suggested to Hay in October, 1902, that Brazil might refund the money invested by the Bolivian Syndicate, the Secretary of State indicated his approval of the idea.[34] A month later Assis Brasil informed Itamaraty that the syndicate agreed to the idea and that the price would be less than a million dollars.[35] Whatever the cost, Assis Brasil felt the money would be well spent to get the syndicate out of South America. Rio-Branco concurred and took steps toward refunding the syndicate's investments in order to eliminate it from the Amazon and to satisfy the State Department's requirement of protecting the "innocent" rights of American investors.[36]

Faced with an increasingly effective Brazilian campaign against its existence, the Bolivian Syndicate despaired. Unable to reach Acre by the Amazon, the company was never able to send its agents there. The syndicate hoped that diplomatic pressure from the United States would force Brazil to open the Amazon, but the State Department's protest was tardy and mild. The syndicate never succeeded in getting approval or support from the American government. Even so, hope did not die easily, and Mr. Whitridge sought a last-minute miracle of intervention. Assis Brasil's major task was to prove to the Bolivian Syndicate that the State Department would not come to its aid.[37] In a moment of discouragement, Whitridge admitted to him that the American government was not disposed to support the Bolivian Syndicate and that Hay had never committed himself to help.[38]

The strategy of Rio-Branco to keep the syndicate and the State Department separated was working well. He knew that the American government's only interest was in seeing that the investors received a just compensation. He also knew that in the last analysis the syndicate would accept an indemnification in return for its contract.[39] Furthermore, he realized that poverty-striken Bolivia could not indemnify the company. The logical conclusion was for Brazil to assume Bolivia's responsibility and to repay the investors.

Cognizant of the diplomatic maneuvers and discouraged by the attitude of the Department of State, Whitridge decided to sell the company's investments in Acre to Brazil. In mid-February of 1903, Whitridge asked Assis Brasil if he had instructions to negotiate.[40] He did, and on February 26 Whitridge agreed to sell the syndicate's rights for $550,000. Assis Brasil telegraphed to Rio-Branco that the syndicate wanted its money at once and it would renounce the contract.[41] The financial arrangements were made through London and the investors received their money on March 10. At that time, Assis Brasil and Whitridge signed the agreement which terminated the Bolivian Syndicate.[42]

As soon as Rio-Branco foresaw the inevitable demise of the syndicate, he reopened the Amazon to international traffic to Bolivia. On February 20, 1903, he informed the American minister:

The situation that obligated the adoption of that expedient has now changed; and therefore, since the Federal Government is desirous of attending as promptly as possible to the interests of commerce, it has, by a decision of this date, reestablished free transit on the Amazon for merchandise between Bolivia and foreign countries.[43]

Both the American and European governments welcomed that announcement.

With the Bolivian Syndicate out of the picture, Rio-Branco could turn his full attention to the boundary dispute with Bolivia. One of his objectives had been to isolate Bolivia from any hope it might have of favorable American intervention which the existence of the syndicate nurtured.[44] With the syndicate gone, Bolivia despaired of receiving any support.[45] As a consequence, shortly thereafter the two governments signed the Treaty of Petrópolis.

After the signing of the treaty, an anonymous **pamphlet** appeared in the United States entitled *Brazil and Bolivia Boundary Settlement*.[46] The object of this publication seemed to be to show Americans that Acre now belonged to Brazil and was no longer open to adventurers. Rio-Branco had closed South America to foreign chartered companies.

A comparison of the contents of diplomatic archives in Washington and Rio de Janeiro with the actions of the two governments reveals that both the United States and Brazil treated openly with each other in the case of the Bolivian Syndicate. The State Department informed Itamaraty on several occasions that Bolivia had requested its support in the boundary question. Furthermore, Minister Thompson mentioned to Rio-Branco that Peru was beginning to solicit American support for its case in the Acre dispute.[47] Affirming it would not intervene in the boundary disputes, the State Department denied any intention of mediating the controversies unless all the parties involved requested such mediation.[48] Rio-Branco appreciated the frank attitude of the American government and counseled Assis Brasil to listen carefully to any advice that the American government might give concerning the Acre boundary dispute.[49] As a matter of fact, he expressed the hope that the United States would be willing to serve as an arbiter if the Acre boundary dispute were ever to come to arbitration.[50]

When the Yankee scare which accompanied the Baron's first months in office ended, the tense atmosphere evaporated and with it most of the Brazilian suspicions of North American intentions in the Amazon. The way became clear for the improvement of relations between the two largest republics of the hemisphere. Rio-Branco took the first positive step toward increasing Brazil's friendship with the United States.

It is not easy to explain his preference for the United States because his education, training, and tastes inclined him toward Europe. Indeed, he chose to travel in Europe as a youth and enjoyed his many years there, particularly in France, as a diplomat. However, sentimental attachments seemed not to have blinded him to diplomatic *Realpolitik* and to the emergence of the United States as a new world power. From youth, Rio-Branco had read North American history and fancied himself well versed in its military history.[51] His first and only visit to the United States was in 1893–95, when he headed the Brazilian delegation in the Missions dispute. During that time he visited New York, Washington, Chicago, and several smaller cities and became acquainted with some governmental leaders. He left no written impressions of or reactions to the United States, and so it is difficult to ascertain his precise feelings, although indications are they were favorable.[52] It is certain that he was gratified that Cleveland awarded Brazil the territorial victory over Argentina, a double pleasure for him because, in addition to the victory for Brazil, it raised him to the rank of a national figure in his homeland. Brazilians who knew him personally or who have studied his policies tend to concur that his residence in and firsthand knowledge of the United States and Cleveland's award in the Missions dispute favorably oriented him toward the United States.[53]

There were perhaps two more reasons for him to be friendly to the United States. He believed that the firm attitude of the United States in favor of arbitration in the Venezuelan–British Guiana boundary controversy in 1895 persuaded France to arbitrate the Amapá dispute rather than to occupy the area militarily. Once submitted to arbitration, Amapá provided Rio-Branco with another brilliant victory. Finally, the hands-off policy of the United States in the Acre dispute built up the chancellor's confidence in the United States and caused him to be friendlier than he might otherwise have been. The combined result of residency in the United States, the Missions award, the indirect support for arbitration of the Amapá dispute, and the hands-off policy in Acre was to dispose him to manifest and express certain pro-American sentiments which were reflected in Brazil's foreign policy.

Rio-Branco's friendliness toward the United States was extremely significant because he had received carte blanche to direct Brazil's foreign policy as he wished. As Rodrigues Alves had promised him, the Ministry of Foreign Relations remained outside of partisan politics. Without any undue extraneous pressures, the popular and influential Baron, recognizing a general trend under way, used his powerful office to complete the change of emphasis in Brazilian diplomacy from Europe to the United States.[54] His goal was for Brazil to imitate the success of the United States and at its side to exercise considerable influence in the world.[55]

His first step toward strengthening relations with Washington was to ratify an extradition treaty of 1897. The exchange of ratifications that took place in April of 1903 was significant as the beginning of a period of positive action aimed at the solidification of friendship. The Baron proved the value of his friendship in the Panama crisis later that year.

THE RECOGNITION OF PANAMA

When Panama rebelled against Colombia and proclaimed its independence on November 3, 1903, world attention focused on the Isthmus. The involvement of the United States in that event was well known, and ten days after the uprising the United States recognized the new state. France extended recognition to Panama on November 18. Recognition by those two major powers ensured Panama's independence.

As tension subsided in Panama, an important question left unanswered was the reaction of the other Latin American nations. Many of these countries had fought separatist movements sometime in the nineteenth century. Mexico had its Yucatan, Guatemala its Los Altos, Ecuador its Guayaquil. Brazil had been particularly susceptible to regional independence movements. The Confederation of the Equator in the northeast and the Ragmuffin Revolt in the south were classic examples. For that reason the United States was apprehensive that Latin America would not accept its new protégé.

Brazilians were fully cognizant of the unfolding drama on the Isthmus. News of the revolt first appeared in the Brazilian newspapers on November 5, and for the next few weeks the journals carried a detailed coverage of the birth of Panama. In long dispatches, Gomes Ferreira, serving as chargé d'affaires in Washington, reported the events to Itamaraty.[56] On November 15, Minister Thompson called on Rio-Branco to inform him of the course of events and of the recognition accorded by the United States.[57] The Brazilian consul in Panama City also reported on the revolution as well as United States and French recognition. He requested instructions to govern his actions.[58]

Brazilian reaction to Panama's independence was generally favorable. Most of the newspapers either commented dispassionately on the course of events or supported the new republic. As early as November 30, the opposition newspaper, *Correio da Manhã,* approved the independence of Panama and the position of the United States and urged the Brazilian government to recognize the newest addition to the Latin American community.[59] The American minister thought the article was significant because it gave the opposition's approval to formal recognition.[60] Public opinion in general seemed indifferent to developments on the distant isthmus, and criticism of the role played by the United States in the revolt was minimal.[61]

Unfavorable reaction to Panama's independence or to the methods by which it was achieved could have inhibited Brazilian-American friendship. Rio-Branco, apparently aware of this danger, gave every indication of using the incident as a means of revealing his friendly intentions toward the United States. He confided to Thompson on November 20 that Brazil would be glad to recognize Panama upon receipt of such a request through traditional channels. He added that his government "heartily" approved of the action of the United

States in the matter.[62] A few days later, President Alves made public his reply to the Colombian president's request for support. It was formal and cool, and counseled Colombia to seek a peaceful solution to its problem.[63]

Perhaps another reason for the approval of the Republic of Panama was the advantage the Brazilians hoped to derive from the projected canal. The union of the Atlantic and Pacific oceans would shorten the maritime distance between the west coast of the United States and Brazilian ports. The Brazilian imagination envisaged an increasing trade over that route. Some thought they foresaw the exchange of California vegetables for tropical fruits and coffee.[64]

In Washington, the recently received Panamanian minister, Philippe Bunau-Varilla, wrote the Brazilian chargé d'affaires on November 27, requesting the recognition of his government.[65] All negotiations concerning Brazil's recognition of Panama were handled through the legations of these two governments in Washington. Rio-Branco informed his diplomatic agent in the American capital that Panama was undeniably independent now and that the best Colombia could hope for would be Panama's assumption of a fair share of the debts.[66]

Rio-Branco consulted with the ministers of foreign relations of Argentina and Chile in order to coordinate the recognition of Panama.[67] At his suggestion, the ABC governments agreed to act jointly after receiving a formal request for recognition. He instructed Gomes Ferreira to inform both Bunau-Varilla and Secretary of State Hay of this decision.[68] According, the Brazilian chargé d'affaires related the news to Minister Bunau-Varilla. Then, Gomes Ferreira spoke with Under Secretary of State Loomis, whom he assured that the ABC nations entertained no intention of forming a league to counter the influence of the United States in Panama.[69] Meanwhile, the Baron had telegraphed his Colombian counterpart to affirm Brazil's desire for friendly relations and to point out that Panama's independence was now an established fact. He counseled the Colombian government not to fight to regain its former department.[70]

While Brazil was coordinating its recognition with that of Argentina and Chile, Peru became the first Latin American country to recognize the new republic. By a letter dated December 18, 1903, Foreign Minister José Pardo informed the Minister of Foreign Relations of Panama of his government's decision.[71] Cuba, Costa Rica, Nicaragua, Guatemala, and Venezuela followed Peru's lead.[72]

After informing the Panamanian government in late December that the ABC powers awaited a letter from the provisional government officially announcing the proclamation of independence, Itamaraty could do nothing but wait. The Panamanian government complied with the formality on January 2, 1904. But the journey from Panama City to Rio de Janeiro was long. The letter went first to the Panamanian legation in Washington, where it was given to the Department of State for delivery to the American legation in Rio de Janeiro, since American legations were authorized to handle Panamanian matters.[73] Thompson delivered the letter to Rio-Branco on February 9.[74]

On receipt of the letter, Rio-Branco telegraphed Buenos Aires and Santiago in order to set a mutually agreeable date for joint recognition, which, at its own request, would include the participation of the Mexican government.[75] Argentina delayed its response to the Baron's request,[76] so that on February 29 Rio-Branco announced to the Plata government that Mexico, Chile, and Brazil would extend joint recognition on March 1,[77] the latest possible date on which Rio-Branco wanted to extend recognition so as not to anger the United States unnecessarily.[78] A last-minute message from Buenos Aires said Argentina would not be able to recognize Panama until March 2.[79] Chile and Mexico went ahead with their plans on March 1; Brazil did likewise on the second; and a further delay in Argentina prevented it from cabling recognition until March 3.

Itamaraty had been ready to welcome the new republic since early December of 1903, but the Baron decided it would be more correct to wait until an official request from Panama had been received and then to coordinate recognition with Argentina and Chile. Those purely administrative delays did not reflect any reservations about the independence of Panama. As Gomes Ferreira, Thompson, and Rio-Branco all informed Secretary of State Hay, Brazil was anxious to demonstrate its friendship toward the United States by the prompt recognition of Panama. The American minister testified in the following manner to the favorable attitude of Rio-Branco toward the American policy:

He spoke quite at length of the attitude of Brazil in matters in which our country was interested, notably Panama, and expressed himself as feeling that the best thing had been done in all controversies in which our Government had been interested.[80]

Brazil's attitude pleased the United States, which was eager to have Panama welcomed into the family of nations.[81]

SETTLEMENT OF THE PERUVIAN-BRAZILIAN CONTROVERSY

Later the same year, the good will of the United States toward Brazil proved its practicality when Minister Thompson ended a stalemate between Rio-Branco and Peruvian Minister Hernán Velarde. The renewed conversations which Thompson established enabled the two nations to settle their dispute in the conference room rather than on the battlefields of Acre.

When Bolivia withdrew from the Acre controversy in 1903, Brazil and Peru remained as claimants of the same area and faced each other across a vague and disputed frontier. Both desired a settlement but neither was willing to cede territory to the other. The area at stake was larger in size than Spain, rich in rubber, and included all the gains Brazil achieved in the Treaty of Petrópolis. Hence, Rio-Branco attributed great importance to the boundary dispute with Peru.[82]

Against Peru alone, the Baron was confident of victory, but if Lima succeeded in obtaining support for its cause from the Department of State, he realized Peru would be a more determined and difficult opponent.[83] Again it was necessary to scrutinize events in Washington because decisions important for Acre could be made there. More and more Rio-Branco realized that Washington was South America's diplomatic battleground. In Washington, Peru sought to strengthen its position against its larger neighbor by obtaining the moral support of the United States. Brazilians considered Peru's quick recognition of Panama as one attempt to court the favor of the United States.[84] Lima, in Rio-Branco's opinion, was intriguing to convey the impression that the United States was friendlier to Peru than to any other South American nation.[85] Such a close association, if it existed or was believed to exist, would add considerable moral power to Peru's case. The *Jornal do Commercio,* always closely linked to the Ministry of Foreign Relations, published accounts of the frequent visits of Peruvian Minister Alvarez Calderón to Secretary of State Hay, and accused Peru of trying to disturb Brazilian-American relations.[86] Cognizant of Peru's maneuvers, Itamaraty determined to counter them. It was necessary to be extremely attentive to the intrigues of the Peruvians there, Rio-Branco warned his diplomatic representative in Washington.[87] One of his objectives was to prevent intimately friendly relations between the United States and Peru.[88]

He thought that the United States would not encourage Peruvian ambitions in the Amazon despite Peruvian boasting to the contrary.[89] However, to be certain the chancellor sought some sort of assurance from Washington. After several conferences with State Department officials, Gomes Ferreira telegraphed Rio-Branco twice to advise that official American policy was "perfect impartiality." [90]

Later, in a longer report, he confirmed that the United States would look upon the new dispute in the Amazon "with the same spirit of impartiality" that it had observed in the past.[91] Although occasionally nervous about possible American interference, the Baron trusted the expressed neutrality of the Department of State. Some weeks later the *Jornal do Commercio* announced confidently, "The American Government will not intervene. . . . The Peruvian intrigues will not have the success here that Lima hoped for." [92]

Although professedly neutral, the Department of State maintained an active interest in the Peruvian-Brazilian parleys in Rio de Janeiro. Washington desired to see a peaceful solution of the dispute.

When those discussions came to a sudden halt in early May because of the heated words and questionable actions of Velarde, Minister Thompson served as the agent through whom arrangements were made to recommence the talks. From Washington, which was kept informed by the Peruvian diplomatic agent there, as well as from Minister Velarde, Thompson received information about Lima's position and desire to reach an amicable settlement.[93] Thompson learned of Brazil's position directly from the Baron.[94] Thus informed, Thompson was a convenient and trusted messenger between the two South American diplomats. Velarde mentioned to Thompson that Peru was ready to come to an agreement and hinted that he would be pleased to confer again with Rio-Branco if the latter would summon him. Thompson outlined Brazil's proposals to the Peruvian and then conveyed the contents of the conversation to the Baron.[95] Later Thompson returned to Velarde with proposals from Itamaraty, and the Peruvian diplomat displayed interest in and concurrence with Rio-Branco's suggestions for a *modus vivendi*.[96] Thompson reported to Itamaraty the conversations with Velarde in the following frank manner:

My aim . . . has been to get Peru to accept your seemingly reasonable terms or conditions and the only suggestions I have made to Mr.

Velarde have been to this end. Knowing this he asked me if an interview between you and him could be arranged and this I was pleased to undertake to do feeling that my suggestion, had it not been well thought of, the interview would not have been sought and that it was likely to lead to an understanding between your government and his.[97]

Rio-Branco was receptive to the American minister's suggestions.

Rio-Branco delayed some days (probably a tactical move) and then summoned the Peruvian minister to confer with him. On June 5 the two men reopened their negotiations, which this time progressed more smoothly. Both confided to Thompson that the interviews indicated an early preliminary agreement would be reached.[98] The result of the new discussions was the *modus vivendi* which brought peace to troubled Acre and which in the definitive settlement of 1909 became a territorial victory for Brazil.

Although the Brazilian newspapers remained silent about Minister Thompson's role in the *modus vivendi,* Rio-Branco was quick to acknowledge the American contribution. He wrote in praise:

In our dispute with Peru, the American Minister, Mr. Thompson, has acted very correctly. . . . To the Peruvian Minister he declared that the Government in Lima ought to accept the conciliatory proposition that I made on May 9, and he said that, in his opinion, the Peruvian counterproposal would be unacceptable to Brazil. As you see, Mr. Thompson, by doing justice to our moderation, created no difficulties for us. On the contrary, he pronounced himself to be frankly on our side.[99]

In that manner, Itamaraty recognized the support lent by the United States, through Minister Thompson, to its successful boundary settlement with Peru.

Before the final treaty with Peru was signed in 1909, the United States supplied another service to Rio-Branco in the person of Professor Moore, who had become a paid counselor to the Brazilian legation. Rio-Branco frequently sought his legal advice, particularly in the Acre disputes. The Baron advised Gomes Ferreira, "It is always wise in these matters to listen to Professor Moore, who can give good counsel." [100] As a significant contribution to the settlement of the dispute, the Columbia lawyer wrote a pamphlet entitled *Brazil and Peru Boundary Question,* which cogently defended Brazil's rights in the dispute with Peru.

The success in Acre brought forth charges of imperialism. From the point of view of the Spanish-American countries, the territorial growth of Brazil at their expense was a clear-cut case of the large neighbor encroaching on the smaller one. Consequently they did not hesitate to label their Portuguese-speaking neighbor an aggressor.[101] More than once Juan Bautista Alberdi, Argentine jurist and political analyst of the nineteenth century, had pointed out the danger to Spanish America posed by Brazilian expansion. In his opinion, internal unrest and political instability within the Spanish-American republics were the greatest allies of Brazil in its constant efforts to extend its boundaries. Failure of the Spanish Americans to unite, Alberdi asserted, encouraged Brazilian imperialism.[102] There was a great deal of wisdom in those observations. Had Alberdi's advice been heeded, Brazil's expansion would have been more difficult. From the Brazilian point of view, however, the demarcation of the boundaries was simply the legal recognition of the occupation by Brazilian nationals of abandoned or neglected territory in the hinterlands. The new boundary lines represented to them the reward for four centuries of Luso-Brazilian penetration into the interior of South America. Brazil never did nor does admit any validity in those Spanish-American accusations. However, their consistency and frequency make it difficult to ignore them. Furthermore, the Baron seemed to encourage those charges by close association with the other hemispheric giant accused of similar acts.

In the final settlement of the dispute in Acre, Brazil found itself cooperating with Washington. The United States, on the one hand, denied moral support to Peru and thereby weakened Peruvian morale, and, on the other hand, openly advised Velarde to accept the Brazilian proposals. This practical application of international friendship pleased the Baron and was additional evidence of the unspoken entente developing between the two nations.

THE ELEVATION OF THE LEGATIONS TO EMBASSIES

Events during the first two years of Rio-Branco's ministry demonstrated the advantages of a foreign policy oriented toward cooperation with the United States. Successfully neutralizing the United States in the controversy with Bolivia, Itamaraty achieved the agility necessary to eliminate the Bolivian Syndicate and to obtain Acre. For its part, the United States was visibly pleased with Brazil's leadership in the recognition of Panamanian independence. The promulgation of the extradition treaty, the exchange of complimentary messages, and the friendly neutrality of the United States toward Brazil in the dispute with Peru indicated the course of reciprocally amiable diplomatic relations which both nations were pursuing. The trend required, according to Rio-Branco, a diplomatic expression of the mutual satisfaction. He thought that the elevation of the legations to embassies by the American and Brazilian governments would be an appropriate demonstration of their growing friendship.

At the turn of the century, an embassy was still a diplomatic rarity found exclusively in the capitals of acknowledged world powers. Washington in 1904 counted only seven embassies,[103] Rio de Janeiro, none. The creation of an embassy in that era was a serious and significant step.

The idea of elevating the Brazilian legation in the United States received its first serious consideration during the Acre controversy. The complex intrigues of the dispute centered in the United States and revealed the need for an embassy in Washington, increasingly a focal point of hemispheric diplomacy. Minister Assis Brasil thought he could have been more effective had he been able to speak directly to President Roosevelt during the Acre crisis. Since he was not an ambassador, protocol required that he be satisfied with talking to the Secretary of State. In a long report dated February 4, 1903, he complained, "Unfortunately I cannot approach the president. Particularly since the embassies were created in this country, a humble Minister Plenipotentiary remains on a very inferior level, and those of our America are on the lowest of all." [104] He continued by indicating the advantages accruing to Brazil if it would establish an embassy in Washington. In that report he planted in the Baron's mind the idea of elevating the Washington legation to an embassy.

Convinced that it would be advantageous for the two largest republics of the hemisphere to exchange ambassadors, Rio-Branco worked to carry out the suggestion of Assis Brasil. Its accomplishment, he thought, would enhance Brazil's prestige, increase commercial exchange, and strengthen diplomatic ties.[105] The American minister to Brazil, speaking about the foreign minister's enthusiasm for the exchange of ambassadors, reported that the higher diplomatic representation signified "a desire on the part of the Administration of Brazilian affairs to court a closer relationship between the two countries." [106] Two leading Rio dailies commented on the importance of Washington in Brazilian diplomacy and on the practicality of strengthening the friendship between the two nations.[107] The chancellor had begun to classify Washington as "number one" for Brazilian diplomacy.[108] As such, it was desirable to establish an embassy there.

The first written reference to his intention to raise the Washington legation to an embassy appeared in the official *Report* of the Ministry of Foreign Relations for 1902–3. In that *Report,* he cryptically wrote:

The increase which I believe most necessary and urgent is the salary of our Minister in Washington. I think that the chief of that legation ought not to receive less than 35:000$ in gold, free of all taxes, and that it would be advisable to give the temporary commission of Ambassador to our Envoys Extraordinary when they serve there.[109]

The *Report* mentioned the subject no further, but those two sentences were sufficient to show that the suggestion of Assis Brasil had taken hold in his mind.

The next written reference to the embassy appeared on November 1, 1904, in the well-informed *Brazilian Review*, an English weekly published in Rio de Janeiro.[110] The editors limited themselves to calling the attention of their readers to the statements of the foreign minister in his annual *Report*. The American minister forwarded the article to the Department of State,[111] apparently the first information received by the American government concerning Itamaraty's desire.

Shortly thereafter, President Roosevelt visited, among others, the elaborate Brazilian pavilion at the St. Louis Fair.[112] While a military band played the national anthems of the two countries, the Brazilian delegation welcomed the jovial Roosevelt to their exhibition. The hosts presented the Chief Executive and Miss Alice Roosevelt with a variety of gifts from the states of Brazil. During the course of the visit, President Roosevelt pleased his hosts by referring to Brazil as a "great and grand nation." [113] Visibly enthusiastic, he announced after a champagne toast:

I am enchanted with the welcome you have just given me; I congratulate your government for the participation of Brazil at St. Louis and for designating you as its representative. For your great nation is reserved a brilliant future toward which, as representative of this Government, I hope to be able to contribute.[114]

Those unexpected words gratified the officials of the Brazilian governemnt and received wide circulation in Brazil. Rio-Branco interpreted them to mean that the time was propitious to suggest the mutual elevation of the diplomatic missions.[115]

The continued success of the rapprochement depended to a large extent on the selection of an able diplomat for Washington after Assis Brasil had departed. Rio-Branco decided to transfer the Brazilian minister in London, Joaquim Nabuco, to Washington.

In Nabuco, the foreign minister saw the ideal diplomat to execute Brazil's new foreign policy.

Nabuco first became acquainted with the United States as a young diplomat. As an aide in the Brazilian legation in 1876–77, he traveled widely and met many North Americans. His brief residency seemed to have impressed him favorably.[116] He became convinced that the United States was emerging as an important world power and thereafter urged closer friendship with that country.[117] Emphatically stating to Graça Aranha, "No one more than I favors a foreign policy based on intimate friendship with the United States," [118] he regarded Washington as Brazil's "principal political observatory." [119] As early as April 2, 1904, prior to the appearance of the foreign minister's *Report*, Nabuco had written to Rio-Branco to express his approval of a policy of "closer and closer approximation to the United States." [120] As a matter of fact, a few of his compatriots criticized him for being too partial to the North Americans.[121] Friendship for the United States, support of the Monroe Doctrine, and dedication to Pan Americanism made him the Baron's logical choice to serve in Washington.[122]

Rio-Branco wanted the impending arrival of Nabuco in Washington to follow the official elevation of the legations to embassies. On December 9 the legation in Washington received word that Joaquim Nabuco would arrive shortly to fill the vacant post of minister. Casually Rio-Branco added that Brazil was disposed to raise the legation to the rank of embassy if the United States reciprocated.[123] No official correspondence exists in the archives either in Rio de Janeiro or Washington concerning the preparations for the elevation of the legations. The arrangements were made informally.

The press played an important role in those informal arrangements. The New York *Herald,* on December 26, 1904, spoke authoritatively and favorably about the proposal to exchange embassies with Brazil.[124] Two days later the *Gazeta de Notícias* and *A Notícia* carried news about the creation of the embassies.[125] The dateline used by the *Gazeta* was "Washington, December 27," and the article went so far as to give the names of Nabuco as Brazilian ambassador and Thompson as American ambassador. The press reports in both nations served as sounding boards indicating a favorable climate of opinion for the reciprocal elevation of the legations.

Still there was no official statement from either government. Rio-Branco, feeling the time was right and anxious to resolve the matter, telegraphed the legation on December 29 to discuss immediately the proposed elevation with the proper officials of the State Department.[126] Before Gomes Ferreira could visit the State Department, Under Secretary of State Loomis sought him out to speak about the matter. Unofficial reports of Brazil's intentions had reached President Roosevelt and he declared his approval.[127] In reporting his conversations to Itamaraty, Gomes Ferreira stated that the American government was "sincerely interested" in mutually raising the ranks of the diplomatic representatives.[128] Rio-Branco cabled back immediately asking for the nearest date on which the reciprocal action could be taken.[129]

After telegraphic consultation, the two governments agreed to appoint their ambassadors simultaneously on January 10. The Brazilian president named Nabuco ambassador on that date. On the same day, Roosevelt sent the name of Thompson, the minister to Rio de Janeiro, to the Senate for confirmation as the new ambassador. The Senate approved the appointment on January 13, 1905, and both presidents signed their ambassadors' credentials on the twenty-first.

The official receptions of the new ambassadors occurred some months later. Amid ceremonial splendor and general enthusiasm, Ambassador Thompson presented his credentials to President Alves on March 16, 1905. President Roosevelt received Ambassador Nabuco on May 24. Emphasizing the cooperation and close relations between the two large republics, Nabuco said in part:

The wishes of the two countries to strengthen still more the bonds of friendship that unite them have met spontaneously together in their idea of raising at the same time the rank of their diplomatic agents in Washington and in Rio de Janeiro. . . . All the wishes of Brazil are indeed for the increase of the immense moral influence that the United States exercises upon the march of civilization.[130]

After making his formal reply, Roosevelt laid aside the prepared text and chatted amiably with the new ambassador. He spoke of his firm conviction that Brazil would play a leading role in the development of South America during the twentieth century and of his desire for the continuance of the harmonious relations between the two countries.[131]

Official and public opinion in Brazil, as in the United States, generally favored the creation of embassies. Rio-Branco spoke of his "pleasure" at the event,[132] and President Alves expressed his opinion that the new embassies would "make even more cordial, if it is possible, the relations of good and ancient friendship which happily exist between our respective countries." [133] The *Diario Oficial* spoke with pride of the new embassies.[134] Similar sentiments were expressed in two notable editorials in *O Paiz*,[135] a newspaper often closely associated with the government. The reception of Ambassador Thompson by the president received favorable comment in the newspapers of Rio de Janeiro.[136] The new American embassy seemed to be a source of pride to the Brazilians, whose national ego was flattered by the attention of their more powerful neighbor.[137]

Within Brazil, disapproval of the new embassies was minimal. Among the major newspapers of the capital, only the *Jornal do Brasil* decried the embassy in Washington. First, it criticized the embassy as "an unjustifiable luxury." [138] Then it attacked the creation of the embassy because the act represented more "bowing and scraping" to the "greatest common enemy . . . North American imperialism." [139] Some of the Baron's habitual critics likewise deprecated the action.

Rio-Branco employed several arguments to counter those criticisms. At first he attributed to the American government the idea of elevating the legations.[140] Another argument that weakened the critics' position was to emphasize the distinction the United States conferred upon Brazil by establishing an embassy in Rio de Janeiro.[141] As a final argument to support the embassies, as well as to clarify Brazil's frank pro-American policy, Rio-Branco, under the pseudonym of J. Penn, wrote the essay "Brazil, the United States, and Monroeism," which first appeared in the *Jornal do Commercio*.[142] The article summarized the relations between the two countries during the nineteenth century and characterized them as friendly and intimate. A tradition of harmony had developed, and the embassies could be regarded as the logical conclusion to a century of mutual friendship. The article, if perhaps generous in its interpretations, was well written and persuasive. The critics of Rio-Branco's policy proved ineffective, and soon nothing more was said against the new embassies.

Later, after the criticism disappeared and the idea of the embassies was accepted by all, the Baron affirmed that the initiative had been his, although the American government had readily supported it. In discussing the elevation of the legations with Thompson, he candidly admitted, "What I suggested . . . was the creation of the two Embassies the same day." [143] In a speech to military officers the following year, the chancellor took the full responsibility for the creation of the Brazilian embassy.[144] Several telegrams to Ambassador Nabuco during the following years further testify to the fact that he originated and encouraged the idea of creating Brazil's first embassy in the United States.[145]

The American embassy in Rio de Janeiro was the only one in

South America. Likewise, Nabuco was the only South American ambassador in Washington. Mexico, which had created its Washington embassy in 1897, was the only other Latin American nation exchanging ambassadors with the United States. That limited number added greatly to the prestige value, and Rio-Branco preferred the number of Latin American embassies in Washington to remain at two.[146]

The creation of the embassies represented more than merely another diplomatic act. It symbolized a new phase in Brazil's diplomatic history.[147] Nabuco understood the importance and implication when he wrote Graça Aranha:

I realize that the title of ambassador is in itself just an announcement—one that has the great advantage of saying everything and requiring nothing. I can see that it is an opening measure. Obviously we are facing the dawn of a new era.[148]

Similar sentiments were expressed by the *Gazeta de Notícias,* which editorialized that the embassy represented in one word a new program in Brazil's foreign relations.[149] Inaugurating a period of more intimate relations with the United States and terminating the former diplomatic emphasis on Europe, the embassy in Washington marked an important shift in Brazilian diplomacy.[150] Washington rather than London henceforth would be the pivotal point of Brazil's diplomatic maneuvering.

Later the same year, President Rodrigues Alves paused in his State of the Union Message to reflect on the Brazilian-American approximation, which had become one of the characteristics of his government's foreign policy. He noted with satisfaction the increasingly cordial relations between the two nations, which he considered as the logical continuation of an historical tendency.[151] As a further gesture of Brazil's friendship, the training vessel, *Benjamin Constant,* put in at Philadelphia on July 28, 1905, to take part in the funeral services for former Secretary of State Hay.

THE *Panther* AFFAIR

While Brazil's relations with the United States continued to improve, relations with Europe suffered a setback in 1905. On November 27 a German naval vessel violated Brazilian sovereignty in the quiet port of Itajaí, Santa Catarina. The first reports told that four officers accompanied by twelve sailors from the *Panther,* already known for sinking a Haitian gunboat and later to play a famous role in the Agadir Incident, disembarked in the early hours of the morning to apprehend a German alleged to have fled Germany in order to evade military service. Their mission, executed with neither the permission nor the knowledge of the Brazilian government, violated the norms of international behavior. Later reports indicated that the incident had been greatly exaggerated.

Brazil resented the offense to its sovereignty. Itamaraty reacted adversely to the "violences practiced in our land in the silence of the night by foreign troops." [152] With headlines condemning the action and demanding retributions, the press of the capital gave vent to jingoistic tirades. Popular reaction suddenly brought to life the anti-German sentiment expressed by one of the Brazilians in Graça Aranha's recently published novel on the Germans in Brazil: "No one can dominate a country if the people do not consent to it. . . . With a box of matches an army can be wiped out and with it all that European riffraff." [153] Defiance was the mood throughout Brazil.

Rio-Branco hastened to register a formal protest with the German government. He summoned the German minister to Itamaraty and requested full satisfaction and a condemnation of the outrage. At the same time, he alerted Minister José Pereira da Costa Mota in Berlin and Ambassador Nabuco in Washington to the gravity of the situation.

Unlike many of his fellow citizens, he never felt that Germany constituted in any way a menace to Brazil. As a matter of fact, he was "well satisfied" with the German immigrants to Brazil and lamented that there were not more of them.[154] His visits to Germany and his brief residence in Berlin had disposed him favorably toward the Germans. In the present crisis, he was confident that the two governments would work out a satisfactory solution within the friendship characteristic of their past relations. The conduct of the German minister in Rio de Janeiro strengthened his confidence. Minister Karl von Treutler expressed the regrets of the imperial government and ordered an inquiry into the incident, promising full satisfaction upon the substantiation of the accusations.[155]

In the belief that Germany and Brazil would come to satisfactory terms without recourse to a third party, the Baron did not request United States intervention in the *Panther* case. He did not consult with the American ambassador in Rio de Janeiro, although he did speak with Ambassador Andrew D. White about the matter. White, who had served as American ambassador in Berlin, 1897–1902, happened to be in the Brazilian capital at the time.[156] Rather than having direct recourse to the American government, Rio-Branco thought it would be wiser to demonstrate to Germany that American public opinion supported Brazil. With that end in mind, he cabled Nabuco, "Try to provoke energetic Monroeist articles against that insult." [157] Such moral support would give him additional maneuvering ability against Germany.

The *Panther* incident excited considerable indignation in the United States, and Nabuco succeeded in augmenting the American news coverage of the affair. Prominent newspapers throughout the country, the Chicago *Tribune*, the Washington *Post*, the Baltimore *Sun*, and the New York *Times*, for example, rallied to Brazil's defense with a unity of support that must have been pleasing to Rio-Branco.[158] *O Paiz* reported to its readers that the *Panther* case was "producing irritation" in the United States against Germany.[159] Americans regarded the insult at Itajaí as another example of the

Kaiser's saber-rattling and were no more disposed to tolerate it in this hemisphere than they had been in the Venezuelan case several years previously.

The incident set off a flurry of diplomatic activity in Washington. On December 9, upon receiving notification from Itamaraty of the event, Nabuco rushed to the State Department to show part of the telegram that had just arrived and to discuss the implications of the incident. His intentions were to give the American officials the Brazilian account of the facts and their point of view. He hoped the State Department would inform the American ambassador in Berlin accordingly. He did not request American intervention.[160] The officials thanked him for the information and expressed interest in a satisfactory solution to the difficulty.[161] Critics of Nabuco have alleged that he exceeded his instructions and requested American intervention. There is no written proof of this charge. To the contrary, Root denied that he made such a request.[162]

On its own initiative, the State Department took several actions which tended to favor Brazil's cause. Root took advantage of a conversation with Speck von Sternberg, the German ambassador, on December 11, to mention the *Panther* case.[163] The German ambassador expressed a belief that his country would make suitable reparations. Both agreed that the incident would close without consequences.[164] In the meantime, Root dispatched a telegram and several letters to the American embassy in Berlin to inform them of the incident and the facts of the case. They contained no instructions to take action.[165] Germany could deduce that the United States was observing with interest the outcome of the incident.[166] If there remained any doubt in the mind of the German Foreign Office about the American position, the preparations being made by the Secretary of State to visit Brazil should have resolved them. On December 7, 1905, the New York *Times* carried the official announcement that Root would journey to Brazil to attend the forthcoming Pan American Congress.[167] The announcement emphasized the increasingly close relations between the two countries and added moral support to Brazil's international stature.

In the American capital, the final event which had direct bearing on the *Panther* case was the visit of Ambassador von Sternberg to Nabuco. On December 18, he called on the Brazilian ambassador to lament the incident and to express his hope that it would not mar German-Brazilian relations. He affirmed that Germany would present its excuses to the Brazilian government.[168]

In Berlin, meantime, Brazilian Minister Mota was remonstrating against the "highhanded" behavior of the captain of the *Panther.* Conferring with Minister of Foreign Relations Baron von Richthofen and Vice-Admiral Büchsel, he energetically demanded German reparations.[169] In his copious correspondence with Mota, Rio-Branco made no mention of recourse to North American support. However, the news published in German papers said that the United States would offer its good offices if Germany and Brazil were unable to settle the *Panther* case peacefully.[170] Deliberately or not, the American presence in the case was felt in Berlin.

Germany and Brazil settled the affair a few months later. Germany apologized for offending Brazilian sovereignty and the Naval Ministry promised to punish the guilty naval officers. Itamaraty expressed its satisfactory with those amends, and the incident was over.

The satisfactory outcome of the *Panther* case added to the growing feeling of good will between Brazil and the United States. Although Brazil did not request American intervention, both parties to the incident were aware of the interest Washington displayed.[171] Rio-Branco felt himself able to make strong demands on Germany because of the existing American-Brazilian solidarity.[172] In an entry confided to his diary, Nabuco humorously summed up Brazil's position:

Right now Brazil proceeds against Germany as France would never dare. And what do we put our trust in? Without the "sea power" (of the U.S.), a German blockade of Rio and Santos would make us "stew in our own juice," which in our case would be coffee juice (very expensive).[173]

The advantage of close friendship with the United States appeared obvious in this case, and Rio-Branco could see the benefits of his foresight in creating an embassy in Washington less than a year before.

The *Panther* case strengthened the Monroe Doctrine and Brazil's regard for it. Official circles in Rio de Janeiro seemed more aware of the practical value which that doctrine possessed.[174] Although the Monroe Doctrine had not been invoked, its presence was felt. There was reassurance in knowing that in an emergency recourse could be had to it. A leading Rio de Janeiro newspaper summed up the Brazilian feeling toward the doctrine in the *Panther* case in an excellent cartoon. In the background stood a ridiculous Kaiser. In the foreground a typical Uncle Sam stood holding a scroll which read "Monroe Doctrine." He was speaking to a handsome Indian who wielded a club on which was inscribed "Force of Right." Said Uncle Sam, "Do you need my services?" Replied the Indian, "Thanks very much, but I can handle it alone." [175] Another newspaper, not known for its friendly attitude toward the United States, concluded that the *Panther* case, of little importance in itself, augured "grave consequences" for Brazil's future by increasing the influence of the United States over its destiny.[176]

Solidarity of North American support in the *Panther* case and announcement of Root's visit to Brazil occurred at the same time that Rio-Branco's efforts to cooperate with Argentina met with reverses. As Argentina voiced disagreement with Brazilian policies, both internal and external, the hopes of Itamaraty for an ABC entente diminished.[177] The Argentine press criticized increasing Brazilian military armament as a threat to its neighbors and as an undesirable means of bringing pressure to bear on them to make territorial concessions.[178] It pointed out that Brazil's foreign policy

toward first Bolivia and then Peru "could not be more dangerous." [179] Later, an editorial in the influential *La Nación* spoke out
harshly "to denounce its [Brazil's] diplomacy of imperialism intent
upon swallowing up the weak." [180] Those criticisms, coupled with a
new and intense disapproval of Brazil's naval improvements program and the recently established embassy in Washington, persuaded
the Baron that cooperation with Argentina would be impossible.[181]
After 1905, he deemphasized his plans for ABC cooperation.

As a countermeasure to deteriorating relations with Argentina,
the Baron reaffirmed Brazil's friendship toward Chile and the
United States. The good will of Washington was more important
than ever as the balance of power shifted in South America. Therefore, Rio-Branco made certain that, by the time the Third Pan
American Conference convened, the Brazilian-American rapprochement was clearly evident for the rest of the hemisphere to see.

THE VISIT OF ROOT

The First Pan American Conference, called by Secretary of State
James G. Blaine, had met in Washington in 1889. Mexico in 1902
had been host to the second reunion. When the governing board of
the International Bureau of the American States began to discuss
the third meeting, the minister of Costa Rica suggested that the
honor of holding the conference be conferred upon Brazil.[182]
Mexico and the United States supported the suggestion, which
Venezuela contested because its president wanted Caracas to receive the honor. Root thought that Rio de Janeiro should be the
city selected and he openly urged its acceptance, an action regarded
in official Brazilian circles as "another significant proof of the
esteem" of the government of the United States.[183] After the final
decision to meet in Rio de Janeiro was made on December 6, 1905,
Root announced his plans to visit Brazil while the conference was in
session. Rio-Branco was particularly gratified that the Latin Ameri-

can delegates would meet in Brazil and that the American Secretary of State would attend.[184]

After Rio de Janeiro had been selected as the site, the date had been set, and plans were under way, the governing body learned to its consternation that the Second Hague Peace Conference would convene at the same time. The conflicting dates disturbed Latin America because the Hague Conference would detract from the importance of the Pan American Conference and because most nations planned to send approximately the same delegates to both conferences. Nabuco conferred with Root about the conflict, and they agreed that the Hague Conference should be postponed in favor of the inter-American meeting. Root discussed the possibility of changing the date of the Peace Conference with the Russian ambassador, to whom President Roosevelt also expressed a hope that the date could be altered. The Russian ambassador spoke with Nabuco about a solution to the conflict. Later, word from The Hague announced that the Peace Conference would be postponed for a year.[185] Thereafter, plans for the Third International Conference of the American States progressed in both Rio de Janeiro and Washington. In order to avoid the lengthy debates and confusion characteristic of the meetings in Washington and Mexico City, the governing board outlined the program and procedures in detail prior to the opening session in Rio de Janeiro. Nabuco and Root cooperated closely in those preparations.[186] Root demonstrated an avid interest in the planning and helped elaborate the program and the rules.[187] In the Brazilian capital, Rio-Branco supervised the tasks of preparation for the conference. Accommodations, banquets, transportation, official receptions, translators, etc., all were provided for to the last detail, which moved the American delegation to comment approvingly that nothing "was left undone by the Brazilian government."[188]

Amid a festive atmosphere in the renovated Rio de Janeiro, an impressive assembly of delegates from nineteen nations gathered in the newly constructed Senate on the evening of July 23 to inaugurate the conference.[189] Opening the first session, the Brazilian foreign minister expressed his hope that the conference would strive "to promote more intimate political relations, to prevent conflicts, and to regulate the friendly solution of international differences by harmonizing the laws of commerce among the people, by facilitating, simplifying, and strengthening the contacts among them." [190] As their first act, the delegates elected Nabuco permanent president of the conference and Root and Rio-Branco honorary presidents.

The conference limited its deliberation to structural changes, administrative planning, and improvements of existing conventions. There were no discussions of any new policies.[191] The majority of the work was done in committees. In its fourteen sessions, the conference considered and adopted fourteen resolutions, four conventions, and three motions which covered the following subjects: the reorganization of the Bureau of the American States, adherence to the principle of arbitration, an extension of the arbitration of pecuniary claims treaty, a resolution concerning the forcible collection of public debts, the formation of a commission to prepare codes of public and private international law, a convention on naturalization, the encouragement of commerce in the Americas, approval of customs regulations and consular laws, the completion of the Pan American railroad, and resolutions on patent and trademark legislation, sanitation regulations, copyright laws, and the practice of learned professions. All the topics were important but none of the resolutions was phrased in such a way as to be controversial.

Nabuco stated that the chief purpose of the meeting should be "to promote harmony." [192] The conference achieved that goal.[193] In doing so, it fulfilled Rio-Branco's hopes for cooperation among the hemispheric nations.

The highlight of the conference was the appearance of Elihu

The Baron of Rio-Branco, Secretary of State Elihu Root, and Ambassador Joaquim Nabuco at the Third Pan American Conference, Rio de Janeiro, 1906

Root, the first visit abroad of an American Secretary of State. Root, a close friend of Nabuco, had decided "spontaneously" to attend and to visit Brazil because of the friendship that neighbor had demonstrated toward the United States.[194] Pleased with that decision, the Brazilian government made elaborate and expensive preparations to receive the distinguished guest:

Unparalleled magnificence marked the banquet given for Root by Rio-Branco, the Minister for Foreign Affairs, on the 28th. Furnishings were specially imported from Paris at a reported cost of $100,000. Eighty covers were spread and Root was driven to the banquet hall in a specially built carriage that had been constructed at a cost of $12,000. It was said that $2,000 was spent to upholster the box at the opera, which the Roots occupied for an hour one evening.[195]

Amid great fanfare, Root arrived in Rio de Janeiro aboard an American warship on July 27. At an official banquet held at Itamaraty the following night, Rio-Branco welcomed his American colleague to Brazil. His remarks emphasized the good relations existing between the two countries:

The enthusiastic and cordial welcome you have received in Brazil must certainly have convinced you that this country is a true friend of your own.

The manifestations of friendship for the United States that you have witnessed come from all the Brazilian people, and not from the official world alone, and it is our earnest desire that this friendship, which has never been disturbed in the past, may continue forever and grow constantly closer and stronger.[196]

The words served as an official statement to all Latin America of the success of the Brazilian-American rapprochement. The presence of Root in Brazil testified to that success.

The delegates held an extraordinary session on the evening of July 31 to receive the Secretary of State. The conciliatory gesture of the United States in opening negotiations with Colombia and the successful efforts of the United States in securing invitations for all the hemispheric nations to the Hague Peace Conference put the delegates in an exceptionally cordial mood to welcome Root. A thunderous applause rang out as he was escorted into the brilliantly illuminated chamber filled to capacity. To the assembly he addressed these words:

> We wish for no victories except those of peace. We wish for no territory except our own, and no sovereignty except over ourselves. We deem the independence and rights of the smallest and weakest member of the family of nations entitled to as much respect as that of the greatest empire, and we deem the observance of that respect to be the chief guarantee for the weak against the oppression of the strong. We neither claim nor desire any rights or privileges of powers that we do not freely concede to every American republic.
>
> We wish to increase our prosperity and to grow in wealth and wisdom of spirit, but our own conception of the true way to accomplish this is not to pull others down and profit by their ruin, but to help all friends to a common prosperity and growth, that we may all become greater and stronger together.[197]

The speech, acclaimed enthusiastically by the delegates, was a new statement of American policy toward Latin America. In it Root set standards which the United States henceforth would try to meet in its relations with the rest of the hemisphere. The reaction of the delegates indicated a continental welcome for the policy, and he himself regarded the speech as a milestone in inter-American relations.[198]

As the applause subsided, Rio-Branco arose to announce that as a tribute to the visit of President Roosevelt to the Brazilian pavilion at the St. Louis Fair (the Senate was a replica of that pavilion) and to perpetuate the memory of Root's visit to Brazil the President had named the building in which they were meeting the Monroe Palace.[199]

Root left the capital for São Paulo on August 3 and later departed from Santos to visit other American republics. Nabuco had urged him to extend his Brazilian visit to include other republics but jokingly warned, "You can flirt with all, but I hope you will wed us."[200] The Third International Conference of the American States closed on August 27, 1906.

The visit to Brazil impressed Root, who welcomed the opportunity to become acquainted with that neighbor and its leaders.[201] His conversations with Rio-Branco enabled him to understand Brazil's foreign policy better.[202] He admired the talent of the Baron.[203] Like President Roosevelt, Root foresaw a great future for Brazil.[204]

The effects of the visit were many. In the first place, Root's selection of Brazil as the first country to be visited by an American Secretary of State was regarded as an honor by his hosts. His presence emphasized the predominance of Brazil among the South American countries,[205] and was testimony to the success of Rio-Branco's policy of approximation. Certainly one direct effect of the visit was the Brazilian reduction of tariffs on some American products. A month after Root's departure, a bill was introduced into the Brazilian Congress to lower tariffs in such a way that only the United States would benefit. The bill was attributed directly to the favorable reaction to Root's visit.[206] His presence and his speech succeeded in removing a great deal of the suspicion and mistrust of the United States felt by some groups within Brazil and throughout Latin America in general.[207] His affable ways charmed one severe critic of the United States, Rubén Darío, the internationally acclaimed poet who represented Nicaragua at the conference—so much so that Darío was even moved to compose a poem favorable to the United States![208] The "Colossus of the North," thanks to Root's sincere and tactful words, appeared more human and less formidable. The most lasting effect undoubtedly was the assurance of American friendship felt by all the delegates and especially the hosts.[209] Nabuco called it "an impression of confidence likely to last long after his passage."[210] The American delegation to the conference likewise noted the positive effect of Root's presence and words on inter-American friendship. They believed that his warm reception portended closer cooperation and harmony in hemispheric relations.[211]

Four years of diplomatic cooperation had diminished Brazilian suspicions of the United States generated by the Acre intrigues. That cooperation had proven valuable to both nations in the recognition of Panama and in the breaking of the Peruvian-Brazilian deadlock over Acre. Those increasingly cordial relations prompted both to exchange ambassadors, and Brazil realized the value and importance of its new, favored position in Washington during the *Panther* case. The culmination of those tightening relations was the visit of Root, whose presence in Brazil can be regarded as the high-water mark in Brazilian-American friendship during the Rio-Branco administration.[212] The visit signified the success of Rio-Branco's policy, supported faithfully and energetically by Nabuco, of aligning the United States and Brazil.

CHAPTER V · THE TRIBULATIONS AND REWARDS OF FRIENDSHIP, 1907–1912

Following Root's visit, there seeemed to be every reason to believe that the relations between the two countries would become even more intimate. In June of 1907, the United States, in the opinion of Rio-Branco, reaffirmed its friendly attentions to Brazil during the Jamestown Exposition.[1] In addition to arranging a display of national products, Brazil dispatched the *Barroso, Riachuelo,* and *Tamoyo,* under the command of Rear Admiral Duarte Huet de Bacellar, to take part in an international naval review there. Nabuco invited the highest ranking officers of the three cruisers to Washington for five days of festivities which included several embassy functions and a dinner offered by Root. The highlight of the visit was a White House reception in which President Roosevelt welcomed the naval officers to the United States.[2] Conversing with Bacellar, Roosevelt expressed his pleasure in the presence of the Brazilian squadron and reviewed the cordial relations between the two nations. He hoped that the future would bring even closer relations and more good will and also touched on one of his favorite themes: Brazil's growth potential.[3] The hospitality shown the officers in Washington and the squadron in Norfolk pleased the Brazilians. That was still the era in which a naval visit, a reception, a banquet, or a prolonged conversation had varied shades of meaning in the diplomatic world. Those distinctions or subtleties, so characteristic of diplomacy prior to World War I, were interpreted as significant signposts indicating the road that relations between two countries might follow. Hence, after such an expression of good will in Washington, it was with a feeling of mutual confidence that Brazil and the United States sent their delegations to the Hague Peace Conference.

THE HAGUE CONFERENCE

Secretary of State John Hay had conceived the idea of inviting all the Latin American nations to the Second International Peace Conference. In 1904, he informed the Brazilian legation of his intention and expressed the hope that Brazil would participate in the conference.[4] In Latin America, only Mexico and Brazil had received invitations to the First Peace Conference in 1899. Mexico attended. Brazil, because of internal preoccupations and disinterest in the agenda, did not send a delegation. Eight years of growing nationalism caused Latin America to be more aware of its position in the world and desirous to enter international politics on a world scale and to send representatives to The Hague. Participation fitted into Rio-Branco's plans to increase Brazil's prestige, and he welcomed the efforts made by the United States to secure invitations for the Latin Americans.

Carrying out the intentions of his predecessor, Root persuaded the European powers to invite all the nations of the Western Hemisphere. Furthermore, when the conflict of dates between The Hague and the Rio de Janeiro conferences occurred, his timely intervention convinced Russia and the Netherlands to postpone the Peace Conference.

After the success of the Rio meeting, the Baron turned his attention to the selection of a delegation for Brazil's debut in an important world conference. He first thought to ask Nabuco to lead the delegation, but before he could make public that intention, the newspapers of the capital began a campaign to nominate Rui Barbosa, a distinguished republican statesman, as the chief delegate. Highly regarded in certain republican circles, Rui Barbosa was well known for his efforts in consolidating the new government after the overthrow of Pedro II. As a candidate for president in 1905, he had demonstrated that he had a wide and loyal following. He counted several influential *carioca* editors among his friends and admirers. In the pages of their papers they clamored for his appointment to lead the Hague delegation. Always sensitive to the press, Rio-Branco acceded to their request and appointed him. Then the chancellor asked Nabuco to accompany Rui Barbosa.[5] The ambassador declined the invitation for several reasons, one of the most interesting of which was an anxiety that some action of the Brazilian delegation might displease the American government and thereby harm his good relations with officials in Washington.[6] Nabuco seemed to have had a premonition that something might go amiss at The Hague to compromise his favorable position in the American capital. Therefore, he limited his participation in the conference to writing informal memorandums and suggestions to Rui Barbosa and Rio-Branco, who jointly were making preparations for the conference.

As the opening date approached, the chancellor worried about the reception the European nations would accord Brazil in its maiden appearance at a global conference. Since one of the reasons for attending was to add luster to Brazil's international prestige, he hoped that Brazil would receive some office or honor at the conference. Fearing that Argentina might obtain honors at Brazil's expense, he spoke of his hopes in a telegram to Nabuco.[7] The Brazilian ambassador went immediately to his friend Root to discuss Brazil's aspirations.[8] After all, a man who had obtained the invitations for Latin America in the first place and had succeeded in changing the date of the conference certainly could arrange an office for Brazil. Understanding the psychology of Latin Americans remarkably well, Root agreed to intervene on behalf of the Brazilians. The American delegation received instructions to favor the Latin Americans and to see that they got some of the offices and honors.[9] Later, Rui Barbosa held the post of *President d'honneur* of the first commission, responsible for the question of arbitration. He was the only Latin American thus distinguished.

The interrelationships, or lack of them, between the State Department, Itamaraty, and the delegations of the United States and Brazil during the conference were curious. One of the most striking features was the temporary absence from the scene of two of the leading supporters of the United States–Brazilian rapprochement. Claiming ill-health and a need for rest, Ambassador Nabuco chose those months to take one of his rare vacations outside of the United States. Perhaps ill-health was the real cause for his absence. One cannot help conjecturing, however, that the ambassador, foreseeing or fearing some friction or disagreement between Brazil and the United States at The Hague, did not want to risk his and Brazil's favored position in Washington by being involved in anything relating to that conference. The one certain way of avoiding such possible involvement was to be absent from Washington during the meeting. Departing for Europe on June 1, he did not return to Washington until October 2, when the important work of the conference had been transacted. The Brazilian embassy during that important period was under the direction of an able but inexperienced chargé d'affaires, Gurgel do Amaral. At the same time, Root was ill and absent from Washington in the isolation of his home in Clinton, New York. Because of their absence, little could be done in Washington during the Peace Conference to coordinate and to further Brazilian-American relations.

Attention to those relations shifted temporarily to The Hague. The Brazilian delegation consisted of twelve members, one of the largest delegations, outnumbering, for example, the eleven-man delegation of the United States, led by Ambassador Joseph H. Choate, and all other Latin American delegations. In early August, the Brazilians gave for their counterparts from the United States a gala banquet at which fraternity was the principal theme.[10] It was the first and last purposeful display of fraternization. Thereafter, neither Choate nor Rui Barbosa seemed to show much enthusiasm about carrying forward the policy of approximation although both had received instructions to do so. Choate seemed oblivious to Root's Latin American policy in general and to approximation with Brazil in particular. Rarely consulting with the sensitive Latin American delegates, he ignored the potential support they could lend American policy.[11] For his part, Rui Barbosa stayed aloof from the American delegates and displayed little inclination to follow Brazil's pro-American tendencies.[12] In The Hague, as in Washington during those months, conditions were inauspicious for cooperation between Brazil and the United States.

The only leader favoring approximation who was on duty, so to speak, during the conference was the Baron of Rio-Branco. He exerted every effort to keep the informal alliance intact during the conference, but receiving little help from Washington, vacated by Nabuco and Root, or from the apparently incompatible delegates at The Hague, he was faced with a greater task than ever. As the correspondence and the nearly 175 telegrams exchanged between them testify, Rio-Branco and Rui Barbosa collaborated intimately during the conference on the major items of business. While there is no evidence of open disagreement, their agreement on certain subjects seemed to be more a matter of convenience than conviction. Rio-Branco directed the broadlines of Brazilian policy at The Hague, but much, of necessity, was left to the discretion of Rui Barbosa. However, there are indications that Rui Barbosa was able to influence Rio-Branco to change or modify certain of his policies. Any generality on this point would be deceptive. The relationship of the two men needs a penetrating study.[13] At any rate, the Baron did not succeed in convincing Rui Barbosa of the value of his policy toward the United States.

Failing to find the accustomed Brazilian-American cooperation at The Hague, Rio-Branco turned to Washington in the hope that a coordination of policy between the Department of State and Itamaraty would be transferred to the respective delegations. He sent Gurgel do Amaral on special missions to the State Department several times and once ordered him to visit Root in Clinton. The chargé d'affaires reported that Root was "embarrassed" by Choate's uncooperative attitude, but because Choate enjoyed special influence with the President, Root felt there was little he could do.[14] Choate apparently used his familiarity with Roosevelt to be independent of State Department policy. The facts reveal, at any rate, that the American delegation was acting without the approval of Root.[15] The information tersely reported in the Brazilian capital was that "Mr. Root is in the interior of the United States and therefore is ignorant of what the Delegates at The Hague are doing." [16] Root's foremost biographer confirms that conclusion.[17] To a great extent Choate and Rui Barbosa were on their own at The Hague, and without the coordinated direction of the advocates of Brazilian-American friendship they were writing their own chapter in the history of the diplomatic relations of their two countries with little regard for the context in which they wrote.

During the opening days of the conference, all the signs seemed to indicate that the customary Brazilian-American cooperation was working well. In one of his first speeches at The Hague, Rui Barbosa supported the proposition of the United States to abolish the right to capture of private property on the high seas in wartime.[18] The two delegations also were in agreement to substitute the Porter Resolution for the Drago Doctrine.

In 1902, Luís María Drago, foreign minister of Argentina, had formulated a doctrine stating that no public debt could serve as the excuse for armed intervention or occupation of territory in the American hemisphere. The doctrine was discussed briefly at the Third Pan American Conference where the delegates resolved to refer the matter to the Peace Conference.[19] Brazil in general and Rio-Branco in particular accorded the doctrine a cool welcome. One Rio newspaper, after attacking Drago's thesis on legal grounds, concluded sarcastically, "The boldness of the Argentine government is really astounding." [20] Rio-Branco held the opinion that the Argentine proposal found no "sympathy" in Brazil.[21] After all, as he explained to Nabuco later, "We pay our debts, and, furthermore, we are creditors to Uruguay and Paraguay." [22] Declining to accept without modification the principles expounded by Drago, General Porter of the American delegation suggested and defended a substitute. According to the Porter Resolution, armed force could be used to collect a debt if the debtor nation refused to arbitrate or to execute the terms of arbitration.[23] In a long and able speech attacking Drago's idea that public debts were an act of sovereignty, Rui Barbosa supported the American resolution.[24] He pointed out:

> The State in borrowing does not exercise its sovereignty, but an act of private law as is the case in so many other contracts in which its personality is divided, that is to say, in which it leaves its political sphere to undertake acts of a civil nature.[25]

The major European nations concurred with his observations. In the final vote, thirty-nine nations favored the Porter Resolution and five abstained. After making several reservations to the proposal, nine Latin American nations cast affirmative ballots, including Argentina.[26] Of the Latin American delegations, only Chile and Brazil upheld the Porter Resolution without reservation.[27] Brazil had discussed the matter with the American delegation outside of the conference hall.[28] Rui Barbosa, perhaps, was following his own convictions, but he also was complying with the instructions of President Pena who wanted Brazil to support the United States in the question of debts.[29]

One of the most important tasks confronting the conference was the creation of an International Court of Justice. The First Hague Peace Conference had established a Court of Arbitration, a panel of judges in which each of the participating nations had an equal voice. The Second Hague Peace Conference sought to expand and to perfect the work of the previous conference. Germany, Great

Britain, and the United States proposed a plan for a seventeen-member court. Nine nations would sit as permanent members of the court. The other nations would share the remaining seats on a rotating basis for a period of time specified by the category into which they were classified.

Classified in the third category beneath smaller and less populous European states, Brazil regarded the plan as unjust. Rio-Branco, his sensitive nationalism injured, thought the plan to be "humiliating" and beneath Brazil's dignity.[30] The inferior treatment accorded Brazil at its first world conference deeply hurt him.[31] His close friend and counselor, Gastão da Cunha, confided to the American ambassador that the Baron considered Brazil's classification as "unfair."[32] On several occasions Ambassador Dudley informed Washington that the court plan had injured Brazilian pride.[33]

North American alignment with the European powers and isolation from Latin America disappointed Rio-Branco. Concentrating on European diplomacy, the United States delegation was running the risk of alienating its recently acquired South American ally.

Having failed to find out the intentions of the United States beforehand and caught unprepared by the seventeen-nation court plan,[34] Rio-Branco found himself at odds with his ally and for the time being in a humiliating position. Brazil's diplomatic goals required a different solution for the structure of the court. Searching for an acceptable court plan, the Baron had but one thought: a permanent seat for Brazil on the tribunal. Uncertainty and desperation caused him to suggest a wide variety of plans, all of which gave his country a permanent seat. On August 4, he proposed a court in which every nation would have the right to nominate a judge, although nations could jointly name one judge from among themselves if they wished. The litigants could select their judges from that panel.[35] On the eleventh, he suggested another plan in which Argentina, Brazil, and Chile each would appoint a judge to the tribunal and the rest of South America would have the right to name one judge.[36] Rio-Branco was beginning to veer away from the idea that each nation had a right to nominate a judge. Modifying his earlier idea of equality still further, the Brazilian chancellor, on the fifteenth, proposed a plan for a twenty-one-nation court in which the fifteen states with a population exceeding ten million inhabitants would have permanent judges and other nations would share the remaining seats on a rotating basis according to assigned categories. That plan, of course, assured populous Brazil of a permanent seat.[37]

The support of the United States was necessary if Brazil hoped to have one of its own plans accepted by the conference. Rio-Branco solicited the approval of the United States for his twenty-one-nation court, which was, after all, only a variation of the seventeen-member court. The Department of State indicated that the American delegation would be instructed to cooperate with the Brazilian delegation in favor of the twenty-one-nation court.[38] However, by this time, the lack of cooperation between the two delegations had become pronounced. The exchange of heated words between Rui Barbosa and Choate during a committee session was an indication of the growing divergence between the two delegations.[39] In Brazil, there was a feeling of deception by the United States because of its attitude at The Hague.[40] Besides that, Rio-Branco was having second thoughts about his latest plan. Satisfactory to Brazil, the plan would be displeasing to the smaller nations.[41] While unsuccessfully expending its efforts to be admitted to the court as a permanent member with the major powers, Brazil was losing the support of the rest of Latin America as well as some smaller European nations.

The realities of the situation showed that the most certain way of assuring Brazil of a permanent seat on the tribunal was through the principle of equality of all nations. Brazil's first proposal to give all nations the right of appointing a judge seemed more natural and correct. Rui Barbosa had stated his preference for the equality of nations, and by August 18, Rio-Branco determined that Brazil should defend that principle.[42] Divergence from the United States could no longer be hidden, and Brazil resolved to break boldly with the American plan and to support equality, a judicially firm position and a popular one with the smaller nations.[43] It became apparent that it was the only plan by which Brazil could hope to gain for itself the coveted permanent seat, one goal of Rio-Branco's policy at The Hague.[44]

Injured pride more than anything else motivated Brazil's support of the equality of nations on that particular occasion.[45] However, it should be noted to the Baron's credit that for some years he had endorsed the principle of equality in theoretical terms. In 1905 he had written, "What America desires is equality in international law . . . and that the sovereignty of its nations be as respected as that of the European nations." [46] Later, at the Third Pan American Conference he affirmed that the weakest and strongest nations must be treated equally before the law.[47] Therefore, after the initial vacillation, it was not entirely inconsistent for the Brazilian delegation to take refuge in the principle of equality. In Rui Barbosa, the chancellor had an eloquent spokesman for equality. In one of his best speeches, the Bahian said:

Without doubt there exist between the various nations differences in culture, in wisdom, in wealth, and in power, but does it follow that there is also a difference with respect to their essential rights? Civil rights are the same for all men as political rights are the same for all citizens. . . . Sovereignty is the elementary right of constituted, independent States and signifies equality in practice as well as in theory. . . . Sovereignty is absolute and knows no classification. Hence, if it is necessary to have a common organ of justice among the States, all the States necessarily must have equal representation in it.[48]

Thereafter, the Brazilian delegation dedicated itself to equality of representation on the court.

Supporting a court plan based on equality, Brazil came into open conflict with the United States, which still advocated the seventeen-nation court. That clash between the two delegations displeased Rio-Branco, who had instructed Rui Barbosa to cooperate with the American representatives. However, regardless of efforts to avoid it, the point had been reached when such cooperation could no longer be honorably given.[49] Both Root and Rio-Branco seemed to lament the failure of cooperation, although nothing exists to prove that their respective delegations at The Hague shared the sentiment. Root made several efforts to placate Brazil by advising Choate to show more consideration for Brazil's point of view.[50] At the same time he asked Rio-Branco to understand that the United States could not act as freely in a world conference as in a hemispheric conference and urged him to compromise with the European demands.[51] The Baron felt he already had compromised too much and believed that the Brazilian plan for permanent judges representing each nation which desired to name one was the suitable solution.[52] The positions of the two nations seemed to be irreconcilable.

Rio-Branco expressed disappointment with the American position because it contradicted previous policy announcements of that government.[53] As the chancellor pointed out to Nabuco, Root and the United States failed to fulfill the obligations made in pronouncements in Rio de Janeiro scarcely a year before.[54] The *Jornal do Commercio* was quick to indicate the inconsistency:

The Delegation of the United States at The Hague is not corresponding to the beautiful words which Secretary of State Root spoke here during the session of July 31 of the Third American Conference when he said, "We understand that the independence and the rights of the smallest and weakest members of the family of nations merit as much respect as those of the largest empires." [55]

Nor was Root's impressive speech before the delegates to the Pan American Conference the only time he had spoken out before representatives of the hemispheric nations in favor of the equality of states. Earlier at the Brazilian embassy in Washington, Root exclaimed, "May the independence, the freedom, and the rights of the weakest be ever respected equally with the rights of the strong-est." [56] Those statements delighted the Latin Americans. Unfortu-nately, much of their effect was undone by the contradictory posi-tion taken by Choate at The Hague. Likewise, the American dele-gation undermined much of the good work accomplished by Root during his tour of South America.[57]

As the separation in the positions of the two delegations contin-ued, it became clear that Brazil was leading the other Latin Ameri-can nations as well as several smaller European nations in a strug-gle for the recognition of equality.[58] That alternative to cooperation with the United States was not unpleasant for Rio-Branco, who as-pired to make Brazil a leader in Latin America. The Hague unex-pectedly gave him an excellent opportunity to assume that role and he took advantage of it. Brazil carried its case for equality to the chancelleries of the other Latin American nations and requested their support.[59] As the debates over the composition of the tribunal continued, the Latin American governments notified Itamaraty of their support.[60] At The Hague the Latin American delegates rallied behind Rui Barbosa.[61] Brazil's prestige among the Latin Americans emerged from the Peace Conference considerably augmented.

The debates over the composition of the International Court of Justice ended in a stalemate. All the delegations agreed that a court should be created, but there was a lack of concurrence about its composition. The conference adjourned without resolving the dead-lock.

A second divergence occurred over the creation of an Interna-tional Prize Court to judge cases of merchant ships captured in war. The conference approved the principle but the procedure for ap-pointing judges to the court caused debates similar to those over the plan for the International Court of Justice. Great Britain pro-posed a scheme to appoint fifteen judges to the court, eight selected by the principal sea powers and seven selected by the other nations on a rotating basis according to their classification. The large, seafaring nations favored the British plan. While approving the idea of the court, as well as a classification of nations, because nations with large merchant navies naturally would have a greater interest and stake in the court, Brazil objected to its classification in the fourth category of merchant marine nations.[62] Under that classification a Brazilian judge would sit for only two out of every six years, which the Brazilians declared to be unjust and arbitrary.[63] Belgium, Portugal, and Rumania, for example, whose merchant navies were smaller that Brazil's, received a higher classification than Brazil.[64] Rui Barbosa argued passionately but ineffectively for a reclassification of Brazil commensurate with its merchant marine tonnage and expanding navy. In the final vote on the creation of the court, twenty-six nations signified their approval and two (Brazil and Turkey) opposed. Fifteen nations abstained.[65] Although approved, the convention never entered into force, and the court was not established.

The United States and Brazilian delegations agreed on the principle of arbitration, but they disagreed on the kind of questions which could be submitted to arbitration. Choate believed that arbitration should cover those legal questions and controversies arising between two nations because of the interpretation of treaties and conventions. He excluded from arbitration questions involving independence, vital interests, and honor.[66] Brazil concurred with those exclusions as far as they went but wanted to extend them considerably. Rui Barbosa thought that no questions affecting independence, vital interests, internal laws or institutions, or territorial integrity should be submitted to arbitration. In any disputes involving inhabited areas, the inhabitants would have to give their consent to arbitration. Furthermore, Brazil held that any recourse to arbitration should be postponed until diplomacy and mediation had been thoroughly exhausted.[67] The Brazilian restrictions were so broad and encompassing that in effect they annulled all possibility of recourse to arbitration.[68] Because of those restrictions, as well as others enunciated in the meetings, the conference failed to write a general treaty of arbitration even of limited scope. Instead the conference settled for a declaration in favor of general arbitration.[69]

Of the four most important issues discussed at The Hague, the Drago Doctrine, the International Court of Justice, the International Prize Court, and compulsory arbitration, the delegations of the United States and Brazil disagreed on three. The disharmony which characterized the relations of the two delegations contradicted the friendly cooperation, apparently unplanned, which the two delegations showed in the discussions of the Drago Doctrine, the capture of private property on the sea, and the approval of periodic meetings of the conference. Rui Barbosa himself sought to deemphasize those issues upon which the two nations had disagreed. He disclaimed those rumors and newspaper articles which implied that he was hostile to the United States.[70] Still, the over-all effect remained after the adjournment that there had been a serious break in the cooperation characteristic of Rio-Branco's foreign policy toward the United States.

Back in Brazil, the role of Rui Barbosa at the conference received full news coverage and popular acclaim.[71] The dispatches ticking off the trans-Atlantic cable repeatedly told of his achievements and brilliance until the newspaper readers must have had the impression that their representative dominated the Peace Conference. The news reports tended to lionize the Brazilian position to the disadvantage of the United States so that an atmosphere of anti-Americanism was created by the press.[72] The critics of Rio-Branco took advantage of the opportunity to point out the insincerity of professed American friendship for Brazil.[73] The general reaction in Brazil was unfavorable to the role played by the United States at The Hague.

The opinions of the Minister of Foreign Relations reflected those sentiments. He thought the United States entirely too willing to shun its friends in Latin America in order to associate with the European powers.[74] The American delegation disappointed him, and in his chagrin he referred to it as "inept."[75] Undoubtedly baffled by the inconsistency between former statements of the United States and the action of its delegation, Rio-Branco must have wondered if his critics could be correct and if the United States had been sincere in its profession of friendship. The chancellor observed, "The American Delegation is out of harmony with the testaments of esteem Brazil received from its government."[76] The difference between what Root said and what Choate did caused confusion and uncertainty in Itamaraty.

The Baron decided that Choate was an "unfaithful interpreter" of American policy and acted without instructions from Root.[77] Thus, Choate, criticized for being hostile to Brazil, bore the blame for the inconsistency between American statements in this continent and actions in Europe.[78] After all, both Root and Roosevelt were absent from Washington and therefore unaware of the actions of their delegate, who knew little about and appreciated less the policy of rapprochement. Such was Rio-Branco's rationalization, which Ambassador Dudley characterized as "a pleasant anxiety to defend and save unimpaired the cordial understanding between the United States and Brazil brought about by Secretary Root's visit to this country."[79] Interpreted from the point of view that Choate had acted without the knowledge of, or instructions from, Washington, the discord at The Hague became an insignificant, although unfortunate, incident in Brazilian-American relations.

While lamenting Choate's actions, Rio-Branco took careful steps to inform Rui Barbosa,[80] Root,[81] and Nabuco[82] that Brazil would continue to cultivate the friendship of the United States. The temporary setback was not to cause any change in the policy of Itamaraty.

Ambassador Nabuco, increasingly becoming the instrument of coordination of the approximation, closely followed Rui Barbosa's actions during the conference.[83] Realizing the beneficial influence such a powerful political figure as Rui Barbosa could have on the relations between the two American nations, Nabuco had solicited his aid in strengthening the approximation.[84] Prior to and during the conference, Nabuco sent him information about the conference and the delegates with the intention of preparing him for his meeting with the Americans. Nabuco rejoiced upon reading of his initial support of Choate on the question of private property at sea and immediately wrote to congratulate him on his speech.[85]

Nabuco's elation quickly turned to disappointment as the opening harmony between the two delegations changed to heated debates over the composition of the International Court.[86] In his opinion, both nations were failing to take advantage of a potentially excellent opportunity to tighten the bonds of friendship. It seemed as though Rio de Janeiro had abandoned the plans for approximation.[87] Nabuco's first reaction was to express antipathy toward Rui Barbosa's position favoring equality. He informed Rio-Branco that had he been a delegate he would have supported a different position.[88] To Rui Barbosa he stated frankly:

I do not think that in the deliberations of mankind in parliament the vote of a fraction of one or two million men ought to have the same weight as the vote of fifty or eighty million. That would not be equality, because no social contract is made without attention to the law of proportion.[89]

Nabuco preferred cooperation with the United States because he felt the real victim of debates would be the friendly relations between the two nations. Brazil, he thought, could not hope to gain any objectives by antagonizing the large powers, and it would be quixotic to try to combat them. Even to succeed in defeating the court plan supported by the United States would achieve little because "to defeat the United States is a foolish victory for any nation."[90] When the court plans ended in a stalemate, Nabuco hoped Brazilian public opinion and the press would not be so unwise as to emphasize the effects of The Hague and thus increase the breach opened by the incompatible delegates.[91] For his own part, Nabuco sought to deemphasize the effects of The Hague, and for that reason he refused to let the embassy publish in English Rui Barbosa's speeches at The Hague.[92]

Later, after his anxieties had been quieted, Nabuco modified his opinion about the equality of nations. He noted the unpopularity of the position of the United States and the support Latin America gave to Brazil's fight for equality. The untenable American position had given Brazil an opportunity to play a significant international role as the champion of equality.[93] Nabuco came to accept the principle of equality as "bound to triumph." [94]

Upon returning to Washington from Europe, Nabuco became aware of the unfavorable American reaction to Brazil's role at the conference. The Americans tended to think Rui Barbosa willfully had led a bloc against them.[95] Even Secretary of State Root registered a mild but apparent dissatisfaction with Brazil's attitude at The Hague.[96] One of the members of the American delegation confided to Nabuco his "disappointment" over Rui Barbosa's behavior, and Nabuco concluded, almost with a sigh of relief, "Fortunately it did not turn out any worse." [97]

Just as Rio-Branco wanted to overlook the temporary disturbance in Brazilian-American relations, Root demonstrated the same intention. Undoubtedly relieved of many anxieties, Nabuco had a "glorious conversation" with the Secretary of State, who attributed no importance to the events at The Hague. When Nabuco inquired if the disagreement at the Peace Conference could be interpreted as a change of American policy, he replied, "On my part, there is not the slightest change," and continued by lauding Brazil and expressing the friendship of the United States.[98] Itamaraty could conclude that the United States agreed that the differences of opinion during the Peace Conference would have no lasting effects on the good relations between the two nations.

THE FLEET VISIT

Occasionally a good diplomatic gesture when relations are strained is to send the navy to show the flag on a friendly visit. When hostile feelings aroused by the Bolivian Syndicate began to appear, the U.S.S. *Iowa* anchored in the Rio harbor for the inauguration of President Rodrigues Alves, a timely call which did much to counteract the anti-American feelings. Similarly, the United States fleet, which paused in 1908 in the Rio harbor on its journey from the Atlantic to the Pacific Ocean, played an especially important role in the relations between the two nations. The fleet visit served as the occasion for both to reaffirm their feelings of solidarity which had been put into question some months before at The Hague.

Nabuco, apparently, first conceived the idea of using the fleet visit as an opportunity to renew the former feeling of confidence between the two nations.[99] In his own words, the "squadron's presence offers us the opportunity to undo the bad impression of The Hague." [100] Rio-Branco was receptive to the suggestion. Assuring Nabuco that the fleet would receive a cordial welcome in Rio de Janeiro, he had certain reservations that the events of The Hague might decrease the usual enthusiasm which could be expected.[101]

Neither need have had any reservations or fears about the reception of the fleet. When the sixteen battleships under the command of Rear Admiral Robley D. Evans steamed into the mountain-ringed harbor on January 12, 1908, the dense crowd lining the shore broke into a tumultuous cheer.[102] A witness to the impressive spectacle recalled the sight:

The majestic warships, white and arrogant . . . entered in an impressive single file, saluting without ceasing so that they were enveloped in the smoke of their own cannons, the salutes were so numerous. The bay was adorned as it never previously had been. Small boats, loaded with the curious, made special trips around those moving fortresses gaily arrayed in our waters, the respectable proof of the increasing power of the United States.[103]

The Brazilians offered their proverbial hospitality to the white-clad visitors. A program of picnics, luncheons, banquets, and balls entertained the high-ranking officers.[104] President Pena informed the officers that Brazil's warm welcome was a demonstration of friendship toward the United States.[105]

When the fleet arrived, President Roosevelt telegraphed a cordial message which delighted the Brazilians. Addressed to President Pena, the message read in part:

The warships of America exist for no other purpose than to protect peace against possible oppression. As between the United States and Brazil these ships are not men-of-war, but are messengers of friendship and good will commissioned to celebrate with you the long-continued and never-to-be broken amity and mutual helpfulness of the two great republics.[106]

Those words, following the disappointment of The Hague, received a hearty welcome and wide circulation in Brazil. They seemed to prove to the Brazilians, as Nabuco already had pointed out less spectacularly in his dispatches, that the United States wished to continue the policy of rapprochement.

To write finis to The Hague, both Rio-Branco and Nabuco tried to persuade Rui Barbosa to make a toast to Brazilian-American friendship at the official banquet honoring the officers of the fleet. Rui Barbosa, under whose responsibility the strain in relations had occurred, would have been the logical person to profess the continuation of the international friendship. Protesting the presence of a military show of might and claiming ill-health, he declined to attend the banquet and to make the toast.[107] Rio-Branco was obliged to excuse him.[108]

The gala banquet in the Monroe Palace on the night of January 20 was the climax of the successful visit of the fleet. Rio-Branco saluted the American nation, president, and fleet in a speech which reflected an intimate knowledge of American history. His words bore no trace of the transient misunderstanding between the two nations a few months before. Describing Brazilian-American friendship as firm, constant, and reciprocal, he unqualifyingly praised "the Great Republic, the pride of the continent." [109] His words complemented those of Roosevelt's telegram and signified that the approximation would continue unchanged.

The reaction to the fleet's visit was very favorable in both countries.[110] The American and Brazilian press concurred that any disagreement at The Hague belonged to the forgotten past. The emphasis now, as it had been before, was on friendship.[111] Apparently Rio-Branco had misjudged the temper of the Brazilians. He seemed more disappointed with The Hague than his compatriots, who quickly forgot the disagreements and eagerly welcomed the United States navy. Reflecting on the significance of the reception of the fleet, Rio-Branco wrote to Dudley, "It shows that the desire always encouraged by the Government of Brazil of constantly strengthening its friendly relations with the United States of America unquestionably has the general support of the Brazilian Nation." [112] In Washington, Nabuco was equally well satisfied with the reception.[113] Vanished were the previous worries about the cordiality of the welcome, and the ambassador revealed his contentment in his diary: "Fortunately it was a great *success* which undoes the impression of The Hague." [114]

Seeking to take advantage of the favorable opinion the fleet's reception created in the United States, Nabuco tried to persuade Rio-Branco to pay an official visit to the United States. The presence of Nabuco, Root, and Roosevelt in Washington undoubtedly ensured him a warm welcome, but he was not enthusiastic about the prospects of undertaking such a long trip. He excused himself on the grounds that neither his health nor the public treasury could permit such a journey.[115] The Baron, once he returned to Rio de Janeiro from Europe, never left the area around the federal capital.

Feeling it obligatory to manage all the details of the ministry personally, he never was absent from his desk for an extended period. He seems to have thought his presence in Rio de Janeiro was indispensable to the success of Brazilian diplomacy. Probably because of those reasons, Nabuco was not successful in convincing him to make the journey.[116] One of the first acts of his successor, Lauro Müller, was to repay the visit of Root.

Grover Cleveland, because of his award favorable to Brazil in the Missions dispute, had enjoyed wide popularity and affection in Brazil. When he died in June, 1908, as a tribute to the man who had given "complete triumph" to Brazil,[117] President Pena ordered the Brazilian flag to fly at half-mast over all public buildings and military installations. Rio-Branco draped in black Cleveland's portrait hanging in Itamaraty, and the Brazilian navy fired a funeral salute.[118] Some months later the name of the town of Bela Vista de Palmas, Paraná, was changed to Clevelandia as a final gesture of Brazil's esteem for the deceased American president.[119]

THE ALSOP CASE

Rio-Branco's foreign policy sought close friendship not only with the United States but also with Chile.[120] With the diplomatic cooperation of those two nations, the Baron felt that Brazil could deal successfully with any intrigues against its interests in the hemisphere.[121] At the same time it was in Brazil's best interest to make certain that friendly relations also existed between its two hemispheric allies. In Rio de Janeiro, Rio-Branco, through the American ambassador, worked to create better understanding between the United States and Chile.[122] Likewise, in Washington, Nabuco, one of whose closest friends was the Chilean minister, Walker Martínez, did his best to encourage good will between Brazil's two closest friends.[123] Friendly relations among the three nations were important for the success of Brazilian diplomacy.

It is understandable, therefore, that news of a pending rupture in Chilean-United States diplomatic relations would disturb Itamaraty. The cause of the threatened rupture was an old claim of an American firm, the Alsop Company. The mining concessions granted the company by Bolivia were not recognized by Chile after the latter obtained in the War of the Pacific the territory in which the concession was located. The Alsop Company got the support of the American government, which sought to settle the matter by arbitration on the condition that Chile accept the principle of the right of the United States to intervene on behalf of a private citizen's claim. When Chile refused to concede that condition, the State Department issued an ultimatum on November 17, 1909: either pay the claims or diplomatic relations would be severed. The United States gave Chile ten days to decide.

Brazil reacted unfavorably to the ultimatum. The Rio press, perhaps with thoughts of the Bolivian Syndicate, denounced the attitude of the United States as threatening and unjust.[124] The incident strengthened Brazilian sympathy for its South American friend.

The Brazilian ambassador and the Minister of Foreign Relations set to work in an effort to prevent the rupture and reestablish understanding. Chilean Minister Cruz informed Nabuco of the events the day after the ultimatum was made. Rio-Branco learned about the ultimatum on the twenty-first. Both took action on that date. Nabuco turned at once to his friend Root, who at the end of the Roosevelt administration had been elected to the Senate. Hearing that he was in Washington for the day, Nabuco dashed off a note asking him, in the name of the Pan American "cause," to intercede with Secretary of State Philander C. Knox to prevent any disruption of relations between Chile and the United States. The ambassador pointed out the adverse reaction in Latin America which a rupture might cause:

I need not tell you that the effect throughout South America would be most discouraging for all the friends of the United States. Friendship and attraction for the United States would be a civilizing influence to all Latin America; fear or distrust, on the contrary, would be a barbarizing influence, as it might bring to power here and there fanatical and violent elements.[125]

At precisely the same time Nabuco was writing those words, Rio-Branco telegraphed his ambassador:

The event . . . will produce the most disagreeable impressions throughout the Americas. Chile is a nation considered respectable by all and is one of the most influential nations of South America. She is thus treated as a small and unimportant country. . . . I cannot understand that a financial claim of this nature is worth more than the continuation of the Pan American policy which the last administration and Root understood and practiced so well and with such success that they uprooted the old prejudices and won for the United States the confidence and good will of the principal Latin American countries.[126]

The action taken by Nabuco and the instructions sent by Rio-Branco, both spontaneous and both done without the knowledge of the other, were in close harmony. They demonstrated a unity of thought between the two diplomats concerning the need to maintain friendly relations between the United States and Chile.

The possible consequences of the Alsop case caused Brazilian diplomats in South America to attempt to find a solution to the deteriorating relations between Chile and the United States. Rio-Branco invited Ambassador Dudley to discuss the Alsop case with him at Itamaraty.[127] In their talks, Rio-Branco expressed sentiments similar to those in his telegram to Nabuco and hoped that a break in diplomatic relations between Santiago and Washington would be avoided.[128] The Brazilian foreign minister conversed daily with the Chilean minister in Rio de Janeiro.[129] In Santiago, the Brazilian minister, Gomes Ferreira, a friend of both Chile and the United States, where he had served for several years, counseled moderation and understanding. However, the principal events occurred in Washington.

After receiving Rio-Branco's telegram ordering him to talk with Secretary of State Knox, Nabuco made an appointment for the afternoon of the twenty-third.[130] Upon arriving at Knox's office, Nabuco was unaware that Root, in answer to his request, had already spoken to the Secretary of State. But the Brazilian ambassador noted at once that any belligerent attitude was absent and that Knox seemed disposed to find a peaceful solution. At that point, Nabuco explained Chile's proposal to name a friendly arbiter to settle the difficulties. According to that proposal, a third party would be selected by mutual consent to judge the Alsop claims and make an award. In effect it was a kind of arbitration without reference to the debated right of the United States to intervene in favor of the claims of a private citizen. Knox immediately approved the suggestion as a convenient solution to the stalemate.[131] The United States formally accepted the Chilean proposal on November 25, and both nations named Edward VII to settle the claims.

Some days later, Nabuco learned of the important role his friend Root had played in the settlement. Just as Root was leaving his apartment on the twenty-first, Nabuco's note arrived. Root called on Knox that afternoon before leaving Washington. Evidently their conversation was the turning point in the Alsop case and resulted in a modification of the harsh United States position. In the words of Root:

I was quite sure from my talk with him that the Chilean matter would be settled without serious difficulty. It would be both deplorable and absurd to have the venerable Alsop case produce such a result.[132]

Root, of course, would not have spoken with Knox had it not been for Nabuco's appeal. Root successfully prepared the Secretary of State to accept the Chilean proposal of a friendly arbiter after Nabuco explained it to him.

Both the United States and Chile appreciated the successful role Brazil played in preventing the break in their relations. Knox sent the Assistant Secretary of State to the Brazilian embassy to thank

Nabuco for his friendly interest in the settlement of the Alsop claim.[133] Later, he twice wrote Nabuco to express his gratitude.[134] Ambassador Dudley formally thanked Rio-Branco for his contributions to the amicable settlement.[135] The American press attributed to "the good office of Baron Rio-Branco . . . an adjustment of the difficulty. . . . He professed timely and not unwelcome mediation."[136] The Chilean ministers in Rio de Janeiro and Washington thanked Nabuco and Rio-Branco for their help.[137] President Pedro Montt sent to Rio-Branco "his thanks and those of the Chilean government for the service of friendship given by Brazil,"[138] and the Chilean government sent a special message of gratitude to the Brazilian government.[139] *El Mercurio,* also, praised Brazilian friendship and thanked the Brazilians for their help.[140]

The Alsop case was one of the great successes of Rio-Branco's hemispheric diplomacy. In it he proved his friendship for both the United States and Chile and gave Brazil a chance for diplomatic leadership in the Americas.

THE FINAL YEARS

Nabuco was able to play in Washington an important role for Brazil in the Alsop case because of the considerable personal prestige he enjoyed. After four years in the American capital, he had become a familiar figure and a close friend to many members of the Washington diplomatic corps and some North American officials, the most important of whom were Root and Roosevelt. A more than occasional visitor at the White House, the ambassador also frequently dined with Root, and together they would go automobile riding in the late afternoon or attend the theater.

Nabuco entered fully into North American life. So friendly did he become with some American politicians that he urged several Republican leaders to include a Pan American plank in their 1908 platform.[141] He crisscrossed the country in a one-man campaign to get to know the United States and to see that North Americans learned something of Brazil. With an excellent command of English, he spoke at universities and clubs throughout the country. Whether at Yale University or the University of Wisconsin or at a civic club in Buffalo, Nabuco demonstrated his intellectual profundity and won friends for Brazil; his cultural campaign was more a novelty in those days than it would have been in later periods of diplomacy. Discoursing on such a familiar subject as Abraham Lincoln or enlightening his listeners on the lesser known Luís de Camões, he pleased his audiences and was a popular speaker.[142] Through that type of activity, he chipped away at the wall of indifference toward Brazil.[143]

Nabuco's successful effort to find a solution for the Alsop case was his final contribution to hemispheric diplomacy and to Brazilian-American friendship. On January 17, 1910, the eminent diplomat died of a cerebral hemorrhage. All Washington, the diplomatic corps as well as government officials, mourned the passing of one of its most respected residents. His funeral was a tribute in which President William H. Taft, Secretary of State Knox, the members of the Supreme Court, congressmen and senators, high military officers, and the diplomatic corps took part.[144] In an unprecedented gesture, President Taft made available an American warship to convey the body back to Brazil and offered his personal yacht to the widow for her return trip. In Brazil, where his compatriots manifested the deepest mourning, those acts of respect were received as "one more proof of the friendship of America for Brazil." [145] Later, the Brazilian Chamber of Deputies, by unanimous resolution, thanked the Congress of the United States "for the affectionate and solicitous attitude of that great nation on the occasion of the death of our glorious compatriot, Joaquim Nabuco." [146]

It is significant, as it is logical, that the years of closest rapprochement between Brazil and the United States during the Rio-Branco ministry were those years when Nabuco served as ambassador.

The only important discord during those five years was at The Hague, and, of course, Nabuco was absent from his post at that time. His greatest achievements as ambassador were persuading Root to attend the Third Pan American Conference, preventing Chile and the United States from breaking diplomatic relations, protecting Brazil's coffee market in the United States, and creating a better understanding of Brazil in the United States. Rio-Branco appreciated Nabuco's important part in the execution of Brazil's new foreign policy and was the first to credit Nabuco with successfully strengthening Brazilian-American relations.[147] While the Baron, rational, cool, and detached, played the role of the grand strategist of the approximation, Nabuco was the warm, personable, somewhat emotional tactician of it. One planned the campaign, the other adapted the master plan to the daily demands.

Finding a substitute for Nabuco was a difficult task, and Rio-Branco spent nearly a year deciding whom he should send to Washington. Finally he named one of his most trusted and closest associates, Domício da Gama, who was then serving as minister in Buenos Aires. Before sailing for the United States in May of 1911, da Gama attended a farewell luncheon President Fonseca gave in his honor. In the presence of high governmental officials, as well as Ambassador Dudley, Rio-Branco made it clear that da Gama was going to Washington to carry on the friendly policy of the government and then raised his glass in a toast to Brazilian-American friendship.[148] A month later, presenting his credentials to President Taft, Ambassador da Gama reaffirmed his country's dedication to that friendship.[149]

Meanwhile, Brazil had welcomed and entertained William Jennings Bryan. Even though he traveled in a purely private capacity, Brazil paid full homage to the distinguished North American. Bryan met and conversed with President Nilo Peçanha, President-elect Hermes da Fonseca, Senator Rui Barbosa, and Rio-Branco, whom he characterized as "one of the ablest public men in South

America, and . . . a good friend of the United States." [150] The government considered his visit, albeit unofficial, another expression of American good will toward Brazil.[151] Feting Bryan at a banquet at Itamaraty, the foreign minister delivered the main address of the evening, a résumé of Brazilian-American diplomatic relations emphasizing the affinities between the two nations.[152]

Those sentiments were embodied in three treaties, concerning naturalization, arbitration, and parcel post, signed during the two-year period following the fleet visit. Of the three, the arbitration treaty was the most significant. Due to Nabuco's efforts, the treaty was signed just two days before Root left the State Department so that the signiture of Brazil's good friend would appear on the treaty, a gesture Root appreciated.[153]

The diplomatic cooperation between the two nations, initiated when Brazil promptly recognized Panama, continued throughout the Rio-Branco ministry and was particularly pronounced during the years 1908–12. For some years, Rio-Branco had been an interested spectator of the deteriorating relations between Venezuela and the United States. In early June of 1908, when a break in Venezuelan-American relations appeared inevitable, Root inquired from Nabuco if Brazil would take charge of United States interests in Venezuela should diplomatic relations be suspended. After consultation with Rio-Branco, Nabuco responded affirmatively.[154] In mid-June, the United States recalled its minister and closed its legation in Caracas.[155] The Brazilian chargé d'affaires in Caracas, Luís Rodrigues de Lorena Ferreira, assumed responsibility for the archives, property, and interests of the United States government. Nabuco telegraphed Rio-Branco nervously that he hoped Lorena had been thoroughly instructed about the importance of his position in Brazilian-American relations.[156] There was no cause for worry. Lorena served the American government well.[157] The reliance of the United States on Brazil was reguarded as a "new success" of the diplomacy of Rio-Branco.[158] When General Juan

Vicente Gómez took control of Venezuela at the end of the year as the new chief of state, one of his first acts was to open negotiations with the government of the United States for the reestablishment of diplomatic relations. Normal relations began again shortly thereafter. The United States was grateful to Brazil for its good offices during the rupture,[159] and the State Department twice expressed its thanks to Rio-Branco.[160]

Just as the United States was settling its differences with Venezuela, Brazilian-Argentine relations were being strained dangerously as a result of the Argentine interception, decoding, falsification, and publication of an official Brazilian telegram being sent to Chile, the communication that became famous as Telegram Number Nine. Foreseeing a possible rupture in diplomatic relations as a consequence, Rio-Branco instructed Nabuco to ask if the United States would take charge of Brazil's interests in Argentina.[161] Expressing hope that no rupture would occur, Root assented to the request and called it "an honor to perform the office of friendship."[162] The reply pleased Rio-Branco.[163] Fortunately the expected break never occurred, but Rio-Branco had the satisfaction of knowing the United States would aid Brazil in a difficult moment by handling Brazilian business in the Argentine capital. There is reason to believe that Rio-Branco felt that the United States offer would strengthen Brazil's position.

Shortly thereafter, Itamaraty and the Department of State coordinated their recognition of two new European governments. When Bulgaria achieved its independence in 1909, Rio-Branco asked the State Department to inform him of the date the United States anticipated recognizing it so that Brazil could extend recognition simultaneously.[164] When the United States telegraphed its recognition on May 4, 1909, Brazil did likewise the following day.[165] The overthrow of the House of Braganza and the proclamation of the Republic of Portugal on October 5, 1910, caused Rio-Branco for a second time to try to coordinate Brazilian-American recognition.[166] His objective was for the two large American republics to acknowledge officially the new European republic on the same day, with Brazil's recognition having precedence by a few hours.[167] Washington was amenable to the idea.[168] However, popular pressure in Brazil favoring immediate recognition was so strong that it forced Rio-Branco to recognize the Portuguese Republic on October 22.[169] Unready and unwilling to act on that date, the United States delayed extending *de facto* recognition until November 11.[170]

In 1910 Rio-Branco cooperated with the United States and Argentine governments in a joint effort to avoid war between Peru and Ecuador over a long-standing boundary dispute. Instructions dispatched by Itamaraty to Quito and Lima told the Brazilian ministers to join with the American and Argentine representatives in recommending the submission of the differences to The Hague Permanent Tribunal.[171] Despite the good intentions of the three largest American republics, the dispute continued and continues today in various forms.

One final demonstration of the good will of the United States toward Rio-Branco was the efforts made by the State Department to encourage Turkey to exchange diplomatic relations with Brazil. Since 1906, Rio-Branco had desired to open diplomatic relations with Turkey because of the large number of Syrians living in Brazil.[172] When the Turkish government continued to respond evasively to his overtures, Rio-Branco asked the United States to approach the government of Constantinople in an effort to persuade the Sultan to send a diplomatic representative to Rio de Janeiro.[173] The United States, on Brazil's behalf, informed the Turkish government that it would be pleased if Turkey would exchange diplomats with Brazil. Despite those efforts the Turks refused to gratify the Baron's wishes.[174]

During the ten-year ministry of Rio-Branco the discord at The Hague stands out as the principal crisis in the friendly Brazilian-

United States diplomatic relations. Its effect was momentary. The two nations reaffirmed their solidarity during the visit of the United States fleet to Rio de Janeiro. Thereafter, cooperation once again characterized their diplomatic relations with each other so that, at the end of the Rio-Branco ministry, Brazil could look back on ten years of intimate diplomatic relations with the United States which were beneficial to both.

CHAPTER VI · THE MONROE DOCTRINE AND PAN AMERICANISM TOO

In the web of events and policies uniting Brazil and the United States diplomatically during the Rio-Branco ministry, few strands were more important than the Monroe Doctrine and Pan Americanism. The foreign policies of the United States and Brazil included both of them, a factor which strengthened the approximation.

The Monroe Doctrine received a mixed, although generally unfavorable, reception in Latin America. The Spanish American nations never officially recognized the doctrine nor gave it hemispheric legitimacy. At best they only tacitly accepted it. Brazil, to the contrary, always accorded the doctrine a cordial welcome.[1] Less than two months after President James Monroe advised Europe on December 3, 1823, to remain aloof from the internal affairs of the Western Hemisphere, the Brazilian government recognized the new doctrine and spoke of an offensive and defensive alliance with the United States.[2] Brazil saw in the doctrine a defense of its newly proclaimed independence and a protection from European aggression.[3] Thereafter, the acceptance of the Monroe Doctrine became an established policy of Brazilian governments.[4]

Accepting the doctrine in principle, Brazil gave its own interpretation to the words of Monroe.[5] As originally presented, the doctrine was a unilateral statement of the United States prohibiting European interference in the affairs of the Western Hemisphere. Refusing to accept the view that the doctrine was a unilateral declaration, Brazil preferred to give Monroe's pronouncement a multilateral interpretation.

During the Rio-Branco period, a majority of the Brazilians upheld the traditional Brazilian view that the Monroe Doctrine required hemispheric cooperation and responsibility. Unwilling to accept the doctrine passively, Rio-Branco and Nabuco sought to share its responsibilities and benefits with the United States by making it a part of hemispheric law enforceable by the cooperative action of the principal republics.[6] In Congress, João Pandiá Calógeras, a firm supporter of the Baron, on numerous occasions declared that a multilateral interpretation of the Monroe Doctrine was an integral part of Brazil's foreign policy.[7] Early in the Rio-Branco ministry, the newspaper *Correio da Manhã* featured an editorial on the doctrine which in many respects exemplified the attitude of the majority of Brazilian leaders.[8] Emphasizing the Brazilian opinion that the doctrine should be multilateral, the editorial stated in part:

If the United States, as the strongest nation on the continent, believes as a matter of fact that it would be to the interest of all the American peoples to effectively prevent the intrusions of Europe; if the Government of the United States is sincere, as we believe it is, then let it do with all the American republics what one government may do with another; let it celebrate with us any treaties which it considers would be useful, with the idea of preserving forever interests which it recognizes as peculiar to the nations of America. Thus, if the protest of Monroe were reduced to a diplomatic formula and consequently to a form having the character of reciprocity, the statement or protest of Monroe would be that of us all. It would be in its fullness a regulating principle of our common action in given emergencies.[9]

To be acceptable to the Brazilians, the Monroe Doctrine had to be the responsibility of the hemisphere, and they, unlike the North Americans, insisted and persisted in giving it a collectivist interpretation.

Regardless of the variance in interpretation between the United States and Brazil, the climate of opinion in Brazil during that period was favorable to the doctrine. Rio-Branco set the mood with his prudent admiration of Monroeism. He stated, "The great service given to the hemisphere by the Monroe Doctrine is the liberty guaranteed to each nation to develop freely." [10] The chancellor believed the doctrine deserved continental support. Ambassador Nabuco was even more enthusiastic than his chief in embracing the doctrine. Of the opinion that the Brazilian acceptance of the North American pronouncement constituted an unofficial alliance between the two republics,[11] Nabuco freely declared himself a "Monroeist," [12] and apparently took pleasure in discussing the Monroe Doctrine with President Roosevelt.[13] Shortly after his arrival in Washington, two leading newspapers, the New York *Times* and the Chicago *Tribune,* featured articles on the ambassador's friendly sentiments toward the Monroe Doctrine.[14] President Afonso Pena spoke favorably of the doctrine.[15] Deputy Dunshee de Abranches, chairman of the congressional committee on diplomacy, was an unmitigated supporter of the Monroe Doctrine and even went so far as to accept the North American interpretation of the doctrine.[16] Others friendly to the doctrine were Clovis Beviláqua, publicist, Alberto Torres, writer, and even Rio-Branco's critic, Oliveira Lima.[17] The last-named, although there were periods in which he was critical of the United States, came to hold the opinion that "the Monroe Doctrine contained a good deal of usefulness." [18] Doubtless one of the most unqualified endorsements of the doctrine was made by the First Secretary of the Brazilian embassy, Gurgel do Amaral, in late 1906. Representing Ambassador Nabuco at the Trans-Mississippi Congress in Kansas City, the Brazilian diplomat, lauding a recent speech by Root on the Monroe Doctrine, stated:

The fundamental principle of the international policy of the United States constitutes also one of the vital principles of the international policy of Brazil. . . . The Monroe Doctrine is . . . an affirmation of peaceful policy, a policy based upon the respect and confidence that all the world ought to have, and really has, towards the younger generations that are building up new countries. . . . It is very gratifying to me to remind any portion of the American public that Brazil has been the first country on earth to recognize fully the Monroe Doctrine. . . . This policy . . . has been invariably devoted to promote, to increase, and to cement the friendship between Brazil and the United States.[19]

The favorable opinion of governmental leaders found an echo in the Brazilian press, which also tended to be sympathetic to the Monroe Doctrine.[20]

Occasionally, however, a critical broadside was fired against the pronouncement of 1823. The *Correio da Manhã,* frequently in opposition to governmental policies, at least once, in 1904, warned against the "Yankee peril" under the vigorous leadership of Theodore Roosevelt.[21] Reflection on some of the implications of the Monroe Doctrine caused the editor of the *Notícias* to ask, "Certainly they [the United States] free us from possible European attempts against the integrity of our territories, but when all is said and done will they not have substituted one peril for another and perhaps a greater?" [22] Those criticisms and doubts represented only a minority opinion; yet, they were always in the background.

Rio-Branco's willingness to use the Monroe Doctrine was proof of Brazil's acceptance of the doctrine.[23] The chancellor showed no reluctance to employ the doctrine when it might serve to strengthen Brazil's international position. An awareness of its value to his foreign policy is evident in such statements as, "The Monroe Doctrine and the respect, mixed with fear, which, by its methods, the United States inspires in the great powers of Europe, have served for many years to prevent Europe from thinking in terms of violence and conquest in our continent." [24] For Brazil's purposes, he considered the doctrine as very "useful," [25] and for that reason he employed it to give himself greater diplomatic maneuverability.

Rio-Branco first discovered its usefulness in the dispute with

France over the Guiana frontier. He understood that French willingness to arbitrate the boundary resulted more from a respect for the Monroe Doctrine (the Venezuelan-British dispute was in the minds of everyone at the time) than from an affinity for the principle of arbitration.[26] Apparently impressed by that lesson in international politics, he did not hesitate to evoke the doctrine during his ministry. His first direct recourse to it was as an argument against the Bolivian Syndicate, which, he pointed out, could fall into European hands and thereby constitute an extracontinental enclave in the heart of South America. Its use against the syndicate won sympathy for his cause in Washington and demonstrated the strength which it could add to Brazilian diplomacy. Later, in March of 1904, when a group of French filibusters in Paris were preparing an invasion of northern Brazil, Rio-Branco telegraphed to the Brazilian legation in Washington:

It would be helpful if some newspapers in that capital or New York would print the news as if it were received from Paris and state that such an attack would not be tolerated by the Monroe Doctrine. I think some articles of that nature would be enough to ridicule and frighten the plotters.[27]

A few days later several leading North American newspapers attacked the adventurers as violaters of the Monroe Doctrine.[28] In the *Panther* case, Rio-Branco once again relied on the moral support of the Monroe Doctrine by requesting Nabuco to enlist newspaper support for Brazil against the apparent German violation of the Monroe Doctrine.[29] The American press unanimously rallied behind Brazil, which caused Nabuco to express his opinion that the Monroe Doctrine was the only guarantee for the independence and integrity of Latin America.[30] The Monroe Doctrine served Rio-Branco well, and by judicious use and support of it he achieved a greater latitude of diplomatic mobility.

Under the energetic leadership of Theodore Roosevelt, the Monroe Doctrine was being expanded during that period. At the turn of the century the United States began to focus its attention on the Caribbean, where the growing pains, irresponsibility, and misbehavior of the smaller republics in that area and consequent threatened European interference in their internal affairs caused concern in Washington. Roosevelt found it necessary to proclaim the possibility of a preventive North American intervention in order to thwart any European meddling. Contained in a message to Congress on December 2, 1904, that announcement became known as the Roosevelt Corollary, an addition to the Monroe Doctrine.[31]

Unlike most of its Spanish-American neighbors, Brazil responded favorably to the corollary.[32] The newspapers in Rio de Janeiro began commenting on Roosevelt's message as early as December 4, and sporadically thereafter editorials discussed the subject. *O Paiz* called the corollary "positive" and felt that the fears of Latin America were "unfounded." [33] *A Notícia* saw no reason for Brazil to be concerned about Roosevelt's statements,[34] and the reporting in the *Jornal do Commercio* was sympathetic to the addition to the Monroe Doctrine.[35] Even the usually querulous *Correio da Manhã* praised the corollary as a restraining force on the misbehavior of the small republics.[36] Just one of the eight newspapers in the capital censured the corollary.[37] The consensus was that Brazil as a large, strong, and progressing country need fear no foreign intervention and should lend its moral support to quieting the turbulent smaller nations.[38]

The realistic Baron saw no reason for Brazil—nor for Argentina and Chile—to be disturbed by the corollary. He understood that the language of the corollary was aimed at the unstable and irresponsible republics whose misbehavior provoked European reprisals and thus necessitated the preventive action of the United States. In itself the corollary posed no menace, and should any of the Latin American republics regard it as such, Rio-Branco pointed out that they themselves had the remedy for the situation: "To try to select honest and provident governments, and by peace and energy to work to progress in wealth and power." [39] The Baron discounted the danger of North American imperialism. When questioned specifically about the Roosevelt Corollary and Central America by an Argentine journalist, the chancellor replied:

If those countries do not know how to govern themselves, if they do not possess those elements necessary to avoid continual revolutions and civil wars that follow one another ceaselessly, they do not have a right to exist and ought to give up their place to a stronger, better organized, more progressive, and more virile nation. [40]

In essence those words were a rephrasing of the Roosevelt Corollary. If any doubts existed about his sentiments concerning the Monroe Doctrine after the Roosevelt addendum, the publication in 1906 of the article "Brazil, the United States, and Monroeism," written by Rio-Branco, and his speech to the military that same year praising the policies of Roosevelt[41] should have removed them. In expressing those sentiments, Rio-Branco was opposing the Drago Doctrine, which offered a certain protection to the less stable nations, and in that context Rui Barbosa spoke and voted against Drago's proposal at The Hague. Ambassador Nabuco was equally emphatic in his support of the Roosevelt Corollary. [42]

There were various reasons why Rio-Branco favored the corollary, but perhaps the most cogent one was that Brazil faced in La Plata a situation analogous to the one faced by the United States in the Caribbean: a large, stable republic neighboring on small turbulent republics. Frequent political chaos in Paraguay and Uruguay embarrassed Brazil, which saw the South American, and more specifically its own, image abroad sullied by much misbehavior. [43] Exasperated by the turmoil in Paraguay in 1905, Rio-Branco suggested that the United States dispatch several warships to Asunción to help restore order. [44] When Rio-Branco admitted that the United States intervention in Cuba in 1906 was "necessary," [45] he possibly was wishing Brazil could do the same under similar circumstances in Paraguay and Uruguay. [46] He gave considerable thought to how responsibility could be imposed on the less stable governments of South America. Exactly at the time Roosevelt announced his corollary, Rio-Branco was thinking of proposing a treaty between Argentina, Brazil, and Chile "with the goal that in case of civil war or insurrection in one of the countries bordering on us, we would try to reestablish, as much as possible, order and peace without detracting from the prestige of the legal government and to prohibit the use of our territories by the revolutionaries." [47] Sentiment in Argentina, as expressed by the press, seemed agreeable to such moral policing by the large South American republics.[48] The objective of this plan was similar to that of the Roosevelt Corollary: the maintenance of stable and responsible governments in Latin America.

Like the corollary, American activity in the Caribbean at that period received only a minimum of criticism in Brazil. The reaction to Roosevelt's conduct in Panama was more favorable than otherwise and intervention in neither Cuba nor Central America aroused hostility.[49] While Spanish America responded violently to the maneuvering of the United States army on the Texas-Mexican border in 1911, Brazil remained silent.[50] Analyzing Spanish America's extreme sensitivity, the *Jornal do Commercio* believed that "Yankee influence" was more "pacific and economic" than political. Then the newspaper posed a rhetorical question which surely would have received caustic answers in some Spanish American capitals:

We . . . have need of foreign capital, immigration, initiative, and money. If, when these auxiliaries came to us from Europe, they did not menace us, why should they menace us now when they come from the United States also? [51]

Clearly, as that responsible paper showed, Brazil's attitude toward the Latin American policy of the United States was serene, self-confident, and sympathetic.

Favorable toward the Monroe Doctrine throughout his ministry, the Baron sought to define it in a general manner acceptable to the United States and Latin America without offending Europe, to which Brazil still had strong sentimental ties and vital commercial links. Knowing Nabuco's enthusiasm for the doctrine, the chancellor charged his ambassador with the responsibility of formulating such a definition.[52] Nabuco sought a definition that would make the doctrine acceptable to all the Latin American nations.[53] After his appointment in early 1909 to head the Brazilian delegation to the Fourth Pan American Conference in Buenos Aires,[54] he suggested to Rio-Branco that Brazil propose there a resolution endorsing the Monroe Doctrine.[55] The Baron concurred and requested the ambassador to frame the resolution.[56] The untimely death of Nabuco prior to the conference required the chancellor to select another chairman for the Brazilian delegation. Fortunately Nabuco already had phrased the resolution, and the Brazilian delegation sailed for Buenos Aires intent upon carrying out Nabuco's original plans.

The Brazilian strategy was to discuss the resolution secretly with Argentina and Chile. With their support, Brazil would present the resolution to the entire assembly of hemispheric delegates for their endorsement. As written by Nabuco, the resolution read:

The long stretch of time since the declaration of the Monroe Doctrine enables us to recognize in it a permanent factor for international peace on the American continent. On this account, while celebrating the first efforts to gain her independence, Latin America sends to her great northern sister the expression of her gratitude for that noble and disinterested initiative that has been of such great benefit to the world.[57]

With an appreciation of the sensitivities of the Spanish American nations, Nabuco had been extremely cautious in phrasing it. The resolution seemed sufficiently moderate to ensure a two-thirds approval or, with good luck, possibly the desired unanimous approval of the conference.

The secret discussions among the ABC delegations began in mid-July. By the twenty-first, word about the talks and their content had leaked out to the press and other delegations, which registered some concern that they had been excluded from the preliminary discussions. The chief delegate from the Dominican Republic noted in his official report, in an exclamation of surprise, that his delegation never received information about the resolution until the Buenos Aires newspapers began to comment on it on July 21.[58] Even the State Department was taken by surprise—albeit a pleasant one.[59]

The ABC discussions of the Nabuco resolution continued until July 24, when, owing to mounting opposition, it was shelved quietly and never appeared on the official program of the conference. Within the tripartite discussions, Chile showed reluctance to accept the resolution without changes.[60] Some of the other delegates voiced reservations about the whole idea and expressed their intention to make additions or corrections.[61] The probability of a full-scale debate of the Monroe Doctrine, a potentially volatile subject which might detract from the desired harmony of the conference, prompted Brazil and Argentina, with the approval of the United States,[62] to drop the resolution. Consequently the Fourth Pan American Conference never debated it.

Despite the failure to give hemispheric sanction and legitimacy to the Monroe Doctrine, the conference treated it with great respect. Argentina, not to be outdone by the initiative taken by its neighbor, made great efforts to demonstrate its support of the doctrine. In opening and closing the conference prominent Argentine delegates lauded the ideas of Monroe.[63] At the final session, Luís Toledo Herrarte, delegate from Guatemala, also praised the doctrine before the delegates.[64] Still, it was Brazil, in formulating a resolution favorable to the doctrine and introducing it to ABC discussion, that most convincingly evidenced its friendly regard for the historic proclamation. It was another manifestation, perhaps for the benefit of the Spanish American nations, of the close association between Brazil and the United States. At any rate, Brazil emerged from the conference as the warmest supporter of the doctrine and, as such, closely linked to the United States.

Contrary to what happened in most Latin American countries,

the Monroe Doctrine always received a hospitable reception in Brazil. An issue which frequently served as cause for disagreement between the United States and Spanish America proved to be one more bond uniting the United States and Brazil. Rio-Branco chose to emphasize the positive side of the doctrine and to employ it when it best served the interests of Brazilian policy. Although the definition of the meaning of the pronouncement might differ in Rio de Janeiro and Washington, the variance never detracted from the general harmony characterizing the approximation. Diplomatic relations between the two countries were more cordial because of the Monroe Doctrine.

In his dedication to and encouragement of Pan Americanism, Rio-Branco also harmonized his foreign policy with the policy of the United States. At about the same time the two republics developed a more lively interest in the Pan American movement. With Blaine's call for the First Pan American Conference in 1889, the United States had begun to take a penetrating second look at the other nations of the hemisphere. The frontier conquered and industrialization an economic fact, the United States had more time to concentrate its energy on hemispheric affairs. A few years later, Rio-Branco began to focus the principal attention of his country on the New World rather than the Old.

The changing emphasis in Brazilian foreign policy meant that closer relations with neighbors in the Western Hemisphere received a new impetus. To the delegates of the Third Pan American Conference, Rio-Branco outlined Brazil's intentions to strengthen its relations with all the nations of the continent, particularly with its immediate neighbors.[65] In his declared support for friendly relations among the hemispheric nations (more often than not foes rather than friends), he became one of the precursors of modern, practical Pan Americanism. His five official speeches on Pan American themes demonstrated that dedication to hemispheric cooperation and repeatedly expressed the hope that the nations of the Western Hemisphere would live in harmony, toward which goal he pledged his country. A convincing proof of the sincerity of Brazil's Pan American policy was the consistent support of it not only in the public and official speeches made for international consumption but also in the chancellor's private correspondence. A few months before his death, he wrote to Domício da Gama a letter containing his hopes for Pan Americanism:

I express the deep hope which we have that the spirit of cooperation and good will manifested in the American conferences will produce the practical results we all ought to have the desire of seeing realized in America.[66]

Those remarks in that confidential letter, like all his private statements on the subject, concurred with the officially pronounced policy of Itamaraty. He sincerely desired to make the Pan American system work.

Among Brazilians of the period there was considerable similarity in defining Pan Americanism. Rio-Branco defined it as a hemispheric movement "to substitute for unfounded distrust and resentment a growing friendship among all the American peoples." [67] Minister Assis Brasil in a press interview in Buenos Aires spoke of Pan Americanism as "a policy of cordiality and intimacy for all the republics of the continent," characterized by "friendship," "fraternity," "peace," "harmony," and "frank approximation." [68] On the occasion of the Third Pan American Conference, Arthur Orlando's book, *Pan-Americanismo*, appeared in support of hemispheric solidarity. He wrote: "Pan Americanism is a work of fraternization between Pan Latinism and Pan Saxonism, awaking among all the people of America the idea and the sentiment of a common destiny." [69] To Oliveira Lima, on occasion a harsh critic of individual nations of the hemisphere, Pan Americanism was "international harmony with a mutual respect." [70] Pan Americanism was an idea in republican Brazil virtually without serious opponents, and in the broad, somewhat sentimental definition of it, Brazil's fraternal goals once again coincided with those of the United States.

Rio-Branco's contributions to Pan Americanism were impressive. At times his efforts concentrated on details such as urging the United States to establish a legation in Asunción[71] or advising Root to extend his visit to Brazil to other South American countries in order to avoid undue jealousies.[72] Of greater significance to incipient Pan Americanism were his three principal contributions toward its growth. First, by settling the various frontiers with Spanish America, he eliminated causes for disputes and opened the way for better understanding between Spanish and Portuguese America, a requisite for the development and success of Pan Americanism. He customarily handled the negotiations in such a way that the litigant governments remained friendly after signing the boundary treaties.[73] Second, he conducted a highly successful Pan American conference. Debates had stultified the first two conferences. In contrast, the brief and well-planned third conference consolidated and gave permanence to the Pan American movement.[74] Third, he succeeded in harmonizing Spanish America and the United States. That achievement was particularly notable at the Rio conference where, thanks to a great extent to the Baron's diplomacy, the United States was accepted more by the rest of the continent and old suspicions and resentments were mitigated.[75] Through those three contributions, Rio-Branco gave pragmatic form to the Brazilian sentiments favoring Pan Americanism.

Pan Americanism and Monroeism, integral parts of the Baron's foreign policy, were not regarded by the Brazilians as separate, unconnected goals. To the Baron they were practically one and the same. Pan Americanism was the continental, multilateral expression of the Monroe Doctrine; Pan Americanism gave solidarity to the Monroe Doctrine; and the Monroe Doctrine expressed the basic aims of Pan Americanism.[76] The desire of the Brazilian government to have the Fourth Pan American Conference endorse the Monroe Doctrine illustrated perfectly the unification of Pan Americanism and Monroeism in the thinking of Itamaraty. The United States, and most certainly Spanish America, might have separated the two, but to the Baron they were inextricably intertwined. In that respect Brazil was a precursor of the present efforts, which began after World War II, to Pan-Americanize the Monroe Doctrine and thereby make the doctrine palatable throughout Latin America.

In the final analysis it matters little if the technical definitions of those two "isms," Pan Americanism and Monroeism, varied in the lexicons of Itamaraty and the Department of State because regardless of any variance they harmonized. The two governments never had occasion to debate semantics. Despite a slight difference in motives, both endorsed the Monroe Doctrine and Pan Americanism and thereby created a unity of policy and action which benefited the Brazilian-American rapprochement.

CHAPTER VII · THE
REASONS WHY

Throughout his ten-year ministry, Rio-Branco demonstrated his sincere friendship for the United States. In fact, even before he took office, he expressed his admiration for that country.[1] Barely a month after taking up his duties at Itamaraty, he announced his intention "to be always in accord with the government of Washington," [2] a statement he repeated to the American minister the following month.[3] Despite vicissitudes in Brazilian-American relations during the ensuing decade, the chancellor maintained a consistently pro-American policy, based on "frankness" and "friendship," [4] in an effort to strengthen progressively the good relations between the two countries.[5] Such a policy he considered to be in the best interest of Brazil.[6] Indeed, it was a "necessary friendship" that helped to ensure the successful execution of the basic aims of Brazil's foreign policy.[7]

The new emphasis Rio-Branco gave to friendship with the United States signified a major shift in Brazil's traditional foreign policy, from Europe to the Western Hemisphere, a shift of diplomatic focal points from London to Washington. Under the empire, economic ties and sentiments linked Brazil closely to Portugal and to Great Britain, particularly the latter. The proclamation of the republic accented an already discernible tendency to align Brazil with the United States and to deemphasize relations with former monarchial mentors. The Baron accelerated that general trend. A realist with a world-wide vision of diplomacy, he understood that the changing times called for a new foreign policy in which the United

States would play a more important role than Great Britain. Breaking with the past, he announced, "Washington is our most important post."[8] That recognition signified for Brazil the shift of its diplomatic axis. Two nearly simultaneous events further dramatized the shift: the unfavorable decision of the king of Italy in the Guiana boundary dispute, which disappointed the Brazilians and cooled their ardor toward Europe,[9] and the elevation of the Brazilian legation in Washington to an embassy.

The shift in diplomatic emphasis that Rio-Branco brought to Itamaraty did not go unnoticed within Brazil. One of the first to note the change was, not surprisingly, the *Jornal do Commercio,* more often than not a mouthpiece for Itamaraty. It observed:

> It appears to us that the axis of the new international policy of Brazil . . . has shifted.
> . . . All feel that ever since the founding of the nation no act of Brazilian international life has had more importance than our diplomatic approximation with the United States. For having accomplished this, the Baron of Rio-Branco gave our country a position in the world such as it never has had before.[10]

Those were observations and sentiments shared by such distinguished contemporaries of Rio-Branco as Araujo Jorge and Calógeras.[11]

In both countries supporters of the increasing rapprochement foresaw as its logical conclusion an alliance between Brazil and the United States. Brazilians tended to speculate more than North Americans about some form of possible alliance. Brazilian newspapers, for example, devoted considerably more coverage and editorials to the topic than did their North American counterparts, and high-ranking governmental officials in Rio de Janeiro spoke oftener and more favorably about such an alliance than did officials in Washington. There was just a sufficient number of allusions made in Washington to some kind of special agreement to keep the topic alive and to encourage Brazilian speculation.

"Our powerful sister and ally of the North" were the words Rio-Branco used when he referred to the United States as early as 1902.[12] Perhaps the Baron was overly enthusiastic when he employed that phrase or perhaps some wishful thinking took verbal form. The statement gives a possible clue to what might have been on the Baron's mind when he returned to Brazil to take up his new duties. At any rate, he waited several more years before he took any action that might be construed as giving substance to those words.

The elevation of the legations to embassies seems to have been his first public effort to give expression to his expectations of some formal understanding between the two countries. As a matter of fact, the elevation precipitated the initial discussion of a possible alliance. *O Paiz* equated the creation of the new embassies to the signing of an *entente cordiale* between the two nations,[13] an opinion not at all uncommon in the political circles of Rio de Janeiro. Some months later the same newspaper commented again in a similar manner,[14] joined then by the *Gazeta de Notícias,* which spoke of an unwritten understanding guiding the two nations.[15] While the papers conjectured, Itamaraty maintained a discreet silence on the subject. No immediate comment was forthcoming from Washington either, although the North American minister sent the newspaper clippings about an alliance to the Department of State.

Months later, sounding as if the United States were interested in some kind of formal understanding between the two governments, Washington issued a series of curious statements. Secretary of State Elihu Root had just been sworn in and was inaugurating a new policy toward Latin America. At once sensitive to the changes, Ambassador Nabuco dutifully reported to his superior the increasing interest of the United States in Latin America which seemed to indicate a period of closer cooperation between the two areas.[16] While formulating this new policy, Root called Nabuco into his office for a private conversation on continental affairs, the contents of which

Nabuco telegraphed to Rio-Branco in a message marked, "very Confidential. To be deciphered only with special authorization." [17] Under such an intriguing security classification, Nabuco related Root's proposal for a triple entente between the United States, Brazil, and Mexico to enforce the Monroe Doctrine in this hemisphere. A few days later, President Roosevelt discussed the same subject with Nabuco.[18] Attributing great importance to the conversation, Nabuco concluded that the United States wanted to see Brazil become the most influential nation in South America. Later that month, while laying the groundwork for the Secretary of State's visit to Brazil, Root and Nabuco exchanged letters in which Root once again spoke of the good effects that would result from the increase of Brazil's "influence" throughout the hemisphere and expressed a hope for a "union of influence" between Brazil and the United States in this hemisphere.[19] Nabuco, of course, informed Rio-Branco of those attitudes.[20] The statements must have had the effect of encouraging official Brazilian hopes for a closer, formal agreement with Washington. Nabuco continued thinking thereafter about some form of "tacit alliance" between Brazil and the United States.[21]

Root's visit to Brazil increased speculation about a possible alliance. From Washington, Nabuco suggested to Rio-Branco that the Secretary's presence in Rio de Janeiro would be an excellent opportunity to formulate the basis for an entente.[22] Before the Secretary's departure, the Washington *Star* carried the headline, "Why Root Goes South. Real Purpose of His Trip to Brazil Will Seek an Alliance." [23] Claiming as its source of information "the highest authority," the article asserted:

It is the President's intention, in view of the close relations between the Republic of Brazil and the United States, to arrange an informal— but none the less strong—alliance with Brazil, and to relegate to her the policy of the Monroe Doctrine in South America.

As it turned out, the *Star*'s reporter seems to have been well informed. In one of his speeches in Rio de Janeiro, Secretary of State Root hinted about such an informal alliance in these words:

Let the United States of North America and the United States of Brazil join hands, not in formal written treaties of alliance, but in the universal sympathy and confidence and esteem of their peoples.[24]

Given the traditional policy of the United States on foreign alliances, the suggestion of an unwritten alliance was about as far as the Secretary of State could reasonably be expected to go. It was enough to continue to encourage within Brazil meditation on, thoughts about, and comments on an alliance—formal or informal—between the two countries. Apparently the Chilean minister in Rio de Janeiro at the time was impressed enough at the growing ties between the two countries to speak of Brazil as "practically the ally" of the United States.[25] After animating the Brazilians about the possibility of an informal alliance or some such nebulous arrangement, Root returned to Washington not to mention the subject again. Nor did any other North American official speak thereafter about any such type of alliance or understanding.

In Brazil, on the other hand, talk of an entente with Washington lasted for several more years, and Rio-Branco continued to favor the establishment of some kind of accord between the two countries.[26] The disagreement at The Hague temporarily stopped Brazilian speculation about an alliance, but the fleet visit in 1908 revived it. Once again journalists and eminent Brazilians joined Rio-Branco and Nabuco in conjecturing about a possible alliance.[27] Oliveira Lima believed a "tacit agreement" existed between Brazil and the United States,[28] and Dunshee de Abranches spoke of a "perfect alliance" "without need of a treaty." [29] Such speculation continued until the end of the Rio-Branco ministry.[30]

Talk about an alliance between Brazil and the United States was a direct result of the shift of Brazil's diplomatic axis from London to

Washington under Rio-Branco's policy to accelerate the rapprochement between the two countries. That the talk was considerable and continuous and was reciprocated to a certain degree by Washington meant that Rio-Branco had successfully carried out Brazil's shift of diplomatic emphasis. Rio-Branco did not bring about that major change in Brazilian diplomacy without serious consideration. A series of historical, commercial, and political reasons firmly supported his action.

Probably the most oft-quoted reason for the rapprochement was historical. None of the Brazilian leaders of the period, certainly Rio-Branco included, would have admitted that the policy of approximation was an innovation. They claimed they were carrying out a traditional policy of friendship.[31] In that claim there was a good deal of truth—or sentimentality at any rate. Although the past provided several historical arguments in favor of the theory of traditional friendship, a close scrutiny reveals that 1889, only thirteen years before Rio-Branco's ministry, marked the real beginning of continuously close relations between Brazil and the United States. As Rio-Branco showed in his article, "Brazil, the United States, and Monroeism," he had a sentimental view of Brazilian-American relations and preferred to emphasize only the positive aspects of them. He chose to find in the past the basis for the approximation, and the fact that he repeatedly emphasized the historical affinities of the two nations as the reason for the approximation gave the historical reason considerable importance. North America's early recognition of Brazilian independence, the welcome accorded Pedro II, and the protection given the republic always stirred up sentimental feelings in Brazil, and all taken together provided the basis for the historical friendship that was one of the reasons for Rio-Branco's policy of approximation with the United States.

More convincing were the commercial reasons for the growing friendship. Statistics of the period vary erratically, but no matter which ones are selected they demonstrate one fact: the preponderant role of the United States as the chief customer of Brazil's exports. As shown in Chapter III, the United States was the single largest buyer of Brazil's three major exports: coffee, rubber, and cocoa. In 1904 the United States bought about 50 percent of Brazil's exports, whereas Great Britain and Germany, Brazil's two other principal markets, together took only about 30 percent of the exports.[32] Statistics from the last years of the Rio-Branco ministry reaffirmed that trend. In 1909 the United States bought 40 percent of Brazil's exports and in 1910 and 1911, 36 percent. The percentage of exports going to England fell from 24 in 1910 to 15 in 1911.[33] During the Rio-Branco ministry, the predominance of the United States as Brazil's most important market, a trend clearly discernible during the last half of the nineteenth century, became an established fact of Brazilian economics.

Brazil during the Rio-Branco period prospered in direct ratio to coffee sales abroad. Coffee encountered no native competitor in the North American market, where the beverage enjoyed increasing popularity. The Brazilian *fazendeiro* supplied the coffee the North American consumer demanded, a simple law of economics at work. Production of coffee in Brazil and its consumption in the United States, a complementary act, economically welded Brazil to the United States.[34] Since the United States consistently purchased most of the coffee, the North American coffee drinker literally held in his cup the fate of Brazil's prosperity, making the American consumer the arbiter of Brazil's economic fortunes. Practical economics required friendly relations toward the chief consumer or, at worst, a policy that would not alienate the market.

Another commercial factor encouraging the approximation was that the exports of both nations complemented each other.[35] Brazil sold tropical and semitropical products on the world market. The United States sold manufactured goods and raw produce from temperate zones. No economic interests clashed—as they did between Argentina and the United States, both of which exported wheat and flour and competed for the same foreign markets.

The rapid economic growth of the United States, its expanding industrialization, and its increasing manufacturing efficiency excited the admiration of Brazil, whose businessmen, industrialists, bankers, and economists were beginning to look more and more to the north as an example.[36] After all, the United States was adequate proof that a new nation carved out of the wilderness of a new continent could rise to the economic level of, or even surpass, the nations of Europe. The broad and general historical and geographical similarities that Brazil shared with the United States made it a more valid model to follow than Europe.

The interplay of economic and political diplomacy did not escape Rio-Branco.[37] On two occasions when the chancellor explained the basis for the approximation with the United States, he emphasized the importance commerce played in Brazilian-American relations. "The United States is the principal market for our coffee," he pointed out once,[38] and later, in an interview, he listed as one of the two reasons for the approximation "the exchange of commercial products." [39]

Other commentators on Brazilian diplomacy agreed with Rio-Branco that commercial reasons contributed significantly to the rapprochement. The principal link between the two countries, according to the Chilean minister in Rio de Janeiro, was commercial.[40] Joaquim Nabuco and Oliveira Lima attributed to commerce one of the chief reasons for the approximation.[41] Various newspaper editorials in the Brazilian capital voiced the same opinion.[42]

Political forces were also at work to effect the approximation. Since the inconfidência in 1789, Brazilians had admired and hoped to emulate the North American form of government.[43] In a huge and diverse country like Brazil, federalism, as perfected in the United States, fascinated and attracted many, but as long as Brazil maintained a parliamentary monarchy, the governmental example followed was highly centralized Great Britain.[44] Once the republic was established, however, Brazil looked elsewhere for its model and focused attention on Washington. The principal author of the Constitution of 1891, Rui Barbosa, confessed readily to following the Constitution of the United States as his model.[45] A comparison of the two documents reveals unmistakable similarities, the most striking of which is federalism. Structurally the new Brazilian government closely resembled the North American.[46]

The newly created similarities between the hitherto diverse governments gave the two countries more in common than before.[47] President de Moraes and Rui Barbosa both paid tribute to the government and Constitution of the United States as an inspiration for Brazilian republicanism.[48] Rui Barbosa believed that the adaptation of the Constitution of 1787 brought in its wake "an intimate approximation between us," [49] a conclusion with which Rio-Branco thoroughly agreed.[50]

Practical international politics of the hemisphere further dictated that Brazil should be friendly toward the United States. Spanish-speaking countries surrounded Brazil on three sides. Brazil had fought against several of them and had experienced boundary problems with all of them. Throughout the nineteenth century, the power politics of South America had taught Brazil to be suspicious of her Spanish-speaking neighbors.[51] Rio-Branco, constantly wary of their intrigues, neither liked nor trusted them. The chancellor regarded the Peruvians as a "very false and pretentious people," [52] and the Paraguayans as "not to be trusted because, in the end, they are not sincere friends." [53] But most of his antipathy was saved for the Argentines, whom he accused of "envy and ill-will" [54] and "intrigue." [55] Both North American and Chilean diplomats in Rio de Janeiro noted among the Brazilians from the highest governmental officials down to the man in the street a marked disdain for the Argentines.[56] The private remarks of Rio-Branco revealed the depth of this dislike for Spanish America in general. Minister Thompson passed on to Secretary of State Hay an indication of those sentiments:

From things said to me on various occasions it is certain Baron Rio-Branco has no little ill-feeling for Argentina, Peru, and Bolivia, and no liking for any of the South American countries other than his own, unless it may be Chile. . . . During the late trouble between Brazil and Peru, he said to me "no Spanish-speaking country is good and no person of Spanish blood can be trusted." [57]

Several years later Rio-Branco repeated essentially the same idea to Ambassador Dudley.[58] The Baron believed that within the Latin American community of nations Brazil lived in an "atmosphere of hate and prejudices" created by her jealous neighbors.[59] Mutual suspicions between Spanish-speaking countries and their single Portuguese-speaking neighbor ran deep. The single exception was Chile, a country that never bordered on Brazil but did flank Brazil's chief rival, Argentina. Those two reasons explain the traditional friendship between Brazil and Chile.[60]

Since geography placed Spanish and Portuguese America together, Rio-Branco, a pragmatist in diplomacy, found it expedient to live as harmoniously as possible with his neighbors, and despite his personal feelings he did as much as possible to maintain friendly relations with them. His Pan American sentiments were genuine. However, a distinction must be drawn between Rio-Branco's policy of official friendliness toward Spanish-speaking America and his private reservations and distrust, realizing that the latter undoubtedly influenced many of his decisions and formed the context in which he directed Brazil's foreign policy.

Rio-Branco's distrust of Spanish America and the consequent feeling of isolation in the hemisphere prompted him to look toward another such isolated country, the United States.[61] Both countries differed from Spanish America in language, history, size, and ethnic background. Because of those differences, they stood apart from the eighteen-nation fraternity of Spanish-speaking nations into which neither was accepted.[62] As the Baron pointed out, the Spanish Americans disliked Brazilians and North Americans equally.[63] Consequently it was natural for the two "outcasts" to become better friends.[64] Closer relations with the United States became one of Rio-Branco's ways to offset Brazil's feeling of solitude or ostracism in South America.[65] Seemingly a similar desire to avoid isolation within the hemisphere encouraged Theodore Roosevelt to embrace Brazil more cordially than he might otherwise have done.[66] Thus, exclusion by the Spanish American republics became another cause for the rapprochement between Brazil and the United States.

The aggrandisement of Brazil by increasing its prestige abroad was a primary foreign policy goal of Rio-Branco. Having spent a good portion of his life outside of Brazil, the chancellor was acutely conscious of the importance of creating and maintaining a good name for Brazil in the world.[67] He announced his intention to the hemisphere: "Today . . . the Brazilian Nation only desires to aggrandize itself through fruitful works of peace." [68] That ambition took some strange forms. He expensively augmented Nabuco's allowance so that the ambassador could live in Washington on a level with the ambassadors from important European states.[69] The anecdotes about Rio-Branco's concern with Brazil's prestige are legion but one is sufficient to illustrate the point. While making preparations to entertain a distinguished foreign visitor to Brazil, Rio-Branco requested a luxury coach of the Central Railroad to transport the guest. On second thought, he spoke personally with the employees who would accompany the visitor, and after making several recommendations he finally advised them: "There is no need to say that this is the only luxury coach we own. It is preferable that he assume that we have others even fancier." [70] Such constant attention to minute detail helped him to achieve his goal. Chilean and Argentine observers credited the Baron with raising Brazil's prestige in the world.[71] The national press agreed,[72] as do historians.[73]

One of the methods Rio-Branco used to aggrandize Brazil was through close association with the United States, whose prestige and power after the Spanish-American War had reached a new height. Friendship with the United States "would be better than the largest army or navy," Nabuco believed.[74] He reasoned in favor of the approximation as a means of national defense.[75] Rio-Branco agreed.[76] The informal alliance strengthened Brazil's position vis-à-vis Europe and improved its position in South America.[77] Brazil's support of the Monroe Doctrine was a guarantee against unwarranted European intervention. Diplomatic primacy over the other South American representatives in Washington meant that in any dispute with those nations Brazil at best could count on the moral support of the United States, at worst Washington could be neutralized so that Brazil could maneuver diplomatically in South America without fear of any pressure from the Department of State.[78] Brazil's diplomacy in Acre was proof that Rio-Branco succeeded in neutralizing the potential power of Washington (in the dispute with Bolivia) and in using Washington's diplomatic pressure (in the dispute with Peru) to Brazil's advantage. Whether or not an actual agreement existed mattered little to the Baron as long as other countries believed such an arrangement, because their belief in such an accord improved Brazil's diplomatic position by increasing its maneuverability in the South American diplomatic chess game.[79] The conclusion was that close association with the United States strengthened Brazil's international position.[80]

At the same time Rio-Branco used his favorable position in Washington to increase Brazil's prestige.[81] Secretary Root's preference for Rio de Janeiro had been one of the deciding factors in selecting that city for the meeting of the Third Pan American Conference. His presence at the meeting added measurably to its importance and success. When questions of prestige were at stake, the Baron did not hesitate to use the good offices of the Secretary of State. He asked Root to intervene to make sure that Rui Barbosa received an office at the Hague Peace Conference. "Because of Brazil's great political and commercial importance," he was anxious that Rio de Janeiro, as a matter of prestige, boast of the largest foreign diplomatic corps in Latin America.[82] Understandably, therefore, he was disturbed when Turkey refused to send a minister to Brazil, and as a result he requested that the United States put pressure on Turkey to exchange diplomats with Brazil.

In identifying themselves with the United States for purposes of national aggrandizement, Brazilians liked to think of themselves as the South American counterpart of the United States. Explicit in the analogy was a pretension to a moral hegemony over South America similar to that exercised by the United States over the Caribbean. Size, population, and potentiality supported Brazil's self-comparison with the United States. As one Brazilian commentator expressed it: "In the American continent there are two foci of civilization, one in the north, the other in the south." [83] He implied that the two giants should divide the continent into two spheres of influence and mutually support each other. Those aspirations received an impetus from Rio-Branco, who spoke of the "beneficial influence" the United States and Brazil jointly could exercise over the rest of Latin America.[84] Such aspirations received encouragement from the nationalists[85] and struck an enthusiastic note in the press of Rio de Janeiro.

The press, not at all bashful about discussing Brazil's dreams of South American hegemony, displayed its exhilarating tendencies. The *Gazeta de Notícias* found similarities between the position of the United States in the Northern Hemisphere and Brazil in the Southern.[86] *A Imprensa* allowed that Brazil had "the necessary preeminence to speak in the name of this part of the continent," [87] an opinion shared by the *Jornal do Commercio*.[88] Most explicit were these remarks from *O Paiz*:

> Our duties and responsibilities on the continent are increasing day by day. . . .
> . . . Brazil has the transcendent obligations of assuring the autonomy and progress of the continent from the line of the equator south.[89]

On another occasion, in an article written to commemorate the elevation of the legations and inspired by Rio-Branco, *O Paiz* continued:

> So long as history is prepared to receive Brazil as the Ambassador of South American fraternity, it is just that the United States should receive us from now on as equals in the guarding of the destinies of the American continent.[90]

The United States seemed willing to acknowledge Brazil's preeminence in South America. No evidence exists that any United States official tried to deride Brazil's ambitions. To the contrary, several high officials encouraged Itamaraty's aspirations. President Roosevelt hoped that Brazil would be strong enough to guard the Monroe Doctrine in South America,[91] and Secretary of State Hay refused to accede to Brazil's request that the United States intervene in Uruguay and Paraguay claiming that Brazil should use its own offices there.[92] Minister William I. Buchanan, one of the outstanding Latin American specialists in the State Department, passed through Brazil in 1902 on his return to Washington after serving for six years as minister in Buenos Aires. The visit to Brazil impressed him so much that he wrote in the New York *Herald*:

> They [the Brazilians] are proud of the growth and increasing power of their own country, are fully alive to the fact that their territory is as great as ours, and are keenly jealous of the supremacy for themselves in South America which the United States boasts in the northern continent.[93]

William Jennings Bryan expressed similar ideas after his visit to Brazil some years later.[94] The New York *Times* and the New York *Daily Tribune* also concurred.[95] Among responsible North American authorities, Brazil found a climate of opinion favorable to its claim of moral hegemony over South America.

While Brazil stood apart from Spanish America, it was never as isolated from the Spanish-speaking nations as the United States. Brazil might have been relegated to the role of a half-sister, but the United States could never hope for any closer relationship with Spanish America than that of a very distant cousin. Standing as intermediary between Spanish America and the United States, Rio-Branco took advantage of his position to serve both as an interpreter of United States policy to Latin America and as a link between Latin America and the United States. His intimate relations with Washington gave him better claim to those roles than any other Latin American had, and he exploited those roles for Brazil's benefit.

The policies of the United States in the Caribbean were extremely unpopular throughout Spanish America. The Roosevelt Corollary, the Big Stick, Dollar Diplomacy, and intervention created an atmosphere of distrust, suspicion, and dislike in Latin America, more specifically in Spanish America. Realizing that none of these policies was intended for Brazil and understanding the reasons for them, Rio-Branco tended to interpret them in the most favorable light possible.[96] To the statesmen in Washington he generally attributed altruistic motives or found excuses for their action.[97] "Faith" in the "good intentions" of the United States government characterized Rio-Branco's attitude toward North American policies.[98] Because of that attitude, Brazilian diplomats gave to the Spanish American foreign ministries favorable explanations of the Washington policies.[99] In that way, Rio-Branco became an interpreter of North American policy in Spanish America, and in a limited sense Brazil became the link between Spanish America and the United States.[100] Functioning as a buffer between North American action and Spanish American reaction, particularly in South America, seemed to serve a dual purpose for Itamaraty: Brazil gave the impression to the Spanish American countries of sufficient intimacy with the United States to be able to interpret its policies and to the United States of being indispensable in preparing Spanish America to receive and even to accept its policies. Both roles augmented Brazil's prestige.

Not satisfied to serve only as a link between the United States and Spanish America in policy matters, Rio-Branco developed that role further and raised it to a more practical plane, so that on several occasions he intervened directly in the diplomatic relations between the United States and Spanish American countries to avoid a crisis or to speed along some worthy cause. Those cases of practical diplomatic assistance established Brazil as a bridge for diplomatic traffic between South and North America. A few examples illustrate a decade of activity. In 1906 Rio-Branco telegraphed Nabuco to persuade Root to exclude arbitration from the agenda of the Third Pan American Conference since that topic was anathema to Chile.[101] In 1908 Rio-Branco tried to persuade the United States to establish a legation in Asunción, the only Latin American capital without a North American minister.[102] During the same year, Rio-Branco ordered Nabuco to help the Chileans in their boundary dispute with Peru by convincing Washington that Chile's proposals were just.[103] And of course in 1909 Brazil's timely intervention prevented a rupture of Chilean-American diplomatic relations over the Alsop claims. As these examples indicate, Rio-Branco successfully served as a diplomatic nexus between South America and the United States.

As a diplomatic link between South America and the United States, as an interpreter of North American policy and action in Latin America, as a close associate of the United States, and as the self-elected South American counterpart of the United States, Brazil was carrying out policies helpful to its primary goal of aggrandizement. Identification with the United States in those various ways gave Brazil a certain amount of power and prestige which in turn improved its image abroad. The desire for aggrandizement was one of the political reasons for the new emphasis on friendship with the United States.

A study of the causation of the Brazilian-American rapprochement would be incomplete if it did not take into account the human factor. A group of leaders, both in Rio de Janeiro and in Washington, worked diligently in favor of greater friendship and better understanding between the two republics. The rapprochement prospered in direct proportion to the support the national leaders gave it.

Notable among a large percentage of Brazilian leaders during the first decade of the twentieth century was a pro-United States feeling.[104] Rodrigues Alves in the presidency, Rio-Branco in the cabinet, Nabuco in the diplomatic service, Dunshee de Abranches in the Chamber of Deputies, José Carlos Rodrigues in journalism, and Graça Aranha in literature exemplified that current in Brazilian leadership. Those men inherited, to a certain extent, the enthusiasm of Salvador de Mendonça for the United States, particularly as manifested in the last decade of the nineteenth century. The principal Brazilian newspapers, with some exceptions, shared the friendly feelings of the national leaders for the United States. Public opinion, too, as reflected in the press as well as in the popular demonstrations for Root, Bryan, and the North American fleet, supported the pro-American policy.

It takes two to make a friendship, and Brazil found in Secretary of State Elihu Root a North American statesman sympathetic to the approximation. There is reason to think that Root wanted Brazil to be the keystone of his Latin American policy and the center of North American diplomacy in South America.[105] Urging the two countries to get to know each other better,[106] he expressed the policy of the United States toward Brazil to be "firm, sincere and helpful friendship." [107] He believed in and worked for the rapprochement, and the measure of his sincerity was evident in the host of unpublicized details to which he attended in order to bring together Brazil and the United States. An excellent case in point was a gala dinner Nabuco offered in early 1906. Admiral George Dewey had turned down an invitation, but the Secretary of State wrote him to reconsider: "The dinner has an important bearing upon the new rapprochement we are endeavoring to bring about between the United States and Brazil." [108] Dewey attended. Root also spoke about the ambassador's dinner at a cabinet meeting and urged everyone to attend.[109]

Because of his friendly and understanding policy toward Brazil and the immense popularity of his visit there in 1906, Root enjoyed prestige and esteem in Brazil at that time unequaled by any other North American. In 1907, when Cook's in Rio de Janeiro was advertising a tour to the United States for Brazilians, they referred to it as an opportunity to visit "the land of Washington and of Root." [110] Root came to be considered as Brazil's true friend in the United States, a statesman who understood and appreciated Brazil.

Theodore Roosevelt, President of the United States during the first six years of Rio-Branco's ministry, actively supported his Secretary's policy toward Brazil. From all indications Roosevelt seemed to be on closer personal terms with Nabuco than with any other South American, or for that matter Latin American, diplomat. His cordiality in greeting the Brazilian naval officers in 1907, his hearty welcome to Nabuco in 1905, and, above all else, his effervescent enthusiasm at the Brazilian pavilion at the St. Louis Fair of 1904 illustrated his continuing interest in and good will toward Brazil. His visit to Brazil in 1913 reaffirmed his former demonstrations of friendship and prompted him to write a favorable book about the giant republic.[111]

During the first decade of the century, four ranking statesmen,

Rio-Branco and Nabuco in Brazil and Root and Roosevelt in the United States, encouraged and carried out the approximation, a goal they believed would benefit their respective nations. More than anyone else they left their stamp upon the diplomacy of the period and the diplomatic relations between the two countries. A history of those relations cannot be understood without taking into account that human or personal factor responsible for formulating and executing policy.

In summary, the reasons for Brazil's approximation with the United States fall into three categories: historical, commercial, and political. There always had been in Brazil an attitude of sentimental or traditional friendship toward the United States; Rio-Branco capitalized upon it. Commercially the United States was Brazil's best market and increasing trade was tightening the economic bonds. Their external trade was complementary and hence there were few reasons for economic rivalry. Also, the United States was beginning to serve as an economic model for Brazil. Politically the reasons for the intimate friendship were the isolation of the two countries in a Spanish-speaking hemisphere, Rio-Branco's dislike and distrust of Spanish America which caused him to rely more on the United States, the political model the United States furnished republican Brazil, and Rio-Branco's policy of aggrandizement. Strengthening those reasons was the activity of the statesmen in both republics who favored and encouraged the approximation.

The positive aspects of Brazil's policy toward the United States have been emphasized without the desire of showing Rio-Branco as obsequious or as a lackey of American policy. He was clever enough to use North American policy and diplomacy for his own ends and goals. He seldom agreed one hundred percent with American diplomacy, which he challenged or disagreed with when he felt he could not support it. Regardless of how friendly he showed himself, he seemed to have a nagging distrust of North American intentions toward the Amazon, one of his touchiest points.[112] As late as 1905, he viewed with suspicion a group of North American tourists ascending the Amazon[113] and he seemed to nourish a certain fear of the United States in that area.[114] The classic example of his disagreement with the United States was The Hague. When it became apparent that the North American position under Choate was detrimental to Brazilian interests, Rio-Branco vociferously opposed it. Later, beneath the surface of the Alsop case, there was little doubt that Brazil sympathized with Chile. At that time he began to manifest antipathy toward Knox's Dollar Diplomacy.[115] Those negative aspects of his relations with the United States were the occasional exceptions to the general agreement between Washington and Rio de Janeiro. The Baron expressed it in these words: "Our small difference of opinion on secondary points ought not to disguise our warm and sincere friendship for the United States." [116] Although occasional disagreements did occur, the salient characteristic of Brazilian-American relations during Rio-Branco's ministry was friendship.

With the intention of presenting the Brazilian point of view, Brazilian attitudes have been purposely emphasized in this chapter. As has been pointed out, in the rapprochement between the two countries the advantages to Brazil were varied and numerous. However, the presentation does need at least some brief balancing. The international friendship conferred some impressive advantages on the United States too. Brazil's leadership in coordinating the major Latin American nations' recognition of Panama and in preventing a diplomatic break between Chile and the United States was appreciated in Washington. Brazilian friendship also served as a guarantee that no South American alliance would be formed to oppose the United States.[117] It was very convenient for the United States to have a friendly, strong, and able power supporting its interests in inter-American conferences[118] and within the Bureau of the Pan American Union.[119] President Roosevelt summed up the appreciation of the United States for Rio-Branco's friendly diplomacy when he told Nabuco that, because of the convincing example of Brazil, Latin America had adopted a different, a more amiable, attitude toward the United States.[120] Approximation conferred advantages on both parties.

CHAPTER VIII · FOREIGN
REACTIONS TO THE ALLIANCE

FOREIGN REACTIONS to the shift of Brazil's diplomatic axis from Europe to the United States varied considerably: in Europe it seemed to have gone unnoticed—nor would it become clearly apparent to the Europeans until after World War I—while in South America, sensitive to all subtleties, real or imagined, of continental diplomatic maneuverings, the change was noted almost at once. Chile, Brazil's closest South American friend, accepted, even welcomed, the rapprochement; Argentina, Brazil's chief rival, reacted adversely.

Because of the keen, traditional rivalry between Brazil and Argentina for supremacy in South America, it would be worth while to analyze carefully Argentine reaction to the approximation as it affected the Argentine position in the hemisphere. To do so requires a brief survey of the diplomatic relations between the two countries.

The rivalry between Spanish-speaking Argentina and Portuguese-speaking Brazil had its roots in the colonial period when the Spaniards and Portuguese disputed the lands drained by the Paraná-Paraguay-Plata river system. Wars, boundary disputes, and intrigues during the nineteenth century accentuated their natural rivalry.[1] Argentina felt that the larger size and population of Brazil were offset by the richer Pampas land, a healthier Argentine climate, a greater number of European immigrants to, and a faster rate of economic development of, the Plata area. To support that thesis, *La Prensa* published this informative chart of comparative data based on conditions in 1906:[2]

	Argentina	*Brazil*
Area in square miles	1,135,840	3,218,130
Population	5,570,000	14,333,915
Inhabitants per square mile	5	4 1/2
Mestizos, Negroes, Indians	30,000	8,031,717
National income	£20,000,000	£20,000,000
Public debt	£94,000,000	£176,000,000
Exports	£80,000,000	£39,000,000
Imports	£41,000,000	£26,000,000
International Commerce per inhabitant	£18.2.8	£4.10.8
Miles of railroad	13,500	10,500
Miles of telegraph lines	30,000	15,000
Warship tonnage	36,000	22,500

Although showing Brazil to have a greater area and population, the statistics also showed that Brazil had more mestizos, Indians, and Negroes as well as a higher public debt than Argentina. On the other hand, the smaller nation had more railroads, telegraph lines, and trade than its larger neighbor. In short, the table reflected a complacency which the Argentines felt toward the Brazilians. But even those smug comparisons did not set the Argentine mind at rest. An always conscious worry lingered that despite all statistics Brazil *might* be superior. In other words, the Argentines could not rely on a statistical chart, although they could take some comfort from it.

Brazil, for its part, manifested an uneasiness about its southern neighbor. Argentina was the only nation capable of offering serious competition for the coveted rank of first power of South America and as such was Brazil's chief rival. Size and population, it was realized, did not guarantee Brazil's superiority over its rival. Brazilian jingoes warned of the "treacherous and aggressive policy" of Argentina, and in order to find reasons to distrust their southern neighbor, they reached as far back as 1825 to a nearly forgotten

Argentine committee which sought Bolivar's aid to invade Brazil.[3] A detailed study of subsequent history furnished chauvinists with an overabundance of material to keep Brazil's suspicions alerted to its southern boundary.

Rio-Branco had been aware of that rivalry from early childhood. Visits to the Plata area and a detailed study of Argentine-Brazilian relations made him sensitive to any changes or movements in Argentina. As early as 1882, he was genuinely distressed because Argentina was emerging stronger militarily than Brazil. "We have no squadron, no torpedoes, no army, and the Argentines have all this," he lamented, imagining his country at the complete mercy of Argentina.[4] He thought that the only way to avoid "a very grave situation" was to arm Brazil, especially to augment the navy, to meet the Argentine threat.[5] He formed his ideas of military preparedness against Argentina early and kept them throughout his life.

When Rio-Branco began his ministry, relations between Argentina and Brazil were friendly. President Julio A. Roca (1898–1904) had visited Brazil in 1899 and had displayed ample evidence of his fraternal feelings toward Brazil, where he was regarded, thereafter, as a true friend. President Campos Salles returned the visit amid pomp and acclaim. It was the first time the presidents of the two neighboring countries had exchanged visits. Those cordial relations continued during the first years of the Rio-Branco ministry despite the fact that Argentina was obviously nervous and sensitive about Brazil's expansion into Acre.[6] Putting aside his prejudices, Rio-Branco, at least during the first two and one-half years of his ministry, worked for a good understanding between the two countries.[7]

Rio-Branco's exterior warmth toward Argentina, and vice versa, cooled rapidly after early 1905. The Argentines harshly and vociferously criticized the Brazilian naval expansion program and the new Brazilian embassy in Washington. Such criticism wounded the hypersensitive Baron. Also, he was suspicious of Argentina's increasing friendship with Peru, Brazil's archenemy in South America at that time, and attempts to woo Paraguay from Brazil's sphere of influence. The chancellor concluded that President Manuel Quintana (1904–6) was hostile toward Brazil and that Brazil should abandon any hopes of friendly understanding with Argentina.[8] Vice-President José Figueroa Alcorta's succession to the presidency in March, 1906, to complete the six-year mandate of the deceased Quintana, and Estanislau Zeballos' appointment to head the foreign ministry in December of the same year, both of whom, particularly the latter, Rio-Branco regarded as implacable foes of Brazil,[9] ended all pretense of cordiality between the two nations.[10]

Zeballos and Rio-Branco, the two opponents in the Missions dispute in Washington and dedicated enemies by 1906, faced each other in the perennial struggle for South American supremacy. An always tense situation worsened, and as long as those two proud and talented rivals headed their respective foreign offices, the establishment of good relations between the two countries was impossible.[11] The press in both nations took up the rivalry and competed with each other to vilify the other nation. The habitual dislike of the people of one country for the other took on excited tones of vituperation.[12]

Zeballos initiated the new crisis in relations with Brazil by failing to appoint a minister to fill the vacant post in the legation in Rio de Janeiro. After nearly a year had elapsed, Rio-Branco, in September of 1907, recalled the Brazilian minister in Buenos Aires until such time as Argentina would appoint a minister to Rio de Janeiro. Shortly thereafter, Julio Fernández arrived in Brazil as the new minister. By that time, however, relations had reached their nadir. Rivalry in the Plata, accentuated by the Argentine-Uruguayan dispute over Martin García Island and shifting political winds in Paraguay, broke out anew.[13] Meanwhile, with the encouragement of Rio-Branco and several highly qualified ministers of the navy, the rather weak Brazilian navy, especially considering the extensive coastline it had to defend, began to expand quickly. With Zeballos as foreign minister, Rio-Branco regarded war with better prepared Argentina as a real possibility and wanted the navy ready for any emergency.[14] In his turn, Zeballos felt that an arming Brazil would become stronger than Argentina unless new armaments were purchased.[15] The "war hawks" soon got into the act, and the result of their cries and the naval arms race was talk of war.

The climax came in mid-1908 with the scandal of Telegram Number Nine, a confidential and coded telegram sent by Rio-Branco to the Brazilian legation in Santiago. The telegram passed through Buenos Aires where officials of the foreign ministry copied and decoded it, after which Zeballos publicly announced the contents. According to the Argentine decoding, Brazil was plotting with Chile and the United States against Argentina. That revelation aroused the nationalistic fury of the Argentines against Brazil and shocked and angered Rio-Branco, who pointed out that the telegram had been decoded falsely. To prove his accusation, Rio-Branco published the text of the telegram and the Brazilian code. An impartial examination of the telegram showed that its contents never mentioned the United States and spoke only of Argentine efforts to alienate friendly Brazil and Chile from each other.[16] Zeballos had stooped to falsehood to discredit his Brazilian rival and was caught in the act. His many political enemies in Argentina and most of the responsible press of Buenos Aires made full use of his *faux pas* to demand his dismissal or resignation. Under that pressure, Zeballos resigned as foreign minister on June 20, 1908.[17]

The resignation of Zeballos removed a major obstacle to the improvement of Argentine-Brazilian relations. However, Brazil did not consider his resignation sufficient, and before undertaking to ameliorate relations it demanded that an adequate explanation be given for the use of a forged document against the Brazilian government or it would sever diplomatic relations with Argentina. The Argentine government eventually gave an indirect explanation, which, coupled with Zeballos' resignation, prompted Itamaraty, after some exceedingly tense moments, to withdraw its threat to sever diplomatic relations with its neighbor.

Thereafter, under the aegis of the new Argentine foreign minister, Victoriano de la Plaza, and with the renewed cooperation of Rio-Branco, Argentine-Brazilian relations began to improve.[18] President-elect Roque Saenz Peña visited Brazil in August, 1910, with the principal intention of tightening relations between the two countries. He promised, "We recognize and we regret the lack of friendliness which has existed, and it will be our aim to promote mutual good-will and cordial friendship between the two countries."[19] The Argentines also sent a special representation and two warships to Rio de Janeiro for the inauguration of President Hermes da Fonseca in 1910. In the meantime, Brazil and Argentina peacefully settled the question of ownership of various islands in the Uruguay and Iguaçú rivers. In 1910 the eminent Argentine diplomat, Manuel Gorostiaga, could discern correctly that there was a shift toward more harmonious relations between the two neighbors,[20] and Rio-Branco was being regarded again as a friend of Argentina.[21] In 1912 the Argentine minister in Rio de Janeiro confirmed the progress in the trend toward better relations which Gorostiaga noted two years earlier. He wrote, "The feeling of true harmony and confidence toward our country becomes more accentuated each day."[22] The death of Rio-Branco the same year evoked genuine official mourning in Argentina.[23]

With that general outline of diplomatic relations as a background, Argentine reaction to the Brazilian-American rapprochement is more meaningful. In the struggle of the two countries for hegemony in South America and, thus, supremacy over each other, close association with the United States was important and was regarded as an advantage for the favored nation. It was thought that the nation more closely linked with the United States would be in the more advantageous position in South America. Hence, there was, manifesting itself in various degrees and forms at different times, rivalry between the two nations for the esteem and support of the United States. It was not that the Argentines particularly cherished a closer rapprochement; rather they were disturbed to see their neighbor strengthened by such a close friendship. In the end, lack of enthusiasm for the United States caused Argentina to back off from a suffocating embrace with the "Colossus of the North" and to resign itself to the idea that an amorphous entente bound Brazil and the United States together to its exclusion.[24]

Argentine leaders noted early in the Rio-Branco ministry that their neighbor was becoming ever more closely associated with the United States. Early in 1904, in a speech before the Senate, Hipólito Irigoyen observed that "great interests and reasons" were drawing Brazil and the United States together.[25] Manuel Gorostiaga, minister to Brazil between 1899 and 1906, the crucial years of Brazil's diplomatic shift, later wrote about the "new ties of cordiality" existent between Brazil and the United States.[26] By early 1905, there were already complaints in Buenos Aires that Brazil and the United States were allied to divide the hemisphere among themselves.[27] Thereafter, Argentina displayed jealousy and sensitiveness toward the Brazilian-American approximation.[28]

From 1906 until the end of the Rio-Branco ministry there was constant speculation in Argentina about a formal Brazilian-American alliance.[29] During that period, the Argentines did not associate Brazil with any European power, such as with Great Britain during the nineteenth century, but repeatedly with the United States to the degree where the Argentine minister in Rio de Janeiro could officially inform his government of an impending accord between the two giant republics.[30] Even though the Argentines occasionally tried to dismiss the potential threat of a Brazilian-American alliance by rationalizing that the United States was not such a great friend of Brazil as Itamaraty would like to believe,[31] the alliance remained a specter which haunted the Argentine government.

Argentina reacted negatively in general to Brazil's diplomatic maneuvers and in particular to the approximation. There was no lack of criticism of Itamaraty's isthmian policy,[32] and its role at the Peace Conference.[33] Perhaps the single most notable reaction was to the mutual elevation of the legations to embassies.[34] *La Nación* greeted the announcement of the elevation with a scathing editorial, highly critical of Brazil,[35] which seemed to indicate that Rio-Branco's diplomatic victory took Argentina by surprise.[36] Argentina complained of its dissatisfaction with the unfounded—in the opinion of Buenos Aires—preference of the United States for Brazil,[37] and there was no lack of rumors that it also hoped to exchange ambassadors with the United States.[38]

As relations cooled and consequently as the struggle for South American supremacy became more open, Argentine reaction to the approximation became bitter and more critical. The Argentines hoped that Buenos Aires could be selected as the seat of the Third Pan American Conference[39] and were offended because Rio de Janeiro received the honor.[40] They were chagrined with the United States for supporting Brazil in its bid to be the host.[41] Some talk of not attending even circulated.[42] Making the most of an unpleasant situation, the Argentines rationalized that once Root arrived in Buenos Aires, following his visit to Brazil, he would soon discover which was the most powerful and advanced country in South America.[43] However, whatever Mr. Root had to say to the Argentines at the official banquet in Buenos Aires, they would have had to read it in their newspapers the next day because the speech was completely drowned out by "the screeching laments of a cat stuck in the main chandelier" of the hall.[44]

As Root had found it mandatory to visit Buenos Aires after scheduling a visit to Rio de Janeiro, so it was necessary that part of the United States fleet call at the Argentine capital in 1908 after anchoring in Guanabara Bay. The Argentines were so distressed that the fleet would visit Rio de Janeiro and then continue on to the Pacific Ocean with no Argentine stop that North American naval officials had to revamp their plans and send the torpedo flotilla to Buenos Aires in order to keep peace in the South American family.[45]

Later, in the Alsop case, Brazil once again got the diplomatic edge on Argentina. The Argentine government saw the dispute as an opportunity to befriend Chile and woo its favor. Unfortunately for the Argentine cause, their minister did not receive instructions from his government until November 25, 1909, and did not speak with the Secretary of State about the Alsop case until the next day.[46] By that time, of course, Nabuco already had prevented the rupture of Chilean-American diplomatic relations and had gained an impressive diplomatic victory for his country. Brazil's early and successful intervention in the Alsop case and the public expressions of gratitude from both the United States and Chile angered Argentina.[47]

The aspect of the approximation which caused the sharpest and most prolonged reaction in Argentina was the tariff preferences Brazil conceded to the United States. Indeed, Argentine exports to both Brazil and the United States were under a disadvantage. In addition to the tariff reductions Brazil gave to the United States and not to Argentina, only 17 percent of Argentine exports to the United States entered duty-free as compared with 99 percent of Brazil's exports.[48] But it was the Brazilian tariff concession on flour which most distressed the Argentines. Their twenty-five flour mills depended upon exportation for prosperity. A threat to their foreign markets would harm the Argentine economy.[49] Blaming the tariff concessions on "the pressure which the United States exerts on the economic policy" of Brazil,[50] the Argentines began to complain when the first reductions were made in 1904[51] and continued complaining right on through the 1911 concessions.[52] At times the Argentines tried to explain rationally to themselves the real reasons for the concessions: the United States bought fifteen times more from Brazil than Argentina did.[53] At other times, they explained them as a new commercial shift in North American policy to dominate all South American markets.[54] They kept up a vigorous campaign in Brazil to win the same tariff concessions for their products, but Rio-Branco icily turned a deaf ear toward his South American rival.[55] After all, helping Argentina to prosperity was not a goal of his foreign policy.

It would be neither fair nor correct to say that Argentina, alone, felt pangs of jealousy because of Brazil's close association with the United States. Jealousy is a double-edged sword, and Brazil jealously guarded its position of preeminence before the United States. If the United States must have a favorite among the Spanish-speaking nations, Brazil preferred that that country be distant from Brazil, namely, Mexico.[56] Certainly, from the Brazilian point of view, it should not be Argentina, which Rio-Branco carefully sought to keep isolated from the United States as a jealous mistress strives to keep temptations out of the path of her lover.[57] An excellent example of that Brazilian jealousy manifested itself as the result of the visit of an Argentine naval training ship, *Sarmiento,* to the United States in mid-1904. When the officers of the ship were introduced to President Roosevelt, the expansive chief of state spoke animatedly with them about the role Argentina could play in the world. The Argentines interpreted those words to mean that President Roosevelt authorized or encouraged them to assume the leadership of South America. The event distracted Itamaraty for some time, but Rio-Branco preferred to interpret the incident as a product more of Argentine pride than of North American sincerity.[58] The significance of the *Sarmiento* affair was that it showed Brazil to be hypersensitive to any Argentine-American entente and just as jealous of its position with the United States as Argentina was of the Brazilian-American approximation.

Contrary to the erratic variations characterizing Argentine-Brazilian relations, Chile maintained its usual cordial relations with Brazil during the Rio-Branco period. The Chileans were particularly happy that the Baron remained for such a long time as foreign minister because they regarded him as a "sincere and dedicated friend," [59] whose death they deeply mourned.[60] Throughout the decade, the diplomatic reports from Rio de Janeiro spoke of the true and enthusiastic friendship displayed by all Brazilians, even in the remote corners of their vast country, for Chile.[61] That warm show of friendship naturally tightened the bonds between Chile and Brazil.

At that particular period in its history, Chile needed a good friend on the South American continent. Its position in South America was a delicate one. The troublesome boundary with Argentina was settled in 1902, but habitual Chilean suspicion and fear of Argentina made it an uneasy neighbor. The boundary with Peru was a sore spot which had occasioned blood, bickering, and brooding and would continue to do so. Bolivia already was importuning, then demanding, then threatening Chile for a corridor to the sea. In short, Chile was isolated or, worse than that, surrounded by enemies whose open dislike could easily turn into open warfare.[62] For those reasons, Chile appreciated the friendship offered by Brazil, a traditional friendship which amounted almost to an alliance.[63]

Out of necessity, the Chilean Foreign Ministry paid close attention to Itamaraty's diplomatic maneuvering and consequently sent an exceptionally able group of diplomats to Rio de Janeiro during the Baron's ministry. Careful observers, they were particularly alert to any change in the balance of power in South America.[64] Studying the shifting sands of South American diplomacy with microscopic care, they noted at once the new orientation of Brazil's foreign policy. As soon as Rio-Branco announced he would send an ambassador to Washington, the Chilean minister in Rio de Janeiro understood the significance of that move. Commenting on the shift in Brazil's foreign policy, he wrote, "The Government of Brazil has understood the need to give greater emphasis to its relations with the United States of America because such a policy better serves its interests and its international position." [65]

The Chileans also understood the reasons and motives for the approximation. They recognized that it would increase Brazil's diplomatic position and strength in South America, the Western Hemisphere, and Europe.[66] "The systematic adhesion of Brazil to North American policy" helped Brazil to realize its ambition to play the role in South America that the United States played in North America.[67] In that context, the penetrating observations of a Chilean diplomat were as follows:

The United States exercises a preponderant influence over the general directions of the policy of this Republic [Brazil]. Traditionally, and even more so in recent years, Brazil has carried out a valiantly absorbent policy in South America with imperialist aspirations, but always under the vigilance and with the declared support of the United States. Brazil believes itself, because of its enormous size, population, geographical position, and evident rich future, to be the country destined to exercise in South America part of the hegemony which the United States now exercises over all America. That line of thought has the publicly declared approval of the United States. Brazilian politicians do not hide their thoughts and they have stated them in public documents. Quite the opposite of Argentina, which frequently confronts the United States face to face, Brazil is an echo of what is done and said in the North and naturally takes advantage of the friendship of the United States to liquidate pending business with Colombia, Ecuador, and Peru with complete freedom of action and in harmony with its ambitions.[68]

Being the only South American country not bordering on Brazil at the time, Chile could and did take a dispassionate view of

Brazilian expansion. Thus, the Chilean minister spoke frankly, even approvingly, of Brazil's "absorbent policy" and "imperialist aspirations." With clearness of vision and honest perspective, the report correctly analyzed Brazil's reasons for the approximation and showed that Chile appreciated Brazil's new diplomatic role. In fact, the Chileans seemed perfectly willing to concede an imperialist role to their friend. At any rate, the Chilean minister in Rio de Janeiro at least once referred to Brazil as "the first nation in South America, destined to exercise in South America part of the hegemony that the United States exercises in all America." [69]

Chileans had adequate reasons to praise the approximation as a victory of good sense and "very clear diplomatic vision" [70] because it strengthened their close friend and semiofficial ally. A strong Brazil represented Chile's principal hope of escape from its isolated and dangerous position in the southwest corner of the continent.[71] Logically the stronger Brazil was, the better for Chile. Therefore, after the Chilean diplomats quickly recognized the approximation, the government applauded and approved it.

More research is necessary before the reaction to the approximation throughout the remainder of Latin America will be known. At least one source has stated that all Latin American diplomats regarded the exchange of ambassadors between Brazil and the United States as an important step in inter-American relations,[72] and, for the moment anyway, the embassies seemed to evoke some jealousy among Brazil's neighbors.[73]

If Latin Americans reacted to the shift in Brazil's foreign policy from Europe to the United States, Europeans did not. It would seem that, concentrating on their own continental affairs, colonial adventures, and war preparations, they failed to see the important change in the international position of South America's largest country. More than likely they were unprepared to note such changes in the still distant and exotic Southern Hemisphere. At any rate, Brazil turned from Europe to the United States without the

Europeans noticing it, and they probably did not really realize it until after World War I.

The shift should have affected England most. During the last colonial decade and the first national decade of Brazilian history, Great Britain tightly fastened its influence on Brazil. The English exercised important economic and political power in Brazil throughout the remainder of the nineteenth century. Meanwhile, the Brazilians eagerly sought to free themselves from the harsher aspects of British control.[74] Nonetheless, Britain was able to maintain its influence until the end of the century. By that time, the English had become increasingly involved in European complications and more interested in Africa than in Latin America. The boundary controversy with Venezuela in 1895 and the Hay-Pauncefote Treaty in 1901 marked the beginning of British withdrawal from the Caribbean and their first recognition of the pre-eminence of the United States in Latin America. During the period from 1895 through World War I, the United States came to replace Great Britain in Latin America.

That generalization holds true for Brazil too. During the Rio-Branco ministry, the United States replaced, as was evident would happen for some decades, Britain's political influence in Brazil. By that time, the United States was also ready to challenge England's commercial supremacy in Brazil.[75] Since the end of the Civil War, the United States had been Brazil's best market; and after the turn of the century, North American merchants, firmly supported by their government, strove to increase their sales to Brazil. However, the English guarded their commercial hold more tenaciously than they had their political, and it was not until World War I that the United States finally succeeded in replacing Great Britain in the economic sphere.[76]

Although the British recognized that Brazil and the United States were the two principal powers in the New World,[77] they did not seem to attribute great importance to the diplomatic links between the two hemispheric nations. When Rio de Janeiro and Washington exchanged ambassadors, *The Times* sedately recognized the event but declined to comment on it.[78] However, if the *Morning Post* of London could be regarded as a bellwether of the rest of the press, the British seemed to have approved of the establishment of a Brazilian embassy in Washington as a wise move of "considerable suggestiveness and significance," to wit, the emergence of Brazil into the "political primacy of Latin America." [79] That might imply, although it certainly did not state, that Brazil had shifted its diplomatic axis from London to Washington. The article probably would have been a little less congratulatory had the English realized the full significance of the new embassy.

An Englishman who quickly understood one aspect of that significance was Sir William Haggard, British minister to Brazil, who arrived in December, 1906, and stayed throughout the Rio-Branco period. He grew to dislike the idea of being a mere minister in Rio de Janeiro where the only ambassador, his North American colleague, outranked and overshadowed the rest of the diplomatic corps.[80] In fact, the British colony in the Brazilian capital seemed to regard the special rank of the American ambassador as a "sign of the times." [81] In other words, they thought that the United States was just beginning to discover Brazil, but as Vice-Consul Hambloch told it, that discovery was primarily commercial, that is, a desire on the part of the North American business community to expand more vigorously into the European-dominated Brazilian market.[82]

That opinion was well expressed in *The South American Journal,* doubtless the most representative publication of English interest in Latin American affairs at the time. The *Journal* early announced Brazil's intention (or hope) of elevating its Washington legation to an embassy[83] and, when the act was consummated, carried the full text of Nabuco's address and Roosevelt's reply—without any commentary.[84] The weekly paper, as usual, demonstrated a more lively interest in North American economic, as contrasted with political, penetration of Brazil. At the same time the editors were scarcely recognizing a diplomatic event of importance for the hemisphere, they were covering in complete detail in five articles the visit of some North American investors to Brazil.[85] It was not difficult to see where the *Journal*'s interest lay.

Clearly Great Britain was much more interested in Brazil commercially than politically and was more susceptible to economic rather than political changes. Aware of "the extraordinary disparity between the United States exports to and imports from Brazil" and of the North American desire to balance that trade,[86] the British, although somewhat wary, still did not regard the United States as their principal commercial threat and surely not as a replacement. British merchants appeared to be considerably more concerned about German competition in Brazil than North American.[87] J. C. Oakenfall in his books on Brazil during this period placed emphasis on commerce and seemed to disregard any North American threat.[88] Three other English Brazilianists, Ernest Hambloch, Frank Bennett, and Charles Domville-Fife, did likewise.[89] Germany appeared to most Englishmen as the principal competitor in the Brazilian market, with the United States running a poor third.

Vice-Consul Hambloch went so far as to accuse Rio-Branco of being pro-German in his outlook,[90] an attitude which, if true, would have favored German commercial interests. At any rate, he understood that Rio-Branco was not an Anglophile. Rio-Branco's long stay in Liverpool had not endeared England to him, and he had escaped to the more familiar atmosphere of the continent for long periods whenever possible. Rio-Branco's possible anti-English sentiments showed themselves on several occasions. He did not like the British minister, Sir William Haggard. In fact, the two diplomats had long periods during which they were not on speaking terms.[91] When the renowned James Bryce, jurist, historian, and British ambassador to the United States, visited Brazil, Rio-Branco did not go out of his way to welcome him although Itamaraty had rolled out the red carpet for less distinguished South American and European visitors.

In his turn, Bryce, otherwise an observant traveler, failed to note or to make note of the Brazilian-American approximation in his commentaries on the Brazilian government in 1910.[92] In that, he probably exemplified the British failure to understand immediately the rapprochement and its political and economic implications.

Before a definite judgment can be made on British sensitivity to the approximation, it will be necessary to peruse the diplomatic dispatches sent to the Foreign Office. The final answer is there. Prior conclusions must necessarily be tentative. From British travelers and newspapers of the period, however, certain, albeit limited, conclusions can be drawn. The first is that the British were considerably more preoccupied during the Rio-Branco ministry with their commercial rather than their political relations with Brazil. The second is that the British did not comprehend Brazil's shift of its diplomatic axis to Washington.

There were also three French observers on the Brazilian scene in the latter part of the Rio-Branco period. All three, Baron d'Anthouard, Pierre Denis, and Georges Clemenceau, failed to see the diplomatic shift which had so recently occurred in the country they were studying. In fact, d'Anthouard flatly claimed that Brazil, despite the excellent market offered by the United States, was more concerned with Europe, particularly France.[93] Culturally he was correct, but he underestimated Brazil's attraction to the United States at that period. Although Denis ably discussed the Brazilian desire "to establish her moral hegemony throughout South America,"[94] his book omitted any hint that Brazil was pursuing a significant policy of rapprochement with the United States. The semi-official visitor, Georges Clemenceau, although he talked with most of the government leaders of Brazil, saw no extraordinary relationship between Brazil and the United States. Quite the contrary, he believed the Baron to be completely European oriented.[95]

These examples from European writers are too few and scattered to be conclusive. More extensive research, particularly in European diplomatic archives, would be required before a definite or definitive statement could be made. However, the examples are too consistent to be dismissed summarily. It seems warranted to deduce from them that Europe tended to overlook a major shift, perhaps *the* major shift, in Brazilian diplomacy. The European oversight, as exemplified by France and Great Britain, contrasted sharply with the reaction of South America, as exemplified by Argentina and Chile, to the Brazilian-American approximation. Both of those South American republics reacted immediately although differently. Argentina disliked the rapprochement. Chile approved.

CHAPTER IX · CONCLUSIONS

B<small>Y THE</small> beginning of the twentieth century, Brazil had success-fully made the change from a monarchy dependent on the support of the sugar barons to a republic dependent for its "order and progress" on the coffee industry. Far-reaching economic, political, and social changes in just little more than a decade modified the traditional characteristics of imperial Brazil. It was an especially dramatic change considering the brief period in which long-estab-lished institutions were altered. Such fundamental changes did not take place, of course, without some stress and strain; but by the end of the nineteenth century, or within a decade after the over-throw of the monarchy, Brazil began demonstrating a new vigor, surpassing in many respects the best days of the empire, as the country adjusted to the new economic and political institutions. A new prosperity, which gave rise to accelerated material progress, characterized republican Brazil.

The external policy of Brazil reflected that internal well-being. At peace at home, the Brazilians were ready for a positive foreign policy which would project upon the world scene the interests and goals of the republic. First, there was the ever present question of the un-marked frontiers, a legacy from Portugal, which had to be defined before any new policies could be undertaken. Rio-Branco success-fully solved that four-hundred-year-old problem in a series of arbitrations, negotiations, and treaties which demarcated nine thou-sand miles of frontier from French Guiana in the north to Peru in the west to Uruguay in the south. Once the boundaries were established, Brazil could emphasize a nationalistic desire to exert its leadership over South America and to raise its prestige abroad. Rio-Branco, during his decade-long ministry, accomplished both these purposes. His ability and the optimum internal conditions, particularly if contrasted with those of the neighboring countries at the time, combined to win for Brazil a final victory in its territorial consolidation and to launch the country on its new policy to achieve leadership and prestige.

In those international maneuverings, both in the consolidation of frontiers and in the increase of national prestige, the United States was called upon to play a significant role. Following the overthrow of the monarchy, Brazil began to associate more closely with the United States. The new republican form of government was a frank copy of the American Constitution, and the expanding coffee industry, dependent upon the United States as its principal market, tied Brazilian prosperity and progress closely to the North American economy. Those intimate economic and political ties with the United States were phenomena peculiar to the republic and a change from the former imperial preference for Great Britain. A host of other historical, commercial, and political considerations added to the growing friendship between the United States and Brazil. Under Rio-Branco's purposeful guidance the approximation at times assumed the characteristics of an informal, unwritten alliance between the two giant republics of the New World.

Upon assuming the Ministry of Foreign Relations in 1902, Rio-Branco seemed predisposed to align Brazil as closely as possible with the United States. He understood the trend under way during the last decade of the nineteenth century and accelerated it with the intention of utilizing the newly recognized prestige and power of the United States to achieve certain foreign policy goals. Intimate United States–Brazilian friendship really began with the ministry of Rio-Branco. However, before emphasizing the rapprochement, the Baron found it necessary to eliminate any possible source of friction between the two countries. At that time, the investments of American capitalists in Acre threatened to disturb their relations. Rio-Branco skillfully got rid of the investors by using Brazilian treasury funds to buy out the Bolivian Syndicate. He thereby demonstrated to the State Department that in trying to keep foreign control and influence out of South America his aims coincided with those of the Monroe Doctrine and that the United States could count on him to expound that doctrine in South America. He went on to win the confidence of Washington by quickly signifying his approval of Panamanian independence and by coordinating the major Latin American countries in their joint recognition of that new republic. Pleased with his friendly action, the United States showed its good will toward Brazil by supporting Itamaraty's position in the Acre dispute with Peru. Frequent exchanges of complimentary messages were made between Rio de Janeiro and Washington. Ready for some concrete expression of their fraternity, the two governments mutually raised their legations to embassies. That elevation was an action of extreme importance in an era when there were few embassies and when the exchange of ambassadors signified a great deal more than it would in subsequent diplomatic history. Shortly after the elevation, when it appeared that German belligerency threatened Brazil and the Monroe Doctrine, the United States was ready to come to the aid of its southern friend. Brazil, through forceful and efficient diplomacy, proved itself master of the situation; and Brazilian diplomacy, the Monroe Doctrine, and Brazilian-American friendship emerged as the victors in the *Panther* case.

The apogee of the approximation was the visit of Secretary of State Root in 1906. The diplomatic corps in Washington believed that Ambassador Nabuco was a close enough personal friend of the Secretary of State to be able to persuade him to make his first foreign visit to Brazil. His presence on Brazilian soil was tangible proof of the esteem of the United States. His words about an unwritten alliance and his appearance before the hemispheric delegates at the

Third Pan American Conference were meaningful diplomatic victories for Brazil. His triumphant tour of Brazil and the cordial reception accorded him sealed the bonds of the entente.

The crest of the wave is followed by the trough. The Hague conference followed the Pan American conference. To The Hague, both countries sent delegates who were neither familiar with nor sympathetic toward the rapprochement. The North American delegation was ignorant of or disregarded the primary Brazilian drive to increase its prestige abroad. As a consequence, American policy for the first time during the Rio-Branco period countered a primary Brazilian foreign policy aim. To Brazil the desire for a prestigious permanent seat on the World Court was more important than harmony with the United States at the conference, and the two delegations clashed over the structure of the court. Although both governments professed regret at the disagreement, the rapprochement had been undeniably weakened. Regardless of the excellent relations which followed The Hague, the high point of the Root visit was never again reached during the Rio-Branco period.

A year later, during the visit of the United States fleet, the two nations repledged their friendship to each other. Brazil demonstrated its good will during the United States–Venezuelan diplomatic rupture and the controversy over the Alsop claims. The United States, in its turn, gave anew ample evidence of its high regard for Brazil.

Perhaps even stronger than the political and diplomatic bonds drawing together the two countries were the commercial ties. The United States was by far Brazil's most important market, a fact Rio-Branco recognized when he used his influence to reduce Brazilian tariffs on North American imports. Throughout the Rio-Branco ministry, trade between the two nations continued to grow. The commercial relations alone, particularly on the Brazilian side, were sufficient reason—the practical reason, understandable in dollars and cents—for the approximation.

Although the pattern of friendship was well established by the end of the Rio-Branco period, the unwritten alliance suffered during the last years of his ministry some subtle alterations which prevented a full recovery from the effects of The Hague. Two of the chief architects of the approximation departed from the scene. Root left office in 1909 when the Taft administration took office, and, more importantly, Nabuco died in 1910. Their absence decreased the former enthusiasm for the rapprochement which neither Knox nor da Gama was able to match.

It is an academic question as to who did more to effect the approximation, Nabuco or Rio-Branco. Rio-Branco originally prompted the Brazilian embrace of the United States. He initiated the rapprochement soon after taking office and decided that Nabuco would be the most able Brazilian to fill the new ambassadorial post in Washington. Only after Nabuco arrived in Washington did the approximation take on real life. With more enthusiasm than Rio-Branco, Nabuco worked indefatigably in favor of the rapprochement. Following Nabuco's death, the rapprochement became static or even declined, which leads to the conclusion that, although Rio-Branco initiated and sustained the approximation, Nabuco was the one who pushed it to its farthest limits. In the final analysis valid arguments sustain the claims of both statesmen to the success of the rapprochement. The approximation reached the intensity it did because at the same time Brazil had two extraordinary statesmen, one in Washington, the other in Rio de Janeiro, working together toward the common goal of Brazilian-American friendship. The good will of Root and Roosevelt complemented and facilitated the efforts of the Brazilian foreign minister and ambassador.

The principal characteristic of Brazilian-American diplomatic relations during the Baron's ministry was friendship. In studying the solidification of that friendship it becomes clear that the approximation was more important to Brazil than to the United States and that Brazil took the initiative in effecting it. The diplomatic archives, the newspapers, and the speeches of the statesmen uphold this view. To Brazil, the unwritten alliance was a strong secondary policy upon which the success of the primary goals of frontier demarcation, increased prestige, and South American leadership depended. To the United States, however, the approximation was simply a part of a larger concern with world diplomacy. Unlike Brazil, the United States maintained, even strengthened, its close relations with several nations of Western Europe. Whether the United States was closely aligned with Brazil or not little affected its policy or action in Europe and Asia. On the other hand, within the confines of hemispheric diplomacy, the approximation was a major asset to North American relations with Latin America and for that reason the State Department encouraged it. Nonetheless, the conclusion seems warranted that the approximation more ably and better served Brazilian ends than North American. For that reason, Brazil was more aggressive in pursuing it.

In particular the friendship of Washington proved to be useful in Itamaraty's plans to settle Brazil's boundaries advantageously. Brazil had accepted the existence of Uruguay, Paraguay, and Bolivia as necessary buffer states. After 1828, there had been no serious desire to incorporate any one of them. Yet, if Brazil was tolerant toward the existence of its neighbors, large or small, there was in republican Brazil, as there had been during the empire, a compulsion to expand the frontiers to their farthest limits. The desire was especially strong in the west and north, areas long neglected by Spanish America but within the realm of Luso-Brazilian concern since the expedition of Pedro Teixeira in 1636. Rio-Branco had no intention of surrendering or limiting Brazil's claims to the hinterlands and thereby to territorial expansion. He worked to bring those firmly claimed but vaguely held areas within the undisputed national territory. The Chilean minister in Rio de Janeiro in an objective and by no means accusatory observation termed those efforts as "absorbent" and "imperialist." To the Spanish Americans those "encroachments" represented a continuation of Luso-Brazilian imperialism which began when the Portuguese heedlessly disregarded and crossed the arbitrary Tordesilhas line. To the Brazilian, the territory gained by Rio-Branco's boundary settlements represented a fulfillment of Brazil's "manifest destiny" in South America. The territory belonged to them, or so they reasoned, by exploration and settlement. For that reason they turned a deaf ear to the mounting cries of imperialism directed at them by their neighbors. The only way the Spanish Americans could have hoped to halt Brazil's drive to the Andes was to unite in opposition and to obtain the moral support of the United States to back their position. The usual rivalries prohibited such a union of action on their part, and individually they were uniformly unsuccessful in winning any support from the United States. Rio-Branco played on the disunion of Spanish South America by wooing Chile. More importantly, he succeeded in allying the United States to Brazil's foreign policy and thereby strengthening its territorial claims. The Baron used the United States, and the United States consciously or unconsciously permitted itself to be used, to expand Brazil's borders. Whether under the nomenclature "imperialism" as the Spanish Americans would charge or "manifest destiny" as the Brazilians would rationalize, Brazil, thanks in part to North American moral support, fulfilled its territorial ambitions during the Rio-Branco era.

In the history of Brazilian diplomacy, the long Rio-Branco ministry is notable for two fundamental changes it made in the foreign policy of Brazil. Both changes involved the United States. The first was the change in Brazil's diplomatic axis. The rapprochement gave Brazil the opportunity it had sought for three quarters of a century to escape the domination of Great Britain. Inherited from Portugal was a commercial, financial, and political dependence on Great Britain in which Brazil had never acquiesced. Throughout the nineteenth century, Brazil had made various efforts to escape British dominance, but London by force of circumstances served as the focal point for Brazilian diplomacy. The ministerial post in the capital of the British Empire became the traditional axis of Brazil's diplomacy. The rapid development of the United States in the last half of the nineteenth century and Britain's gradual abdication of its hegemony in Latin America to the United States during the same period indicated a logical, if not inevitable, shift which Brazilian foreign policy should make. By the turn of the century, Washington was becoming more important than London to republican Brazil, awakened to its new role in the hemisphere. Rio-Branco understood and appreciated that change. Desiring to escape from traditional British domination, he realized that times and circumstances were auspicious to consummate the change by creating an embassy in Washington and by transferring his foremost diplomat from the Court of St. James's to the North American capital. Those two actions as well as the course of international events during the 1902–12 decade signified the definite shift of Brazil's diplomatic axis from Europe to the New World, specifically from London to Washington.

The second fundamental change was in the goals of Brazil's foreign policy. Rio-Branco's successful settlement of the boundary disputes freed Brazilian diplomacy from its traditional preoccupation with the demarcation of the frontiers, allowing it to concentrate on problems of leadership and prestige. As in the last years of the era of border diplomacy, Rio-Branco continued to count on close association with the United States as an advantage necessary for the success of the new period of expanded vision in Brazilian diplomacy.

In altering its foreign policy at this time, Brazil was participating in a world-wide trend caused by a breakdown in the diplomatic order in Europe. The nations of the Old World were at the same time reshaping many hoary foreign alliances and policies. Great Britain moved away from its nineteenth-century policy of isolation and closer to France and Russia and signed its first treaty of alliance with a non-European nation, Japan. Germany was maneuvering for a stronger position in central Europe. Russia, whose weakness Japan's quick victory exposed, was looking about for new allies and a new diplomatic position. In short, European diplomacy was more fluid than it had been in many decades and new foreign policies were being shaped on the Continent which would shortly affect the fate of the world. Just as the growth of militarism in Europe found an echo in distant Brazil, so did the changing of foreign policies there have repercussions in Brazil.

As a curious historical parallel, the United States ended its own "era of border diplomacy" at about the same time. With the disappearance of the frontier during the last decade of the nineteenth century, the United States, like the Brazil of Rio-Branco, began to lift its diplomatic vision to new sights. As a result, both became actively interested in the rest of the hemisphere at almost the same time. Fortunately those interests were complementary and did not conflict. Brazil recognized the sphere of influence of the United States in the Caribbean, while the United States did not interfere in Brazil's sphere of influence, Uruguay, Paraguay, and Bolivia. There seems to have been a tacit accord whereby Brazil acknowledged the hegemony of the United States in North America and the United States respected Brazilian pretensions to the hegemony of South America.

In their newly adopted international roles, both nations appreciated the advantages of the Pan American movement and realized that common sense dictated some policy of neighborliness in this hemisphere. In addition to their allegiance to Pan Americanism and without in any way intending to contradict it, both supported the Monroe Doctrine. Their definitions of Pan Americanism and the Monroe Doctrine varied widely, but since those divergent interpretations caused no disagreement, the fact that both Pan Americanism and the doctrine received the support of Itamaraty and the Department of State further united the two governments. In urging that the Monroe Doctrine be made multilateral and the common goal for unified hemispheric action, Rio-Branco became, in effect, a precursor of the modern Pan American movement. The United States finally came to follow the Brazilian interpretation and fusion of the Monroe Doctrine and Pan Americanism only some decades later.

Unlike Brazil, the United States did not enter into the intricate balance of power maneuvering in Latin America at the beginning of the century. It was recognized and accepted that North American power outweighed any combination of states in Latin America, and there was no reason for the United States, as the Colossus of the North, to make alliances within this hemisphere.

On the other hand, within the intra-South American maneuvering for position there were obvious advantages for the South American nation which succeeded in closely associating itself with the United States. At one time or another, all the South American governments tried to get the moral (if not the physical) support of the United States government to further some national cause. Rio-Branco was particularly successful, except at The Hague conference, in enlisting the support of the United States for his various litigations or disputes with other South American countries as well as for his general policy of leadership and prestige. By doing so, he reached beyond the continent to tip the South American balance of power in Brazil's favor. Although he had thought of an ABC approximation several times, he abandoned any intentions for an entente with Argentina after 1905. Thereafter, he fortified Brazil's diplomatic position in South America by emphasizing closer relations with Chile and the United States. Aligned with South America's third power and the hemisphere's first power, Rio-Branco succeeded in shifting the South American balance of power in Brazil's favor. He thereby isolated Brazil's chief rival, Argentina, both within the hemisphere and within South America. Without being fully conscious of Rio-Branco's skillful use of its power and prestige to achieve

Brazilian diplomatic goals, the United States became an important pawn in the struggle for predominance among South American states.

In its fraternal relations with Brazil, the United States found several advantages which made it seem worth while to encourage the approximation. In an era when the United States was losing friends in the hemisphere because of the Big Stick and Dollar Diplomacy and when most Latin American nations looked suspiciously at any North American action, a good friend in the hemisphere was more than welcome—particularly so when it was one of the principal states. The understanding and friendship of Rio-Branco were a pleasant relief from the usual vituperative accusations, whether they were right or wrong, made against the United States by the rest of Latin America.

Rio-Branco encouraged the approximation because of the many advantages it bestowed on Brazil; the United States accepted the approximation because of the benefits accruing from it to the North American policy in Latin America. Brazil saw in the entente with the United States a means to help achieve its diplomatic ends of boundary settlement, South American leadership, and increased prestige in the world. The approximation, which in 1906 seemed to take the shape of an unwritten alliance, was one of the characteristic policies of the Rio-Branco ministry. Those friendly relations encouraged by the Brazilian chancellor are the high-water mark in the history of diplomatic relations between Brazil and the United States, unequaled before the Baron of Rio-Branco and unsurpassed since.

NOTES

ABBREVIATIONS USED
IN THE NOTES

ABR-BI	Arquivo do Barão do Rio-Branco, Itamaraty, Rio de Janeiro
ADC	Arquivo do Museu David Carneiro, Curitiba, Paraná
AHI	Arquivo Histórico de Itamaraty, Rio de Janeiro
AJN	Arquivo de Joaquim Nabuco, Rio de Janeiro
ANCh	Archivo Nacional de Chile, Santiago
ARE, Arg	Archivo del Ministerio de Relaciones Exteriores y Culta de la Argentina, Buenos Aires
ARE, Ch	Archivo del Ministerio de Relaciones Exteriores de Chile, Santiago
ARE, Mex	Archivo de la Secretaría de Relaciones Exteriores del México, Mexico City
ARE, Pan	Archivo de la Secretaría de Relaciones Exteriores de la República del Panamá, Panama City
Casa	Arquivo da Casa de Rui Barbosa, Rio de Janeiro
Revista IHGB	Revista do Instituto Histórico e Geográfico Brasileiro
NA	National Archives of the United States of America, General Records of the Department of State, Washington, D.C.
OL Lib	Oliveira Lima Library, Catholic University of America, Washington, D.C.

NOTES

Chapter I. PEACE, PROGRESS, AND PROSPERITY

1. "Of the Brazilian population, the browns and blacks composed the following proportions: 61.9 percent in 1872; 56.0 percent in 1890; and 35.9 percent in 1940." The conclusion of this official source was that the population tended to become whiter. Conselho Nacional de Estatística, *Contribuições para o Estudo da Demografia do Brasil*, p. 201.

2. Ministério de Agricultura, Direção Geral de Estatística, *Annuaire Statistique du Brésil, 1ere Année, 1908–1912*, Vol. I: *Territorie et Population*, p. 252.

3. Figures for these percentages come from these sources: *Almanaque Brasileiro Garnier*, 1902, p. 82; *Almanaque Brazileiro Garnier*, 1905, p. 73; Ministério da Fazenda, *Foreign Trade*, pp. 46–47.

4. James, *Latin America*, p. 432.

5. Figures for these percentages come from Elliot, *Brazil*, p. 319.

6. James, *Latin America*, p. 432.

7. Ministério da Fazenda, *Foreign Trade*, p. 48.

8. *Ibid.*

9. Ministério da Agricultura, *Synopse*, pp. 70–86.

10. James, *Latin America*, p. 453. The rapid growth of São Paulo was in sharp contrast to the slower growth of its former rival, Recife, Pernambuco, which had a population of 111,556 in 1890 and of 238,-843 in 1920. Ministério da Agricultura, *Synopse*, pp. 92–104. For an excellent study of the growth of São Paulo during this era see Morse, *From Community to Metropolis*, pp. 200–291.

11. Secretaría da Agricultura, Comércio, e Obras Públicas do Estado de São Paulo, *O Café, 1919*, p. 27.

12. Bernstein, *Modern and Contemporary Latin America*, p. 379. Paul Vanorden Shaw, "Men from Rio Grande do Sul," *Brazil Herald* (Rio de Janeiro), July 14, 1962, p. 4.

13. Lorillard to Root, Feb. 4, 1907, NA, Brazilian Dispatches, Vol. 120, No. 103.

14. Lorillard to Root, Jan. 28, 1907, NA, Brazilian Dispatches, Vol. 119, No. 101.

15. João Cruz Costa, *Esbozo,* p. 121.

16. Thompson to Hay, April 6, 1903, NA, Brazilian Dispatches, Vol. 68, No. 8.

17. *Almanaque Brasileiro Garnier,* 1908, p. 81. William Jennings Bryan was equally enthusiastic about the new Rio de Janeiro. See his remarks in "My Visit to Brazil, the Giant of South America," New York *World,* June 19, 1910, Magazine Section, p. 5.

18. Lorillard to Root, Feb. 4, 1907, NA, Brazilian Dispatches, Vol. 120, No. 103. The officials and merchants of the State of Amazonas were particularly bitter about the deference paid to coffee. *Revista da Associação Commercial do Amazonas* (Manaus), Dec., 1910, p. 2, and March, 1911, p. 6. Valorization was an original Brazilian contribution to the science of economics. Since 1906, many countries in the world, including the United States, have employed variations of this economic scheme in an effort to solve economic problems. Freyre, *Ordem e Progresso,* I, lv.

19. Thompson to Root, Aug. 25, 1905, NA, Brazilian Dispatches, Vol. 71, No. 78; Griscom to Root, Nov. 28, 1906, NA, Brazilian Dispatches, Vol. 228, No. 2372/4.

20. *Revista da Associação Commercial do Amazonas* (Manaus), Dec., 1910, p. 2.

21. Elliott, *Brazil,* pp. 187–88.

22. Associação Commercial do Amazonas, *State of the Amazonas,* pp. 40 and 132; Estado do Amazonas, *Relatório,* p. 9.

23. Ferreira Filho, *A Borracha,* p. 7.

24. Associação Commercial do Amazonas, *State of the Amazonas,* p. 38.

25. The legends concerning Manaus during its boom days are innumerable. Two recent books which recount some of them are: Genesino Braga, *Fastígio e Sensibilidade do Amazonas de Ontem* (Manaus, 1960), and João Nogueira de Mata, *Flagrantes de Amazônia* (Manaus, 1960).

26. Elliott, *Brazil,* p. 185.

27. Melby, "Rubber River: An Account of the Rise and Collapse of

the Amazon Boom," *Hispanic American Historical Review,* XXII (August, 1942), 464. Wagley, "Brazil," in *Most of the World,* ed. Ralph Linton, p. 232.

28. Estado do Amazonas, *Leis,* p. 59; Estado do Amazonas, *Relatório,* p. 14.

29. Melby, "Rubber River," *Hispanic American Historical Review,* XII, 463–64.

30. *Brazilian Review* (Rio de Janeiro), Dec. 31, 1907, p. 1482.

31. Elliott, *Brazil,* p. 278.

32. Ministério da Agricultura, *Resumo,* p. 80. More detailed railroad statistics for the period can be found in Ministério de Viação e Obras Públicas, Inspectoria Federal das Estradas, *Estatística das Estradas de Ferro da União, 1902–1912* (Rio de Janeiro, 1903–14).

33. For a history of that agency see David H. Stauffer, "The Origin and Establishment of Brazil's Indian Service: 1889–1910" (unpublished Ph.D. dissertation, Department of History, University of Texas, 1955).

34. Frederic William Ganzert, "The Baron do Rio-Branco and Brazilian Foreign Relations" (unpublished Ph.D. dissertation, Department of History of the University of California, 1933), p. 113.

35. The eminent novelist Erico Veríssimo describes this regional pride and frustration very ably in some of his novels about Rio Grande do Sul. For example, see *O Arquipélago* (Rio de Janeiro, 1962), I, 91.

36. Lima e Silva to Rio-Branco, Dec. 1, 1910, AHI, Ofícios 234/1/10.

37. Dudley to Secretary of State, Nov. 29, 1910, NA, Brazilian Dispatches, No. 832.00/67.

38. Dudley to Secretary of State, Dec. 16, 1910, NA, Brazilian Dispatches, No. 832.00/68.

39. Rives to Secretary of State, Feb. 8, 1912, NA, Brazilian Dispatches, No. 832.002/8.

40. David Carneiro, *Galeria de Ontem e de Hoje,* p. 361. Another aspect of the growing nationalism of the period was the "Buy Brazilian" campaign of local industries. Freyre, *Ordem e Progresso,* I, cxxix.

41. For example, see Bello, *História da República,* I, 260; Besouchet, *Rio-Branco,* pp. 34–35; Lawrence F. Hill, "Reconstruction and Progress," in *Brazil,* ed. Lawrence F. Hill, p. 81; "Brazil's Quarter Century," *The Nation,* XCIX (Nov. 26, 1914), 623.

42. Chargé d'Affaires of Mexico in Brazil to the Ministry of Foreign Relations, Mexico, May 15, 1910, ARE, Mex, Folder 3053-12.

Chapter II. A MAN FOR THE TIMES

1. Oliveira, *Actos Diplomáticos do Brasil*, II, 310.
2. Fernandes Levi Carneiro, *Discursos*, p. 55. During the first week of December, 1902, all the newspapers of Rio de Janeiro and of the other principal cities carried an extensive coverage of Rio-Branco's return.
3. "Luiz Barroso Pereira," *Revista Popular*, XIII (Rio de Janeiro, Jan.–March, 1862), 206–12.
4. "Episódios da Guerra do Prata (1825–28)," *Revista Mensual do Instituto Científico*, II (São Paulo, June, 1864), 83; III (Aug., 1864), 8.
5. *A Noite* (Rio de Janeiro), Feb. 17, 1912, p. 1.
6. Dias, *Pequena Biografia do Barão do Rio-Branco*, p. 56; Assumpção, "Rio-Branco e 'L'Illustration,'" *Revista IHGB*, CLXXXVIII (Rio de Janeiro, July–Sept., 1945), 10–13.
7. "O Esbôço Biográfico do General José de Abreu, Barão do Sêrro Largo," *Revista IHGB*, XXXI, 2ª parte (Rio de Janeiro, 1868), 62–135.
8. Ganzert, "The Baron," p. 7.
9. Viana Filho, *A Vida do Barão do Rio Branco*, p. 42.
10. *Ibid.*, p. 72.
11. Napoleão, *O Segundo*, p. 46.
12. *Ibid.*, p. 119.
13. Gutiérrez, *Hombres*, p. 184.
14. Viana Filho, *A Vida do Barão do Rio Branco*, p. 89.
15. Napoleão, *O Segundo*, p. 31.
16. Viana Filho, *A Vida do Barão do Rio Branco*, p. 143. The editor of the *Encyclopédie*, E. Levasseur, paid tribute to the contribution of Rio-Branco at a banquet on October 3, 1889. Azambuja, "Biografia," *Revista do O Jornal* (Rio de Janeiro), April 22, 1945, p. 7.
17. Azambuja, "Biografia," *Revista do O Jornal*, April 22, 1945, p. 7.
18. *Obras*, Vol. VI.
19. Lyra Filho, *O Barão*, p. 49.
20. Amado, *Rio-Branco*, p. 11.
21. Barreto, *Rio Branco*, p. 53.
22. Rodrigues, *Teoria da História do Brasil*, p. 20.
23. "He is said to have known English and French very well and

possessed a fair understanding of Spanish, German, and Italian." Ganzert, "The Baron," p. 7. "He spoke Spanish with a certain slowness." Bernárdez, *Le Brésil*, p. 163. "He spoke and wrote perfectly several languages, among which were English, French and Spanish." Raul de Rio-Branco, *Reminiscências*, p. 186. It is interesting to note that among his papers is encountered material written in his hand in English. In his small, private notebooks, he made occasional notations in English. This is particularly true for the years he was in the United States, 1893–95.

24. Viana Filho, *A Vida do Barão do Rio Branco*, p. 205.

25. Carlos Sussekind de Mendonça, *Salvador de Mendonça*, pp. 176–86.

26. "Biografia," *Revista do O Jornal*, April 22, 1945, p. 7.

27. *Gazeta de Notícias* (Rio de Janeiro), Feb. 8, 1895, p. 1; Feb. 9, p. 1; *Jornal do Commercio* (Rio de Janeiro), Feb. 7, 1895, p. 1; Feb. 8, p. 1; *O Estado de S. Paulo* (São Paulo), Feb. 8, 1895, p. 1; Feb. 9, p. 1.

28. Viana Filho, *A Vida do Barão do Rio Branco*, p. 205.

29. Barreto, *Rio Branco*, pp. 54–57.

30. Viana Filho, *A Vida do Barão do Rio Branco*, p. 273.

31. *Correio Paulistano* (São Paulo), Dec. 2, 1900, p. 1; *Jornal do Brasil* (Rio de Janeiro), Dec. 2, 1900, p. 1; *Jornal do Commercio* (Rio de Janeiro), Dec. 2, 1900, p. 1.

32. Viana Filho, *A Vida do Barão do Rio Branco*, p. 307.

33. Feijó Bittencourt, "Quem Escreveu e como Escreveu acerca do Barão de Rio Branco," *Revista IHGB*, CLXXXVII (Rio de Janeiro, 1945), 52–53.

34. Napoleão, *O Segundo*, p. 98.

35. *Ibid.*, p. 40.

36. *A Noite* (Rio de Janeiro), Feb. 14, 1912, p. 1.

37. Ganzert, "The Baron," p. 45; A. Teixeira Soares, *O Barão do Rio-Branco e a Diplomacia Brasileira* (Porto Alegre, Brazil, 1946), p. 9.

38. Rio-Branco to Nabuco, Aug. 30, 1902, ABR-BI. In effect those were reiterations of an opinion he had expressed to Nabuco as early as 1891. Rio-Branco to Nabuco, 1891 (letter without day or month), in the possession of Ambassador Maurício Nabuco, AJN.

39. Calmon, *História do Brasil*, V, 251.

40. "Without hiding it, he confessed his love for the army by defending the thesis 'to be strong in order to be peaceful.' " Antunes, *História do Grande Chanceler*, p. 101.

41. Caroline Nabuco, *The Life,* p. 318.

42. Pinto da Rocha, "O Barão do Rio-Branco e o Direito Interna-cional," *Revista Americana,* IV (April, 1913), 31; Calmon, *História Diplomática do Brasil,* p. 53. Raul Bazán Dávila, "El Barón de Rio Branco," manuscript of a speech given by the author when he was Chilean ambassador to Brazil, p. 5.

43. João Frank da Costa, "Rio Branco, Nabuco e o americanismo," *Jornal do Commercio* (Rio de Janeiro), Feb. 18, 1962, 2° caderno, p. 5.

44. Alencar, "Some Postulates of Brazilian Foreign Policy," *Brazilian-American Survey,* XII (1960), 6. Minister of Foreign Relations Afonso Arinos de Mello Franco stated on July 23, 1962, "Foreign policy is an external projection of our national personality in the international sphere." *Brazil Herald* (Rio de Janeiro), July 24, 1962, p. 2. "Foreign policy is nothing more than national policy carried beyond the frontiers." Maurício Nabuco, *Algumas Reflexões sobre Diplomacia,* p. 36. See also Olympio Guilherme, *O Nacionalismo e a Política Internacional do Brasil* (São Paulo, 1957), p. 30.

45. Afonso de Carvalho, *Rio-Branco,* p. 201.

46. Lima, *The Evolution of Brazil,* p. 42.

47. Fleiuss, *Rio-Branco,* p. 12.

48. Those letters are found in the Arquivo Histórico de Itamaraty.

49. Rio-Branco to Brazilian Ambassador, Washington, March 6, 1906, AHI, Teleg. Exp. 235/3/15.

50. Calógeras, *Rio Branco,* p. 19.

51. Abranches, *Rio Branco,* I, 51.

52. Rio-Branco to Brazilian Minister, Washington, Jan. 24, 1903, AHI, Teleg. Exp. 235/3/15. Said President Alves, " 'I resolved then to inter-vene in order to protect our compatriots and to avoid further unnecessary bloodshed.' " Júlio Rocha, *O Acre,* p. 11.

53. Most Brazilian historians agree that the number of Brazilians in Acre at this time probably was near 60,000. Delgado de Carvalho, *História Diplomática,* p. 223. Ganzert at first placed the number at only 15,000. "The Baron," p. 204. Later, however, he stated, "By 1900, there were more than 60,000 Brazilians in the Acre region." "The Boundary Controversy in the Upper Amazon Between Brazil, Bolivia, and Peru, 1903–1909," *Hispanic American Historical Review,* XIV (Nov., 1934), 434. Minister Thompson reported, "Brazil has been immensely aided in

obtaining the present favorable status to herself of this dispute by the fact that the Acre is inhabited solely by Brazilians." Thompson to Hay, March 23, 1903, NA, Brazilian Dispatches, Vol. 68, No. 4. "The population of Acre has grown constantly to the point where it now has around 20,000 inhabitants, of whom 99 percent are Brazilians, according to data published by Bolivia on February 21st of this year [1903]." Júlio Rocha, *O Acre,* p. 8. According to Bolivian Minister of War and Colonization, José Cosío Guzmán, 99 percent of the inhabitants were Brazilians. *El Estado* (La Paz), March 14, 1903, p. 1. The population figures may vary, but all authorities agree that Brazilians, not Bolivians, inhabited the area.

54. *Correio da Manhã* (Rio de Janeiro), March 18, 1904, p. 1.

55. Washington *Post,* Aug. 26, 1903, p. 5. Acre, known officially in Bolivia as *Territorio de Colonias,* had been a constant drain on the impoverished Bolivian budget. Júlio Rocha, *O Acre,* p. 9.   . .

56. Abranches, *Rio Branco,* I, 138; Associação Commercial do Amazonas, *State of the Amazonas,* p. 39; Fleiuss, *Rio-Branco,* p. 20. Figures vary considerably from source to source. Probably none are accurate. The important fact to consider, however, is that all sources claim that rubber-rich Acre quickly paid for itself.

57. Rio-Branco to Brazilian Ambassador, Washington, June (?), 1909, AHI, Teleg. Exp. 235/4/1.

58. *Ibid.*

59. Heitor Lyra, "Europe and the South American Neighbors," in *Brazil,* ed. Lawrence F. Hill, p. 334.

60. Delgado de Carvalho, *História Diplomática,* p. 214.

61. Napoleão, *Rio Branco,* p. 206.

62. There is some difference of opinion as to the exact number of square miles of territory which Rio-Branco obtained for Brazil. However, most authorities agree that it was approximately 342,000 square miles. Viana Filho, *A Vida do Barão do Rio Branco,* p. 420. Centro Cívico Sete de Setembro, *À Memória,* p. 10. Liberato Bittencourt, *Psicologia do Barão do Rio Branco,* p. 31.

63. Angelo do Amaral, "Política Internacional," *Jornal do Commercio* (Rio de Janeiro), Jan. 13, 1910, p. 2.

64. Ganzert, "The Baron," p. 36. I asked several Brazilian historians, Artur Cesar Ferreira Reis, Leandro Tocantins, Luiz Viana Filho, Hélio

Viana, A. G. de Araujo Jorge, and David Carneiro, what they re-garded as the greatest accomplishment of Rio-Branco. They unanimously agreed that it was the settlement of the boundaries.

65. A considerable amount of the diplomatic activity of the 1902–12 period can be reconstructed by studying the lists of diplomats sent and received by Brazil in Campos, *Relações Diplomáticas do Brazil.* Another useful source is the only "annual" *Relatório* which Rio-Branco published during his ministry. Ministério das Relações Exteriores, *Relatório, 1902–1903.* An outline of the principal diplomatic acts for those years can be found in the annual presidential messages delivered on May 3 of each year and published by the Imprensa Nacional.

66. In 1910 Brazil also sent delegations to a large number of inter-national conferences: International Congress of Chambers of Com-merce and of Commercial and Industrial Associations, London; Inter-national Conference of Administrative Sciences, Brussels; International Congress of Physiotherapy, Paris; International Congress of Tropical Agriculture, Brussels; Pan American Scientific Congress, Buenos Aires; International Congress of Railroads, Bern; International Congress of School Hygiene, Paris; International Congress of Public and Private Assistance, Copenhagen; International Congress of Popular Education, Brussels; International Congress of Associations of Inventors and of Industrial Artists, Brussels; International Congress on Assistance to the Insane, Berlin.

67. Chile, Argentina, United States, Portugal, France, Spain, Mexico, Honduras, Venezuela, Panama, Ecuador, Costa Rica, Cuba, Great Britain, Bolivia, Nicaragua, Norway, China, El Salvador, Peru, Sweden, Haiti, Dominican Republic, Colombia, Greece, Russia, Austria-Hungary, Uruguay, Paraguay, Italy, and Denmark. Abranches, *Rio Branco,* II, 23–27.

68. Fernandes Levi Carneiro, *Discursos,* p. 63. Paulo Filho, *Ensaios,* p. 67. The correspondence exchanged between Rio-Branco and Nabuco, AHI, contradicts any assertions that Rio-Branco dominated those under him. Nabuco spoke freely in his letters and suggested policies for U.S.-Brazilian relations. He even threatened to resign if Brazil's policy toward the United States was sharply altered. In one letter, for example, Nabuco thanked Rio-Branco for the "liberty of action" he was given. Nabuco to Rio-Branco, Oct. 12, 1906, ABR-BI.

69. Calógeras, *Rio Branco,* p. 35. Another Brazilian who worked with

Rio-Branco spoke of the relationship between the minister and his subordinates as one of "cooperating closely." Lobo, *Brasilianos & Yankees,* p. 166.

70. Mme Beltrão to Oliveira Lima, June 20, 1905, OL Lib.

71. "Reputações falsas—O Barão do Rio Branco," *O Internacional* (Rio de Janeiro), May 10, 1911, p. 1. In his book *O Brasil e o Internacionalismo,* published to commemorate the first anniversary of Rio-Branco's death, Alcides Gentil, after praising the Baron, went on to criticize his policy for being too friendly to the United States, for not strengthening even more relations with Spanish America, and for opposing the Drago Doctrine.

72. Ameida Brandão to Oliveira Lima, April 15, 1903, OL Lib.

73. Venáncio Filho, *Rio Branco,* p. 48.

74. Reyes to Oliveira Lima, May 3, 1909, OL Lib.

75. Burns, "Rio Branco Visto Pelos Seus Contemporáneos Norteamericanos," *Jornal do Commercio* (Rio de Janeiro), Aug. 11, 1962, p. 4.

76. Lins, *Rio-Branco,* II, 617–21. A Mexican diplomatic official reported that Argentina initially was favorable to the new foreign minister of Brazil. Consul General of Mexico, Buenos Aires, to Minister of Foreign Relations, Mexico, Dec. 7, 1902, ARE, Mex, Folder No. 11-6-105, No. 117. Joaquim D. Cassasus, Mexican ambassador to the United States, to Nabuco, May 16, 1906, enclosed with Gurgel do Amaral to Rio-Branco, June 16, 1906, AHI, Ofícios 234/1/4. Legation of Mexico, Buenos Aires, to Minister of Foreign Relations, Mexico, Feb. 15, 1912, ARE, Mex, Folder 11-4-196, No. 128. Chilean Minister, Rio de Janeiro, to Minister of Foreign Relations, Santiago, Nov. 30, 1902, ANCh, Legation of Chile in Brazil, 1902–3, No. 65; Chilean Minister, Rio de Janeiro, to Minister of Foreign Relations, Santiago, Feb. 29, 1909, ARE, Ch, Oficios received from the Chilean Legation in Brazil, 1904–8, No. 1. Chilean Minister, Rio de Janeiro, to Minister of Foreign Relations, Santiago, July 5, 1909, ANCh, Legation of Chile in Brazil, 1908–9, No. 38.

77. Manuel Bernárdez, *Rio-Branco* (Montevideo, 1909), p. 21.

78. *The United States of Brazil,* p. 81.

79. *South America,* pp. 416–17.

80. New York *Times,* April 23, 1911, Magazine Section, p. 5.

81. Joaquim Nabuco, *The Spirit,* p. 13.

82. Feb. 10, 1912, p. 1.

Chapter III. COMMERCE AS A BACKDROP
FOR DIPLOMACY

1. A summary of the diplomatic events of this period can be found in Hill, *Diplomatic Relations.*

2. Rio-Branco to Brazilian Legation, Washington, Jan. 31, 1905, AHI, Despachos 235/2/5. An account of Pedro II's visit to the United States, his impressions, and the American reaction is given in Argeu Guimarães, *D. Pedro II nos Estados Unidos* (Rio de Janeiro, 1961).

3. Leão, *Salvador de Mendonça,* p. 63.

4. Salvador de Mendonça, *A Situação,* pp. 81–86.

5. Carlos Sussekind de Mendonça, *Salvador de Mendonça,* p. 154.

6. *Ibid.,* pp. 229–33.

7. Salvador de Mendonça, *A Situação,* pp. 247–48.

8. Rio-Branco to Rui Barbosa, Feb. 12, 1890, quoted in Lacombe, *Rio-Branco e Rui Barbosa,* p. 17.

9. Rio-Branco to Homem de Melo, March 19, 1890, ADC; Viana Filho in his *A Vida do Barão do Rio Branco* makes frequent references to Rio-Branco's idyllic desires to become a *fazendeiro.*

10. Rio-Branco to Domício da Gama, Dec. 31, 1911, AHI, Despachos 233/2/8.

11. U.S. Department of Commerce and Labor, Bureau of Manufactures, *Daily Consular and Trade Reports,* I (Aug. 27, 1910), 617; Manchester, *British Preeminence in Brazil,* p. 333.

12. Rodrigues, "The Foundations of Brazil's Foreign Policy," *International Affairs,* XXXVIII (July, 1962), 331–332.

13. Associação Commercial do Amazonas, *State of the Amazonas,* p. 40.

14. Domville-Fife, *The United States of Brazil,* p. 159.

15. E. C. Duley, *North Brazil* (London, 1914), p. 161.

16. Thompson to Rio-Branco, April 28, 1903, AHI, Represent. Estrang. Notas, EUA 280/2/7.

17. *Bulletin of the Pan American Union* (Washington), July, 1911, pp. 60–61.

18. Carlos Sussekind de Mendonça, *Salvador de Mendonça,* p. 218.

19. Janes to Bacon, March 4, 1904, NA, Brazilian Dispatches, 837/59; Gomes Ferreira to Rio-Branco, March 26, 1905, AHI, Ofícios 234/1/3.

20. *Brazilian Review* (Rio de Janeiro), Oct. 25, 1904, p. 693.

21. Dudley to Knox, April 3, 1909, NA, Brazilian Dispatches, 18643/10.

22. Dudley to Secretary of State, April 5, 1909, NA, Brazilian Dispatches, 18843/4.

23. Rio-Branco to Nabuco, Feb. 8, 1909, AHI, Teleg. Exp. 235/4/1.

24. Nabuco to Root, Dec. 30, 1908, NA, Notes from Brazilian Embassy, 637/40.

25. "Dinner with Senator du Pont." Diary of Joaquim Nabuco, AJN (cited hereafter as Nabuco Diary), Jan. 15, 1909. "Later I had a long conversation with Senator Aldrich about the coffee tax. He tells me that it will be enacted only if there is no other way to get revenue." *Ibid.*, Jan. 23, 1909. "Senator Elkins conversing with Quezada about the coffee question said, 'We cannot do anything which would displease Mr. Nabuco.'" *Ibid.*, Feb. 9, 1909. "Dinner with Senator and Mrs. Elkins." *Ibid.*, March 9, 1909. "I have already expressed the substance of your views to many of my associates in the Senate and I have a strong impression that the view will prevail." Root to Nabuco, March 3, 1909, AJN. "The proposed countervailing duty on coffee is now happily disposed of. As you know, it was on account of the suggestions you were kind enough to make to me when I met you at the home of Mr. and Mrs. Jennings that I obtained the facts and presented them to the House." Congressman Douglas to Nabuco, quoted in Caroline Nabuco, *The Life,* p. 351.

26. Nabuco to Knox, March 22, 1909, NA, Notes from Brazilian Embassy, 18643/1.

27. Dudley to Secretary of State, May 5, 1909, NA, Brazilian Dispatches, 18643/4.

28. Nabuco to Rio-Branco, May 5, 1909, AHI, Ofícios 234/1/9.

29. *Ibid.*

30. Stuart, *Latin America,* p. 434.

31. The complete story of the antitrust suit against valorized coffee is treated in detail by Sensabaugh, "The Coffee-Trust Question in United States–Brazilian Relations: 1912–13," *Hispanic American Historical Review,* XXVI (Nov., 1946), 480–96.

32. Estado de Amazonas, *Relatório,* p. 8.

33. Ferreira Filho, *A Borracha,* p. 5; Moog, *Bandeirantes e Pioneiros,* p. 240.

34. Napoleão, *Rio Branco,* p. 151.

35. Thompson to Hay, May 10, 1905, NA, Brazilian Dispatches, 71/30; Griscom to Root, Aug. 29, 1906, NA, Brazilian Dispatches, 836/3; Rio-Branco to Janes, Jan. 25, 1909, enclosed in Janes to Root, Feb. 1, 1909, NA, Brazilian Dispatches, 836/134.

36. Thompson to Hay, July 23, 1903, NA, Brazilian Dispatches, 68/46.

37. Thompson to Hay, May 7 and Dec. 27, 1903, NA, Brazilian Dispatches, 68/17 and 69/103.

38. Thompson to Loomis, June 24, 1904, NA, Brazilian Dispatches, 70/188.

39. *Monthly Bulletin of the International Bureau of American States* (Washington), June, 1904, p. 1483. Itamaraty's official reasons for granting the concessions were worded similarly. Ministério das Relações Exteriores, *Relatório, 1913–1914,* I, 209.

40. Rio-Branco to Dawson, April 18, 1904, enclosed in Dawson to Hay, April 27, 1904, NA, Brazilian Dispatches, 69/142.

41. Rio-Branco to Brazilian Legation, Washington, May 2, 1904, AHI, Teleg. Exp. 235/3/15.

42. Thompson to Loomis, June 24, 1904, NA, Brazilian Dispatches, 70/188.

43. Dawson to Hay, Feb. 15, 1904, NA, Brazilian Dispatches, 89/122.

44. April 23, 1904, p. 1.

45. Dawson to Hay, Feb. 15, 1904, NA, Brazilian Dispatches, 69/122.

46. Thompson to Hay, May 4, 1904, NA, Brazilian Dispatches, 70/143.

47. Rio-Branco to Thompson, May 24, 1904, AHI, Represent. Estrang. Notas, EUA 280/3/16.

48. Thompson to Hay, May 4, 1904, NA, Brazilian Dispatches, 70/143.

49. Adee to Thompson, Feb. 4, 1905, NA, Brazilian Instructions, 18/668.

50. Rio-Branco to Thompson, Dec. 31, 1904, quoted in Thompson to Hay, Jan. 6, 1905, NA, Brazilian Dispatches, 71/248.

51. Thompson to Hay, Jan. 3 and Aug. 21, 1905, NA, Brazilian Dispatches, 71/247 and 71/76.

52. Griscom to Root, Nov. 6, 1906, NA, Brazilian Dispatches, 856/31.

53. Rio-Branco to Brazilian Embassy, Washington, July 5, 1906,

quoted in Gurgel do Amaral to Rio-Branco, July 21, 1906, AHI, Ofícios 254/1/4.

54. Root, *Speeches,* p. 86.

55. Griscom to Root, Nov. 22, 1906, NA, Brazilian Dispatches, 2210/4.

56. The decrees as well as the most pertinent correspondence between the American diplomatic representative in Rio and Itamaraty are reprinted in Ministério das Relações Exteriores, *Relatório, 1912–1913,* Anexo A, pp. 39–49.

57. Dudley to Secretary of State, Jan. 14, 1911, NA, Brazilian Dispatches, 611.3231/180.

58. Feb. 1, 1911, p. 1. The Chilean minister noted that Brazilian tariff concessions to the United States were one way of guaranteeing and protecting Brazil's profitable market in North America. Chilean Minister, Rio de Janeiro, to Minister of Foreign Relations, Santiago, Feb. 9, 1911, ANCh, Chilean Legation in Brazil, 1911, No. 30.

59. Dudley to Root, June 17, 1908, NA, Brazilian Dispatches, 836/116.

60. New Orleans *Times-Democrat,* Jan. 14, 1912, Pan American Mail Section, p. 1.

61. Thompson to Loomis, Feb. 11, 1905, NA, Brazilian Dispatches, 71/265.

62. *Bulletin of the Pan American Union* (Washington), July, 1911, p. 61.

63. Memorandum of M. H. Davis, Oct. 19, 1909, Bureau of Trade Relations, Department of State, NA, Brazilian Dispatches, 836/155.

64. Mello, *Politique Commerciale du Brésil,* p. 74.

65. Baldwin, "The Brazil of Today," *The Outlook,* XCIV (Oct. 21, 1911), 426–27.

66. Chamberlain, "A Letter from Brazil," *Atlantic Monthly,* XC 1911), 821.

67. "American Capital in Brazil," *Scientific American,* LXXX (Jan. 26, 1899), 53; Chamberlain, "Our Neglect of South American Markets," *North American Review,* CLXXXI (July, 1905), 122; Bingham, *Across South America,* p. 24; John M. Turner, *Trade Development in Latin America,* U.S. Department of Commerce Special Agent Series No. 45, pp. 25–41.

68. Bingham, *Across South America,* p. 26.

69. Ministério da Fazenda, *Foreign Trade,* p. 864.

70. New Orleans *Times-Democrat,* Jan. 14, 1912, Pan American Mail Section, p. 1.

71. Dudley to Rio-Branco, May 10, 1910, AHI, Represent. Estrang. Notas, EUA 280/3/10.

72. "The American colony is practically negligible in number as compared to others." E. N. Hurley, *Banking and Credit in Argentina, Brazil, Chile, and Peru,* U.S. Department of Commerce Special Agents Series No. 90, p. 49.

73. *Bulletin of the Pan American Union* (Washington), Feb., 1915, pp. 149–50.

74. Hale, "The South American Situation," *The Reader,* VIII (Oct., 1906), 474.

75. *Bulletin of the Pan American Union* (Washington), Aug., 1916, pp. 316–18.

76. Elliott, *Brazil,* p. 287.

77. Speech of Gurgel do Amaral before the Commercial Club of Kansas City on the occasion of the Trans-Mississippi Congress, Nov. 19, 1906, enclosed in Nabuco to Rio-Branco, Dec. 4, 1906, AHI, Ofícios 234/1/5.

78. Da Gama to Rio-Branco, Jan. 31, 1912, AHI, Ofícios 234/1/13.

79. Elliott, *Brazil,* p. 295.

Chapter IV. FROM SUSPICION TO
FRIENDSHIP, 1902–1906

1. Tocantins, *Formação,* II, 419.

2. Ministério das Relações Exteriores, *Relatório Apresentado ao Presidente da República dos Estados Unidos do Brasil pelo Ministro de Estado das Relações Exteriores* (Rio de Janeiro, 1902), p. 3.

3. *O Paiz* (Rio de Janeiro), Dec. 7, 1902, p. 1.

4. Seeger to Hay, Feb. 12, 1903, NA, Brazilian Dispatches, Vol. 68.

5. *Atlantic Monthly,* Dec., 1902, pp. 826–28; *Harper's Weekly,* May 30, 1903, pp. 919–21.

6. Seeger to Hay, Feb. 12, 1903, NA, Brazilian Dispatches, Vol. 68.

7. New York *Herald,* Dec. 14, 1902, 2d section, p. 5.

8. Seeger to Hay, Feb. 12, 1903, NA, Brazilian Dispatches, Vol. 68.

9. Assis Brasil to Foreign Minister, Nov. 1, 1900, AHI, Ofícios 234/1/1.

10. Lisboa to Minister of Foreign Relations, July 25, 1900, AHI, Ofícios 211/2/11; Lisboa to Minister of Foreign Relations, March 11, 1901, AHI, Ofícios 211/2/11; Lisboa to Minister of Foreign Relations March 26, 1902, AHI, Ofícios 211/2/11.

11. Leon F. Sensabaugh, unpublished manuscript on Brazil, p. 103. That Bolivia put great reliance on the syndicate can be seen in these words of Armayo: "Thanks to the influence of this syndicate, doubtless we will be able to count on the moral support of the Department of State in our questions with Brazil." *Diario Oficial* (Rio de Janeiro), Nov. 15, 1906, p. 6159.

12. Conversation Assis Brasil–Hay, Jan. 26, 1903, enclosed in Assis Brasil to Rio-Branco, Feb. 4, 1903, AHI, Ofícios 234/1/2.

13. Tocantins, *Formação,* III, 565.

14. Bryan to Hay, May 6, 1902, NA, Brazilian Dispatches, 67/413.

15. Hay to Bryan, May 3, 1902, NA, Brazilian Instructions, 18/567.

16. Bryan to Hay, May 30, 1902, NA, Brazilian Dispatches, 67/426.

17. Assis Brasil to Foreign Minister, May 16, 1902, and Jan. 27, 1903, AHI, Teleg. Receb. 235/2/14.

18. Conversation Assis Brasil–Hay, Jan. 26, 1903, enclosed in Assis Brasil to Rio-Branco, Feb. 4, 1903, AHI, Ofícios 234/1/2.

19. Assis Brasil to Rio-Branco, Feb. 4, 1903, AHI, Ofícios 234/1/2.

20. Conversation Assis Brasil–Hay, Jan. 26, 1903, enclosed in Assis Brasil to Rio-Branco, Feb. 4, 1903, AHI, Ofícios 234/1/2.

21. Assis Brasil to Rio-Branco, Oct. 17, 1902, ABR-BI.

22. New York *Herald,* Dec. 14, 1902, 2d section, p. 5; *Diario Oficial* (Rio de Janeiro), Nov. 15, 1906, p. 6165.

23. Memo from Brazilian Legation to Secretary of State, July 16, 1902, NA, Notes from the Brazilian Legation, Vol. 8.

24. Seeger to Rio-Branco, Jan. 21, 1902, AHI, Represent. Estrang. Notas, EUA 280/2/7.

25. Tocantins, *Formação,* III, 566–68.

26. Telegram from Rio-Branco to Brazilian Legation, Lisbon, enclosed in Seeger to Secretary of State, Feb. 4, 1903, NA, Brazilian Dispatches, Vol. 68.

27. Rio-Branco to Brazilian Minister, Washington, Jan. 21, 1903, AHI, Teleg. Exp. 235/3/15.

28. The correspondence from Moore to Rio-Branco is on file in ABR-BI.

29. Rio-Branco to Seeger, Feb. 20, 1903, quoted in Ministério das Relações Exteriores, *Relatório, 1902–1903,* p. 122.

30. Conversation Assis Brasil–Hay, Jan. 26, 1903, enclosed in Assis Brasil to Rio-Branco, Feb. 4, 1903, AHI, Ofícios 234/1/2.

31. Assis Brasil to Rio-Branco, March 19, 1903, AHI, Ofícios 234/1/2.

32. Mendonça to Afonso Pena, Aug. 21, 1906, quoted in Carlos Sussekind de Mendonça, *Salvador de Mendonça,* p. 258.

33. Assis Brasil to Rio-Branco, Oct. 17, 1902, ABR-BI.

34. *Ibid.*

35. Assis Brasil to Minister of Foreign Relations, Nov. 18, 1902, AHI, Ofícios 234/1/1.

36. Seeger to Secretary of State, Jan. 20, 1903, NA, Brazilian Dispatches, Vol. 68.

37. Assis Brasil to Rio-Branco, Feb. 18, 1903, AHI, Ofícios 234/1/2.

38. Assis Brasil to Minister of Foreign Relations, Nov. 18, 1902, AHI, Ofícios 234/1/1.

39. Assis Brasil to Rio-Branco, Oct. 17, 1902, ABR-BI; Assis Brasil to Minister of Foreign Relations, Nov. 18, 1902, AHI, Ofícios 234/1/1.

40. Assis Brasil to Rio-Branco, Feb. 19, 1903, AHI, Ofícios 234/1/2.

41. Assis Brasil to Rio-Branco, March 4, 1903, AHI, Ofícios 234/1/2.

42. Assis Brasil to Rio-Branco, March 14, 1903, AHI, Ofícios 234/1/2.

43. Rio-Branco to U.S. Legation, Feb. 20, 1903, enclosed in Seeger to Hay, March 3, 1903, NA, Brazilian Dispatches, Vol. 68.

44. Rio-Branco to Brazilian Minister, Washington, Feb. 14, 1903, AHI, Teleg. Exp. 235/3/15.

45. Assis Brasil to Rio-Branco, April 2, 1903, AHI, Teleg. Receb. 235/2/14.

46. Published by the Knickerbocker Press, New York City, the booklet bears no date, but the NYC Public Library received a complimentary copy from the Brazilian legation on August 15, 1904. The pamphlet contains 44 pages and a map.

47. Thompson to Hay, July 30, 1903, NA, Brazilian Dispatches, 68/50.

48. Assis Brasil to Rio-Branco, March 19, 1903, AHI, Ofícios 234/1/2. Interview Assis Brasil–Hay, April 15, 1903, enclosed in Lima e Silva to Rio-Branco, May 3, 1903, AHI, Ofícios 234/1/2.

49. May 3, 1903, AHI, Ofícios 234/1/2.

50. *Ibid.*

51. Rio-Branco discussed the action of Admiral David G. Farragut in the Civil War and criticized L. Schneider, author of *The History of the Triple Alliance,* for not knowing U.S. naval history well and making errors in discussing it. Rio-Branco to Homem de Mello, Jan. 23, 1888, ADC. When the North American fleet visited Brazil in 1908, Rio-Branco gave a speech again displaying considerable knowledge of U.S. naval history. *Obras,* IX, 145.

52. In a conversation with Minister Thompson, Rio-Branco reminisced fondly about his stay in the United States. Thompson to Hay, April 6, 1903, NA, Brazilian Dispatches, 68/8.

53. João Frank da Costa, "Rio Branco, Nabuco e o americanismo," *Jornal do Commercio,* Feb. 18, 1962, 2° caderno, p. 5; Fernandes Levi Carneiro, *Discursos,* p. 110; Delgado de Carvalho, *História Diplomática,* pp. 364–65. Araujo Jorge and Moniz de Aragão affirmed to me in conversation that Rio-Branco had spoken well of his sojourn in the United States, and both believed that the favorable decision of Cleveland influenced or disposed his opinions in favor of the United States.

54. Napoleão, *Rio Branco,* p. 181.

55. Rio-Branco to Nabuco, no date, AJN.

56. The first dispatch of Gomes Ferreira on Panama exemplifies the type of reporting thereafter. Gomes Ferreira to Rio-Branco, Nov. 12, 1903, AHI, Ofícios 234/1/2.

57. Thompson to Hay, Nov. 16, 1903, NA, Brazilian Dispatches, 69/82.

58. Pedro Arias to Minister of Foreign Relations, Rio, Nov. 23, 1903, AHI, Consulados Brasileiros, Ofícios 260/1/2.

59. *Correio da Manhã* (Rio de Janeiro), Nov. 30, 1903, p. 1. It is curious to note that after Brazil recognized Panama, the *Correio da Manhã* ran an editorial criticizing the government for so doing. May 8, 1904, p. 1.

60. Thompson to Hay, Dec. 4, 1903, NA, Brazilian Dispatches, 69/94.

61. Thompson to Hay, Nov. 21, 1903, NA, Brazilian Dispatches, 69/88.

62. Thompson to Hay, Nov. 20, 1903, NA, Brazilian Dispatches, 69/87.

63. Thompson to Hay, Nov. 27, 1903, NA, Brazilian Dispatches, 69/93.

64. Arthur Guimarães, *Actualidades,* p. 28. *A Notícia* (Rio de Janeiro), June 3, 1911, p. 1. In one month, April, 1963, Los Angeles was the largest North American export port to Brazil after New York. *Boletim Informativo,* Embassy of Brazil, Washington, D.C., May 23, 1963, p. 2.

65. Gomes Ferreira to Rio-Branco, Nov. 28, 1903, AHI, Ofícios 234/1/2.

66. Rio-Branco to Brazilian Minister, Washington, Dec. 6, 1903, AHI, Teleg. Exp. 235/3/15.

67. C. de Azevedo to Rio-Branco, Jan. 7, 1904, AHI, Ofícios 206/1/2. Rio-Branco also worked with the Argentine and Chilean ministers in Rio de Janeiro to coordinate and to encourage the recognition of Panama. Chilean Minister, Rio de Janeiro, to Minister of Foreign Relations, Santiago, Dec. 10, 1903, ANCh, Chilean Legation in Brazil, 1902–3, No. 77.

68. Rio-Branco to Brazilian Legation, Washington, Dec. 21, 1903, quoted in Gomes Ferreira to Rio-Branco, Jan. 6, 1904, AHI, Ofícios 234/1/2.

69. *Ibid.*

70. Gomes Ferreira to Rio-Branco, Dec. 28, 1903, AHI, Ofícios 234/1/2.

71. *Gaceta Oficial* (Panama), Feb. 10, 1904, p. 2.

72. They extended recognition on the following dates: December 23 and 29, 1903; January 1 and 15 and February 25, 1904.

73. Loomis to Thompson, Jan. 2, 1904, NA, Brazilian Dispatches, 18/633.

74. Dawson to Hay, March 4, 1904, NA, Brazilian Dispatches, 69/126.

75. Gomes Ferreira to Rio-Branco, Jan. 6, 1904, AHI, Ofícios 234/1/2.

76. Dawson to Hay, March 4, 1904, NA, Brazilian Dispatches, 69/126.

77. C. de Azevedo to Rio-Branco, March 13, 1904, AHI, Ofícios 206/1/2. Rio-Branco's role as the coordinator of the recognition of Panama by the major Latin American republics is discussed in Burns, "Rio-Branco e o Reconhecimento do Panamá," *Jornal do Commercio* (Rio de Janeiro), March 1, 1963, pp. 4–5.

78. Chilean Minister, Rio de Janeiro, to Minister of Foreign Relations,

Santiago, Feb. 8, 1904, ANCh, Chilean Legation in Brazil, 1905–6, No. 9.

79. C. de Azevedo to Rio-Branco, March 13, 1904, AHI, Ofícios 206/1/2.

80. Thompson to Hay, Jan. 15, 1905, NA, Brazilian Dispatches, 71/252.

81. After recognizing Panama, Rio-Branco created a Brazilian legation in Panama City in 1906. President Ricardo Arias received the first Brazilian minister, Antônio de Fontaura Xavier, on May 20, 1907. Five days later Panama created a legation in Rio de Janeiro and sent Belisario Porras as minister the following year. ARE, Pan, Brazilian Legation in Panama, Casilla No. 1-A, Vol. 1, Expedientes Nos. 1, 3, and 9.

82. Nabuco to Oliveira Lima, May 24, 1904, OL Lib.

83. Rio-Branco to Nabuco, Jan. 11, 1908, quoted in Nabuco to Rio-Branco, Jan. 15, 1908, AHI, Ofícios 234/1/7.

84. Dawson to Hay, March 19, 1904, NA, Brazilian Dispatches, 169/132; Gomes Ferreira to Rio-Branco, March 31, 1904, AHI, Ofícios 234/1/2.

85. Dawson to Hay, March 19, 1904, NA, Brazilian Dispatches, 169/132.

86. May 26, 27, and 30, 1904, p. 1.

87. Rio-Branco to Gomes Ferreira, June 30, 1904, and Feb. 28, 1905, Despachos 235/2/5.

88. Nabuco to Rio-Branco, Jan. 9, 1908, AHI, Teleg. Receb. 235/3/2; Nabuco to Rio-Branco, Jan. 15, 1908, AHI, Ofícios 234/1/7.

89. Rio-Branco to Brazilian Legation, Washington, April 9, 1904, AHI, Teleg. Exp. 235/3/15.

90. Gomes Ferreira to Rio-Branco, April 16 and 18, 1904, AHI, Teleg. Receb. 235/2/14.

91. Gomes Ferreira to Rio-Branco, April 30, 1904, AHI, Ofícios 234/1/2.

92. May 28, 1904, p. 1.

93. Hay telegraphed Thompson Peru's position. May 10, 1904, NA, Brazilian Dispatches, 18/637.

94. Rio-Branco to American Legation, May 16, 1904, AHI, Represent. Americanas, Notas, EUA 280/3/16.

95. Thompson to Rio-Branco, May 22, 1904, AHI, Represent. Estrang. Notas, EUA 280/2/7.

96. Thompson to Hay, May 27, 1904, NA, Brazilian Dispatches, 70/160.

97. Thompson to Rio-Branco, May 31, 1904, AHI, Represent. Estrang. Notas, EUA 280/2/7.

98. Thompson to Hay, June 22, 1904, NA, Brazilian Dispatches, 70/177.

99. Rio-Branco to Gomes Ferreira, July 7, 1904, AHI, Despachos 235/2/5.

100. Rio-Branco to Gomes Ferreira, July 7, 1904, AHI, Despachos 235/2/5.

101. Accusations of Brazilian imperialism are many. Of recent examples, one of the most outspoken is a Bolivian account of it: Gosálvez, *Proceso del Imperialismo del Brasil.*

102. Carlos Pereyra, *El Pensamiento Político do Alberdi* (Madrid, n.d.), pp. 253–57.

103. Austria-Hungary, France, Germany, Great Britain, Italy, Mexico, and Russia.

104. Assis Brasil to Rio-Branco, Feb. 4, 1903, AHI, Ofícios 234/1/2.

105. *O Paiz* (Rio de Janeiro), Jan. 8, 1905, p. 1. This article is attributed to Rio-Branco and all internal evidence leads to the conclusion that he wrote it. He telegraphed the entire article to Washington. Rio-Branco to Brazilian Legation, Washington, Jan. 8, 1905, AHI, Teleg. Exp. 235/3/15.

106. Thompson to Hay, Jan. 3, 1905, NA, Brazilian Dispatches, 71/247.

107. *Jornal do Commercio* (Rio de Janeiro), Jan. 1, 1905, p. 1. *O Paiz* (Rio de Janeiro), March 17, 1905, p. 1.

108. Graça Aranha to Nabuco, Dec. 27, 1904, quoted in Viana Filho, *A Vida do Barão do Rio Branco,* p. 355.

109. Ministério das Relações Exteriores, *Relatório, 1902–1903,* p. 66.

110. P. 1. The notice was repeated in *The South American Journal* (London), Nov. 26, 1904, p. 568.

111. Richardson to Hay, Nov. 2, 1904, NA, Brazilian Dispatches, 70/227.

112. The Brazilians were exceedingly proud of their participation in

the Fair. Gomes Ferreira to Rio-Branco, Sept. 24, 1904, AHI, Ofícios 234/1/2.

113. *Jornal do Commercio* (Rio de Janeiro), Jan. 1, 1905, p. 1.

114. *O Paiz* (Rio de Janeiro), Jan. 2, 1905, p. 2.

115. Rio-Branco, *Relações Exteriores do Brasil durante a Administração do Presidente Rodrigues Alves,* p. 85.

116. Joaquim Nabuco, *Minha Formação,* p. 159 *et passim.*

117. Caroline Nabuco, *The Life,* p. 307.

118. Elmano Cardim, "A Imprensa na Vida e na Obra de Rio Branco," *Revista IHGB,* CLXXXVIII (July–Sept., 1945), 132.

119. Napoleão, *Rio Branco,* p. 170.

120. ABR-BI.

121. "[Nabuco] is compromising our future in his last minute enthusiasm for the United States." José Veríssimo to Oliveira Lima, May 23, 1906, OL Lib; José Verissímo to Oliveira Lima, April 4, 1910, OL Lib; Carlos de Laet, "Pro Patria," *Jornal do Brasil* (Rio de Janeiro), March 29, 1906, p. 1.

122. Calmon, *Brasil e América,* pp. 82–83.

123. Ganzert, "The Baron," p. 381.

124. P. 9.

125. Both dated Dec. 28, 1904, p. 1.

126. Rio-Branco to Brazilian Legation, Washington, Dec. 29, 1904, AHI, Teleg. Exp. 235/3/15.

127. *Jornal do Commercio* (Rio de Janeiro), Jan. 1, 1905, p. 1.

128. Gomes Ferreira to Rio-Branco, Jan. 30, 1905, AHI, Ofícios 234/1/3.

129. Rio-Branco to Brazilian Legation, Washington, Dec. 31, 1904, AHI, Teleg. Exp. 235/3/15.

130. Brazilian Embassy to Loomis, May 24, 1905, NA, Notes from the Brazilian Legation, Vol. 8.

131. Nabuco to Rio-Branco, May 30, 1905, AHI, Ofícios 234/1/3.

132. Thompson to Hay, Jan. 15, 1905, NA, Brazilian Dispatches, 71/252.

133. Alves to Roosevelt, Jan. 21, 1905, NA, Notes from the Brazilian Legation, Vol. 8; the Brazilian president's official account of the elevation is contained in *Mensagem Apresentada ao Congresso Nacional na Abertura da Terceira Sessão da Quinta Legislativa pelo Presidente da*

República Francisco de Paulo Rodrigues Alves (Rio de Janeiro, 1905), pp. 18–19.

134. Nov. 15, 1906, p. 6171.

135. Jan. 8, 1905, p. 1; Jan. 15, 1905, p. 1.

136. *A Noticia* (Rio de Janeiro), March 16, 1905, p. 1; *Jornal do Commercio* (Rio de Janeiro), March 16, 1905, p. 1; *Gazeta de Notícias* (Rio de Janeiro), March 17, 1905, p. 1.

137. Griscom to Root, July 19, 1906, NA, Brazilian Dispatches, 141/113/2.

138. Jan. 14, 1905, p. 1.

139. Jan. 16, 1905, p. 1.

140. Thompson to Hay, Feb. 1, 1905, NA, Brazilian Dispatches, 71/263.

141. *O Paiz* (Rio de Janeiro), Jan. 26, 1905, p. 1. The editorial on January 26 was the third and last of a series defending and explaining the elevation of the legations. All three articles are favorable to the United States. The other two appeared on p. 1 of the January 8 and 17 editions.

142. May 12, 1906, p. 2. The article has been widely reprinted over the succeeding decades including an English translation circulated by the Brazilian embassy in the United States in 1908.

143. Rio-Branco to Thompson, March 27, 1905, Represent. Estrang. Notas, EUA 280/3/16.

144. "To me only is owed the merit of having proposed the creation of our Embassy in Washington and the appointment to it of Joaquim Nabuco." *Obras,* IX, 102.

145. Rio-Branco to Nabuco, March 2, 1907, and Jan. 22, 1909, AHI, Teleg. Exp. 235/3/15 and 235/4/1.

146. AHI, Rio-Branco to Nabuco, March 2, 1907, AHI, Despachos 235/2/6. When Chile made overtures for an exchange of ambassadors with Washington, it met a cold reception in the United States. Nabuco assured Rio-Branco that such hostility was contrary to the reaction evoked by the exchange of embassies with Brazil. Nabuco to Rio-Branco, Jan. 19, 1907, AHI, Ofícios 234/1/6.

147. Viana Filho, *Rui e Nabuco,* p. 62; Heitor Lyra, "Europe and the South American Neighbors," in *Brazil,* ed. Lawrence F. Hill, p. 336; Fernandes Anibal, *Nabuco, Cidadão do Recife* (Recife, Brazil, 1949), p. 48; Napoleão, *Rio Branco,* p. 160.

148. Caroline Nabuco, *The Life,* p. 307.

149. March 17, 1905, p. 1.

150. Napoleão, *Rio Branco,* p. 159; Mario de Barros e Vasconcellos, *O Barão do Rio-Branco,* p. 100; Napoleão, "A Tribute to Barão do Rio Branco," *Brazil* (July, 1945), p. 9.

151. *Mensagem Apresentada ao Congresso Nacional na Abertura da Primeira Sessão da Sexta Legislatura pelo Presidente da República Francisco da Paula Rodrigues Alves* (Rio de Janeiro, 1906), p. 27.

152. Rio-Branco to Nabuco, Dec. 11, 1905, quoted in Nabuco to Rio-Branco, Dec. 16, 1905, AHI, Ofícios 234/1/3.

153. *Chanãa* (Rio de Janeiro, 1943), pp. 164–65.

154. Rio-Branco to John B. Moore, Nov. 22, 1907, ABR-BI.

155. Richardson to Root, Dec. 20, 1905, NA, Brazilian Dispatches, 72/125.

156. Brazilian Minister, Berlin, to Rio-Branco, Dec. 21, 1905, AHI, Ofícios 202/4/15.

157. Rio-Branco to Nabuco, Dec. 9, 1905, quoted in Nabuco to Rio-Branco, Dec. 16, 1905, AHI, Ofícios 234/1/3.

158. I did not find one U.S. newspaper that failed to support Brazil and to condemn Germany. Many felt that the incident was a challenge to the Monroe Doctrine. A sampling of those opinions will be found in Chicago *Tribune,* Dec. 10; New York *Herald,* Dec. 10; Baltimore *Sun,* Dec. 10; Baltimore *American,* Dec. 10; New York *Sun,* Dec. 10; Washinton *Evening Star,* Dec. 11; Washington *Post,* Dec. 11; and New York *Times,* Dec. 12, 1905.

159. Dec. 11, 1905, p. 1.

160. Nabuco to Root, Dec. 14, 1905, NA, Notes from the Brazilian Legation, Vol. 8.

161. Nabuco to Root, Dec. 11, 1905, NA, Notes from the Brazilian Legation, Vol. 8; Root to Nabuco, Dec. 15, 1905, NA, Notes to the Brazilian Legation, Vol. 7.

162. Root to Nabuco, Dec. 15, 1905, NA, Notes to the Brazilian Legation, Vol. 7.

163. Jessup, *Root,* I, 473.

164. Root to Nabuco, Dec. 11, 1905, NA, Notes to the Brazilian Legation, Vol. 7; Root to Baron von Sternberg, Dec. 11, 1905, NA, Notes to Diplomatic Representative of Germany in the U.S.

165. Acting Secretary of State to U.S. Embassy, Berlin, Dec. 10, 1905,

NA, Telegrams; also letters numbers 440 and 441, Diplomatic Instructions to U.S. Embassy, Berlin, Vol. 22.

166. Chicago *Tribune,* Dec. 11, 1905, pp. 1, 4.

167. P. 1.

168. Nabuco to Rio-Branco, Dec. 19, 1905, AHI, Ofícios 234/1/3.

169. New York *Herald,* Dec. 13, 1905, p. 11.

170. Mota to Rio-Branco, Dec. 21, 1905, AHI, Ofícios 202/4/15.

171. Delgado de Carvalho, *História Diplomática,* pp. 266–67; Calmon, *Brasil e América,* p. 85.

172. Calmon, *História do Brasil,* V, 242.

173. Nabuco Diary, Dec. 12, 1905.

174. Richardson to Root, Dec. 12 and 19, 1905, NA, Brazilian Dispatches, 72/117 and 72/124.

175. *Jornal do Brasil* (Rio de Janeiro), Dec. 12, 1905, p. 1.

176. *L'Etoile du Sud* (Rio de Janeiro), Dec. 17, 1905, p. 2. Page 1 contains an editorial lamenting the increase in prestige accruing to the United States.

177. Rio-Branco to Rui Barbosa, Aug. 28, 1907, Casa, Teleg. No. 447.

178. *La Nación* (Buenos Aires), May 18, 1904, p. 5.

179. *La Prensa* (Buenos Aires), May 3, 1904, p. 4.

180. *La Nación* (Buenos Aires), March 3, 1905, p. 5.

181. Rio-Branco to C. de Azevedo, Feb. 22, 1905, AHI, Despachos 207/4/9.

182. Nabuco to Oliveira Lima, Jan. 8, 1906, OL Lib.

183. *Diario Oficial* (Rio de Janeiro), Nov. 15, 1906, p. 6172.

184. A long article expressing approval of the forthcoming conference has been attributed to Rio-Branco and internal evidence indicates he was the author. *Jornal do Commercio* (Rio de Janeiro), Dec. 11, 1905, p. 2. For a detailed study of that important article see Burns, "Rio-Branco e sua política externa," *Revista de História,* XXVIII (April–June, 1964), 367–82.

185. Nabuco to Rio-Branco, April 10, 1906, AHI, Ofícios 234/1/4; Scott, *The Hague,* p. 97.

186. Oliveira Lima criticized Root's "interference" in the planning of the conference. A series of articles that he wrote in the *Estado de S. Paulo,* March 15, p. 1; March 20, p. 1; April 10, p. 1; April 17, p. 1; and May 1, 1906, p. 1, received the disapprobation of President Rod-

rigues Alves, who thought the articles "extremely improper." Da Gama to Rio Branco, March 22, 1906, ABR-BI.

187. Chicago *Tribune,* July 21, 1906, pp. 1, 6.

188. Inter-American Conference, Rio de Janeiro, *Report of the Delegates,* p. 4.

189. Haiti did not attend for financial reasons. Venezuela did not send a delegation because its government was angry that Rio had been favored over Caracas. J. Paul to Oliveira Lima, Jan. 8, 1906, OL Lib.

190. *Obras,* IX, 86.

191. Wilgus, "The Third International Conference at Rio de Janeiro, 1906," *Hispanic American Historical Review,* XII (Nov., 1932), 451–52.

192. Nabuco to Rio Branco, April 29, 1906, ABR-BI.

193. Rippy, *Latin America in World Politics,* p. 247.

194. Nabuco to Rio-Branco, Dec. 23, 1905, AHI, Ofícios 234/1/3.

195. Jessup, *Root,* I, 479.

196. *Obras,* IX, 91. In its 1908 edition, p. 215, the *Almanaque Brasileiro Garnier* commented in a similar way saying that the enthusiastic reception by the Brazilian people of Root and Nabuco indicated their approval of the approximation.

197. Washington *Post,* Aug. 1, 1906, p. 1.

198. Jessup, *Root,* I, 480. "I made a speech at the Conference Tuesday evening . . . which I designed to be the formulation of the true *raison d'être* of the Conference, and the true theory of relations between the American Republics. It was exceedingly well received, and I think will serve to clarify the ideas of a good many people in the Conference and out of it, who did not really know what the object of the Conference was." Root to Roosevelt, Aug. 2, 1906, NA, 194/FW.

199. ABR-BI, $\frac{34.6}{\text{IX}}$ 50/2ª/1.

200. Nabuco Diary, Feb. 9, 1906.

201. Root to Nabuco, Aug. 9, 1906, AJN.

202. A. G. de Araujo Jorge, secretary of Rio-Branco from 1906 to his death, stated in an interview on December 14, 1962, Rio de Janeiro, that during Root's visit in Rio de Janeiro the Secretary of State and Rio-Branco were together frequently and conversed at length during numerous formal and informal meetings.

203. Root to Roosevelt, Aug. 2, 1906, NA, 194/FW.

204. *Ibid.*

205. Wilgus, *A Brief Survey,* p. 13; Richardson to Root, Dec. 1, 1905, NA, Brazilian Dispatches, 2/113.

206. Griscom to Root, Aug. 31, 1906, NA, Brazilian Dispatches, 194/ 47.

207. Stuart, *Latin America,* p. 433; Perkins, *Hands Off,* p. 318.

208. Fred P. Ellison, "Rubén Darío and Brazil," *Hispania* (March, 1964), pp. 27–28.

209. Griscom to Root, Aug. 31, 1906, NA, Brazilian Dispatches, 194/47.

210. Wilgus, "The Third International Conference at Rio de Janeiro, 1906," *Hispanic American Historical Review,* XII (Nov., 1932), 441.

211. Inter-American Conference, Rio de Janeiro, *Report of the Delegates,* p. 23.

212. Ganzert, "The Baron do Rio Branco, Joaquim Nabuco and the Growth of Brazilian-American Friendship, 1900–1910," *Hispanic American Historical Review,* XXII (Aug., 1942), 444.

Chapter V. THE TRIBULATIONS AND REWARDS OF FRIENDSHIP, 1907–1912

1. Rio-Branco to Nabuco, Jan. 18, 1908, AHI, Teleg. Exp. 235/4/1.

2. Washington *Post,* May 16, 1907, p. 4.

3. *Jornal do Commercio* (Rio de Janeiro), May 17, 1907, p. 1.

4. Gomes Ferreira to Rio-Branco, Nov. 30, 1904, AHI, Ofícios 234/ 1/2.

5. Rio-Branco to Nabuco, March 2, 1907, AHI, Teleg. Exp. 235/ 3/15.

6. Nabuco to Rio-Branco, March 5, 1907, AHI, Teleg. Receb. 235/ 3/1.

7. Rio-Branco to Nabuco, May 20, 1907, quoted in Nabuco to Rio-Branco, May 27, 1907, AHI, Ofícios 234/1/6.

8. Nabuco to Secretary of State, May 25, 1907, NA, Notes from Brazilian Embassy, 40/290.

9. Hill to Root, May 29, 1907, NA, Hague Dispatches, 40/305; Jessup, *Root,* II, 68–69.

10. Lemgruber Kropf to Rio-Branco, Aug. 15, 1907, AHI, Ofícios 210/3/15. Rui Barbosa to Rio-Branco, Aug. 9, 1907, Casa, Telegram.

11. Stead, *O Brazil em Haya,* p. 24.

12. Rui Barbosa to Rio-Branco, Aug. 5, 1907, Casa, Telegram. Dudley to Root, Sept. 11, 1907, NA, Brazilian Dispatches, 40/539. The American with whom Rui Barbosa seemed to have had the closest relations was William I. Buchanan, a diplomat with considerable Latin American experience. For Rui Barbosa's relations with Buchanan see Rui Barbosa to Rio-Branco, July 14, Aug. 16, and Aug. 18, 1907, Casa, Telegrams.

13. Opinions of Brazilian historians can be found in the following: Viana Filho, *A Vida do Barão do Rio Branco* p. 383; Lacombe, *Rio-Branco e Rui Barbosa*, pp. 83–87; Accioly, "O Barao do Rio Branco e a 2ª Conferencia da Haia," *Revista IHGB*, CLXXXVII (April–June, 1945), 67–68; Luís Gurgel do Amaral, *O Meu Velho Itamarati*, p. 247; Napoleão, *O Segundo*, p. 122; Venáncio Filho, *Rio Branco*, p. 49; Delgado de Carvalho, *História Diplomática*, p. 251. Rio-Branco told the Chilean minister that Rui Barbosa acted strictly under orders. Chilean Minister, Rio de Janeiro, to Minister of Foreign Relations, Santiago, Dec. 10, 1907, ARE, Ch, Oficios received from the Chilean Legation in Brazil, 1904–8, No. 69.

14. Gurgel do Amaral to Rio-Branco, Aug. 14, and Sept. 3, 1907 AHI, Ofícios 234/1/7.

15. Jessup, *Root*, II, 76–77; Washington *Post*, Aug. 28, 1907, p. 4.

16. *Brazilian Review* (Rio de Janeiro), Aug. 27, 1907, p. 1000.

17. Jessup, *Root*, II, 76–77.

18. Accioly, "Rui Barbosa na Segunda Conferência da Haia," *Revista IHGB*, CCXXXVII (Oct.–Dec., 1957), 165.

19. McGann, *Argentina*, p. 248. Rippy, *Latin America in World Politics*, p. 248.

20. *Correio da Manhã* (Rio de Janeiro), March 30, 1903, p. 1.

21. Rio-Branco to Assis Brasil, March 29, 1906, AHI, Dispachos 207/4/9.

22. Accioly, "O Barão do Rio Branco e a 2ª Conferência da Haia," *Revista IHGB*, CLXXXVII (April–June, 1945), p. 73.

23. Rippy, *Latin America in World Politics*, p. 264; Turner, *Ruy Barbosa*, p. 140.

24. Scott, *The Hague*, pp. 204, 411; Hull, *Two Hague Conferences*, p. 361.

25 Ganzert, "The Baron," pp. 419–20.

26. Hull, *Two Hague Conferences*, p. 370.

27. McGann, *Argentina,* p. 266.

28. Rui Barbosa to Rio-Branco, July 9, 1907, Casa, Telegram.

29. Rio-Branco to Rui Barbosa, June 18, 1907, Casa, Pasta Cartas e Ofícios, No. 314.

30. Rio-Branco to Rui Barbosa, Aug. 4 and Aug. 5, 1907, Casa, Telegrams; Dudley to Root, Dec. 14, 1907, NA, 2098/88; Rui Barbosa referred to the court plan as a "bitter humiliation" in Rui Barbosa to Rio-Branco, Aug. 3, 1907, Casa, Telegram.

31. Rio-Branco to Nabuco, Jan. 11, 1908, AHI, Teleg. Exp. 235/4/1.

32. Dudley to Root, Sept. 11, 1907, NA, Brazilian Dispatches, 40/539.

33. Dudley to Root, Aug. 26 and Sept. 11, 1907, NA, Brazilian Dispatches, 40/476 and 40/539.

34. Rio-Branco had not been informed ahead of time of any U.S. policies to be followed at The Hague. Chilean Minister, Rio de Janeiro, to Minister of Foreign Relations, Santiago, June 1, 1907, ARE, Ch, Oficios received from the Chilean Legation in Brazil, 1904–8, No. 5.

35. Rio-Branco to Rui Barbosa, Aug. 4, 1907, Casa, Telegram.

36. Rio-Branco to Rui Barbosa, Aug. 12, 1907, Casa, Telegram.

37. Gurgel do Amaral to Rio-Branco, Aug. 15, 1907, AHI, Teleg. Receb. 235/3/1C.

38. Gurgel do Amaral to Rio-Branco, Aug. 16, 1907, AHI, Teleg. Receb. 235/3/1C.

39. Dudley to Root, Sept. 11, 1907, NA, Brazilian Dispatches, 40/539.

40. Chilean Minister, Rio de Janeiro, to Minister of Foreign Relations, Santiago, Sept. 16, 1907, ARE, Ch, Oficios received from the Chilean Legation in Brazil, 1904–8, No. 6.

41. Rio-Branco to Rui Barbosa, Aug. 16, 1907, Casa, Telegram.

42. Rio-Branco to Rui Barbosa, Aug. 28, 1907, Casa, Telegram. Rui Barbosa spoke out strongly in favor of a plan of equality of states and supported that principle before Rio-Branco was converted to it. Rui Barbosa to Rio-Branco, Aug. 17, 1907, Casa, Telegram.

43. Rio-Branco to Rui Barbosa, Aug. 18 and 26, 1907, Casa, Telegram.

44. Rio-Branco to Rui Barbosa, Aug. 15, 1907, Casa, Telegram.

45. Chilean Minister, Rio de Janeiro, to Minister of Foreign Relations, Santiago, Sept. 16, 1907, ARE, Ch, Oficios received from the Chilean Legation in Brazil, 1904–8, No. 6.

46. *Jornal do Commercio* (Rio de Janeiro), Dec. 11, 1905, p. 2.

47. *Obras,* IX, 86.

48. *Jornal do Commercio* (Rio de Janeiro), Oct. 16, 1907, p. 1.

49. *Brazilian Review* (Rio de Janeiro), Jan. 7, 1908, p. 13.

50. Jessup, *Root,* II, 77.

51. Root to Dudley, Sept. 3, 1907, NA, Brazilian Instructions, 40/436.

52. Memo dated Sept. 5, 1907, to U.S. Ambassador in Rio for transmission to Washington, AHI, Represent. Estrang. Notas, EUA 280/3/16.

53. Rio-Branco to Rui Barbosa, Aug. 20, 1907, Casa, Telegram.

54. Rio-Branco to Nabuco, Jan. 11, 1908, AHI, Teleg. Exp. 235/4/1.

55. Aug. 19, 1907, p. 3.

56. Washington *Evening Star,* Feb. 20, 1906, p. 2. Nabuco commented on those statements as follows, "Those are true declarations of an international political character." Nabuco to Rio-Branco, Feb. 23, 1906, AHI, Ofícios 234/1/4.

57. Rio-Branco to Rui Barbosa, Aug. 31, 1907, Casa, Telegram.

58. *Brazilian Review* (Rio de Janeiro), Sept. 3, 1907, p. 1204; Napoleão, *Rio Branco,* p. 192; New York *Herald,* Aug. 21, 1907, p. 9.

59. In the case of Panama, for example, Rio-Branco sent a long explanation of the inequity of the seventeen-member court and requested support for Brazil's plan of equal representation. ARE, Pan, Legación del Brasil en el Panamá, Casilla No. 1-A, Vol. I, Exp. No. 4.

60. Rio-Branco to Rui Barbosa, no date, Casa, Pasta Telegrams.

61. Rui Barbosa telegraphed triumphantly to Nabuco that Brazil had the support of "nearly all the Latin American nations." Nabuco Diary, Sept. 6, 1907,

62. Ganzert, "The Baron," p. 413.

63. Hull, *The United States and Latin America at The Hague,* p. 11; Hull, *Two Hague Conferences,* p. 446.

64. Hull, *Two Hague Conferences,* p. 444.

65. Accioly, "O Barão do Rio Branco e a 2ª Conferência da Haia," *Revista IHGB,* CLXXXVII (April–June, 1945), 85.

66. Scott, *The Hague,* p. 335.

67. *Ibid.,* p. 338; Ganzert, "The Baron," p. 423.

68. Accioly, "Rui Barbosa na Segunda Conferência da Haia," *Revista IHGB,* CCXXXVII (Oct.–Dec., 1957), 173.

69. Lawrence, *International Problems,* p. 76.

70. Hull, *Two Hague Conferences,* p. 426; *Jornal do Commercio* (Rio de Janeiro), Oct. 16, 1907, p. 1.

71. An example of the laudatory comment on Rui Barbosa's contributions would be the *Diario da Bahia* (Salvador, Bahia), Aug. 29, 1907, p. 1.

72. Chamberlin to Assistant Secretary of State, Sept. 24, 1907, NA, Brazilian Consular Reports, 1113/5. In late 1964, R. Magalhães Jr. published a critical study of Rui Barbosa entitled *Rui, O Homem e o Mito.* The book reevaluates his role in Brazilian public life and presents a much more balanced picture of his activity at The Hague. The book stirred up considerable controversy within Brazil, where Rui Barbosa has been accepted unquestionably as a national hero. To get the flavor of the controversy see *Manchete* (Rio de Janeiro), Jan. 16, 1965, pp. 84–85, or *Fatos & Fotos* (Brasília), Jan. 30, 1965, pp. 44–45.

73. Lorena Ferreira to Mrs. Oliveira Lima, Aug. 30, 1907, OL Lib.

74. Rio-Branco to Rui Barbosa, Aug. 18, 1907, Casa, Telegram. Rio-Branco to Nabuco, Oct. 15, 1907, AHI, Despachos 235/2/7.

75. Rio-Branco to Nabuco, Jan. 11, 1908, AHI, Teleg. Exp. 235/4/1.

76. Rio-Branco to Rui Barbosa, Aug. 16, 1907, Casa, Telegram.

77. Rio-Branco to Nabuco, Jan. 5, 1908, quoted in Nabuco to Rio-Branco, Jan. 15, 1908, Ofícios 234/1/7.

78. Dudley to Root, Sept. 7 and 11, 1907, NA, Brazilian Dispatches, 40/446 and 40/5939.

79. Dudley to Root, Aug. 26, 1907, NA, Brazilian Dispatches, 40/476; Rio-Branco to Nabuco, Jan. 11, 1908, AHI, Teleg. Exp. 235/4/1.

80. Rio-Branco to Rui Barbosa, Aug. 27, 1907, Casa, Telegram.

81. Dudley to Secretary of State, Aug. 26, 1907, NA, Brazilian Dispatches, 40/436.

82. Rio-Branco to Nabuco, Oct. (exact day unclear), 1907, AHI, Teleg. Exp. 235/3/15.

83. Viana Filho, *Rui e Nabuco,* p. 80.

84. Nabuco to Rui Barbosa, Oct. 15, 1906, Casa, Pasta J. Nabuco.

85. Nabuco to Rui Barbosa, June 29, 1907, Casa, Pasta J. Nabuco.

86. Viana Filho, *Rui e Nabuco,* p. 80.

87. "I feel myself completely isolated. The Hague ended what little

sympathy that American approximation inspired there for one moment. I seem to be preaching in the desert." Nabuco Diary, Aug. 18, 1908.

88. Nabuco to Rio-Branco, Aug. 17, 1907, ABR-BI.

89. Nabuco to Rui-Barbosa, Aug. 26, 1907, Casa, Pasta J. Nabuco.

90. Nabuco Diary, Sept. 4, 1907.

91. *Ibid.,* Sept. 5, 1907.

92. *Ibid.,* Nov. 5, 1907.

93. Nabuco to Rui Barbosa, April 11, 1908, Casa, Pasta J. Nabuco.

94. Joaquim Nabuco, *The Spirit,* p. 12.

95. Nabuco to Rui Barbosa, Aug. 3, 1908, Casa, Pasta J. Nabuco.

96. Nabuco to Rio-Branco, Dec. 2, 1907, AHI, Teleg. Receb. 235/3/1C.

97. Nabuco Diary, Jan. 8, 1908.

98. Nabuco to Rio-Branco, Jan. 15, 1908, AHI, Ofícios 234/1/7.

99. *Ibid.*

100. Nabuco to Rio-Branco, Jan. 10, 1908, quoted in Nabuco to Rio-Branco, Jan. 15, 1908, AHI, Ofícios 234/1/7.

101. Rio-Branco to Nabuco, Jan. 5, 1908, quoted in Nabuco to Rio-Branco, Jan. 15, 1908, AHI, Ofícios 234/1/7; Rio-Branco to Nabuco, Jan. 11, 1908, Teleg. Exp. 235/4/1.

102. Washington *Post,* Jan. 13, 1908, p. 1.

103. Luís Gurgel do Amaral, *O Meu Velho Itamaratí,* p. 256.

104. *Brazilian Review* (Rio de Janeiro), Jan. 21, 1908, pp. 71–72, and Jan. 28, 1908, p. 105. A possible reason for the extravagant reception was the rumor in Rio of a gala reception planned for the fleet in Peru. Chilean Minister, Rio de Janeiro, to Minister of Foreign Relations, Santiago, Dec. 23, 1907, ARE, Ch, Oficios received from the Chilean Legation in Brazil, 1904–8, No. 71.

105. *Brazilian Review* (Rio de Janeiro), Jan. 21, 1908, p. 71.

106. Washington *Post,* Jan. 16, 1908, p. 1.

107. Viana Filho, *Rui e Nabuco,* pp. 92–93.

108. Unsigned, unaddressed memo penciled in English in Rio-Branco's handwriting. ABR-BI, $\frac{34.6}{IX}$ 5°/2ª/1.

109. *Obras,* IX, 143–46.

110. Root to Nabuco, Jan. 23, 1908, AJN.

111. New York *Herald,* Jan. 14, 1908, p. 1; *O Paiz* (Rio de Janeiro), Jan. 18, 1908, p. 1.

112. Rio-Branco to Ambassador Dudley, Feb. 5, 1908, AHI, Represent. Estrang. Notas, EUA 280/3/16.

113. Nabuco to Rio-Branco, Jan. 22, 1908, AHI, Teleg. Receb. 235/3/2.

114. Feb. 8, 1908.

115. Ambassador José Joaquím Moniz de Aragao told me during an interview on December 13, 1962, Rio de Janeiro, that Rio-Branco had expressed to him a desire to visit the United States but that reasons of health prevented him from realizing his desire.

116. Nabuco to Rio-Branco, May 29, 1908, AHI, Ofícios 234/1/8.

117. Nabuco to Rio-Branco, June 29, 1908, AHI, Ofícios 234/1/8.

118. New York *Herald,* June 26, 1908, p. 4.

119. Dudley to Knox, June 7, 1909, NA, Brazilian Dispatches, 20469.

120. Chilean Minister, Rio de Janeiro, to Minister of Foreign Relations, Santiago, July 20 and Nov. 8, 1908, ARE, Ch, Oficios received from the Chilean Legation in Brazil, 1904–8, Nos. 8, 13.

121. Rio-Branco to Nabuco, Nov. 23, 1909, AHI, Teleg. Exp. 235/4/1.

122. Thompson to Hay, Jan. 15, 1905, NA, Brazilian Dispatches, 71/252; Chilean Minister, Rio de Janeiro, to Minister of Foreign Relations, Santiago, Feb. 29, 1909, ARE, Ch, Oficios received from the Chilean Legation in Brazil, 1904–8, No. 1; Chilean Minister, Rio de Janeiro, to Minister of Foreign Relations, Santiago, Sept. 14, 1910, ANCh, Chilean Legation in Brazil, 1910, No. 112.

123. Nabuco to Rui Barbosa, no date (1906?), Casa, Pasta J. Nabuco; Nabuco Diary, May 2, 1906.

124. *Gazeta de Notícias, Correio da Manhã, O Paiz, A Tribune,* and *A Notícia* (Rio de Janeiro), Nov. 26, 1909; Dudley to Secretary of State, Nov. 26, 1909, NA, 1154/249.

125. Nabuco to Root, Nov. 21, 1909, enclosed in Nabuco to Rio-Branco, Dec. 1, 1909, AHI, Ofícios 234/1/9.

126. Rio-Branco to Nabuco, Nov. 21, 1909, AHI, Teleg. Exp. 235/4/1.

127. Dudley to Secretary of State, Nov. 26, 1909, NA, Brazilian Dispatches, 1154/249; Rio-Branco to Nabuco, Nov. 23, 1909, AHI, Teleg. Exp. 235/4/1.

128. Dudley to Secretary of State, Nov. 23, 1909, NA, Brazilian Dispatches, 1154/205.

129. Chilean Minister, Rio de Janeiro, to Minister of Foreign Rela-

tions, Santiago, Nov. 29, 1909, ANCh, Chilean Legation in Brazil, 1909, No. 198.

130. Nabuco to Secretary of State, Nov. 23, 1909, NA, Notes from Brazilian Legation, 7329/7.

131. Nabuco to Rio-Branco, Dec. 1, 1909, AHI, Ofícios 234/1/9; Nabuco Diary, Nov. 23, 1909.

132. Root to Nabuco, Nov. 29, 1909, enclosed in Nabuco to Rio-Branco, Dec. 1, 1909, AHI, Ofícios 234/1/9.

133. Nabuco to Rio-Branco, Dec. 1, 1909, AHI, Ofícios 234/1/9.

134. Knox to Nabuco, Dec. 1 and 4, 1909, NA, Notes to Brazilian Embassy, 1154/127 and 1154/223.

135. Dudley to Rio-Branco, Nov. 27, 1909, AHI, Represent. Estrang. Notas, EUA 280/2/9.

136. Chicago *Record-Herald,* Dec. 1, 1909, p. 1. Said the Washington *Times,* "This Government would have been in a most embarrassing position had it not been for the timely and acceptable interference of Baron de Rio-Branco. . . . He saw the difficulty and made the suggestion that some outside ruler settle the claim. . . . The State Department, according to the unofficial explanation of the sad affair, accepted Branco's advice and thanked him very kindly." Nov. 30, 1909, p. 2.

137. Chilean Minister, Washington, to Minister of Foreign Relations, Santiago, Nov. 27, 1909, ANCh, Chilean Legation in the United States, 1909, No. 197.

138. *Jornal do Commercio* (Rio de Janeiro), Nov. 29, 1907, p. 1.

139. *Ibid.,* Dec. 9, 1909, p. 1.

140. *El Mercurio* (Santiago), Nov. 27, 1909, p. 3.

141. Nabuco Diary, June 10, 1908.

142. Ganzert, "The Baron," p. 392.

143. Caroline Nabuco, *The Life,* p. 318.

144. *Evening News* (Newark), Jan. 20, 1910, p. 2.

145. Rio-Branco, *Obras,* IX, 237; Rio-Branco to Chermont, Jan. 21 (?), 1910, AHI, Teleg. Exp. 235/4/1; Dudley to Secretary of State, Jan. 20, 1910, NA, Brazilian Dispatches, 4737/38.

146. 61st Congress, 2d Session, House of Representatives, Document No. 954.

147. *Monthly Bulletin of the International Bureau of American States* (Washington), Jan., 1907, p. 114.

148. New York *Herald,* May 21, 1911, p. 12.

149. Da Gama to Rio-Branco, June 19, 1911, AHI, Ofícios 234/1/12.

150. William Jennings Bryan, "My Visit to Brazil, the Giant of South America," New York *World,* June 19, 1910, Magazine Section, p. 5.

151. *Jornal do Commercio* (Rio de Janeiro), March 12, 1910, p. 2.

152. *Obras,* IX, 235–38.

153. Nabuco to Rio-Branco, Jan. 23, 1909, AHI, Teleg. Receb. 235/3/3.

154. Nabuco to Rio-Branco, June 18, 1908, AHI, Ofícios 234/1/8.

155. Root to Sleeper, June 13, 1908, NA, Venezuelan Instructions, 4832/9a.

156. Nabuco to Rio-Branco, June 18, 1908, AHI, Ofícios 234/1/8.

157. Buchanan to Secretary of State, Jan. 2, 1909, NA, Venezuelan Dispatches, 15363/10.

158. *O Paiz* (Rio de Janeiro), June 29, 1908, p. 1.

159. New York *Daily Tribune,* June 26, 1908, p. 6.

160. Knox to Rio-Branco, Feb. 23, 1909, AHI, Diversos no Exterior, 278/2/16. Adee to Dudley, June 25, 1908, NA, Brazilian Instructions, 4832/8.

161. Nabuco to Root, Dec. 11, 1908, NA, Notes from Brazilian Embassy, 16972/1.

162. Root to Nabuco, Dec. 12, 1908, NA, Notes to Brazilian Embassy, 16972/5; Nabuco to Rio-Branco, Dec. 15, 1908, AHI, Ofícios 234/1/8; Root also volunteered to try to settle the misunderstandings. Root to Nabuco, Dec. 6, 1908, AJN.

163. Dudley to Knox, April 3, 1909, NA, Brazilian Dispatches, 2761/32; Rio-Branco to da Gama, Dec. 15, 1908, ABR-BI.

164. Dudley to Secretary of State, April 23, 1909, NA, Brazilian Dispatches, 5072/47.

165. Dudley to Knox, May 9, 1909, NA, Brazilian Dispatches, 5072/47.

166. Dudley to Secretary of State, Oct. 6, 1910, NA, Brazilian Dispatches, 853.00/86.

167. Dudley to Secretary of State, Oct. 16, 1910, NA, Brazilian Dispatches, 853.00/102.

168. Adee to Dudley, Oct. 13, 1910, NA, Brazilian Instructions, 853.00/100.

169. Dudley to Secretary of State, Oct. 27, 1910, NA, Brazilian Dispatches, 853.00/135.

170. The United States did not grant full recognition to the Portuguese Republic until June 19, 1911, on the occasion of the first meeting of the Constituent Assembly. Lorillard to Secretary of State, June 19, 1911, NA, Brazilian Dispatches, 853.00/206.

171. Dudley to Secretary of State, Dec. 30, 1910, NA, Brazilian Dispatches, 722.2315/525.

172. Rio-Branco to Nabuco, March 26, 1906, AHI, Despachos 235/2/6.

173. Rio-Branco to Dudley, May 6, 1911, AHI, Represent. Estrang. Notas, EUA 280/4/2.

174. Carter to Secretary of State, May 30, 1911, NA, Turkish Dispatches, 701.3267/2.

Chapter VI. THE MONROE DOCTRINE AND
PAN AMERICANISM TOO

1. Alvarez, *The Monroe Doctrine,* p. 285. In his discussion of opinions about the Monroe Doctrine in Latin America, David Y. Thomas contrasts the favorable Brazilian views with the less favorable ones of Spanish America. *One Hundred Years,* pp. 369–98. Similar observations are found in Hart, *The Monroe Doctrine,* pp. 252–55.

2. Perkins, *The Monroe Doctrine,* pp. 195–97; Joaquim Nabuco, *The Spirit,* p. 10; Thomas, *One Hundred Years,* pp. 45, 405.

3. Lima, *The Relations of Brazil with the United States,* p. 5.

4. Afonso de Carvalho, *Rio-Branco,* p. 215; *O Jacobino,* an ultraliberal newspaper of the early days of the republic, carried on its masthead the motto "America for the Americans—Monroe."

5. Calógeras, *Estudos,* p. 255.

6. Lins, *Rio-Branco,* II, 497; João Frank de Costa, "Rio Branco, Nabuco e o americanismo," *Jornal do Commercio,* Feb. 18, 1962, 2° caderno, p. 5.

7. Calógeras, *Rio Branco,* pp. 47, 58; Calógeras, *Estudos,* pp. 232, 255.

8. Thompson to Hay, April 16, 1903, NA, Brazilian Dispatches, 68/11.

9. Rocha Pomba, "A doutrina de Monroe," *Correio da Manhã* (Rio de Janeiro), March 30, 1903, p. 1.

10. *Jornal do Commercio* (Rio de Janeiro), Dec. 11, 1905, p. 2.

11. Hilton, "Joaquim Nabuco e os Estados Unidos," *Revista do Instituto Brasil–Estados Unidos,* VII (July–Dec., 1949), 35.

12. Caroline Nabuco, *The Life,* p. 307.

13. Nabuco Diary, Nov. 10, 1905.

14. July 15, 1905, p. 6; July 10, 1905, p. 1.

15. Washington *Post,* Jan. 17, 1908, p. 7.

16. Abranches, *Brazil and the Monroe Doctrine.*

17. C. A. McCarthy, "Latin American Attitudes Toward the Monroe Doctrine as Shown by Argentina, Brazil, and Chile" (unpublished Master's essay, Department of History, Columbia University, 1929), pp. 26–29.

18. *Ibid.,* p. 28.

19. Speech given Nov. 21, 1906, enclosed in Nabuco to Rio-Branco, Dec. 4, 1906, AHI, Ofícios 234/1/5.

20. Thompson to Hay, July 28, 1903, NA, Brazilian Dispatches, 68/49.

21. June 11, 1904, p. 1.

22. Sept. 27, 1905, p. 1.

23. The Chilean minister in Rio thought that Rio-Branco put much more faith and reliance in the Monroe Doctrine than "he publicly confessed." Chilean Minister, Rio de Janeiro, to Minister of Foreign Relations, Santiago, March 30, 1906, ARE, Ch, Oficios received from the Chilean Legation in Brazil, 1904–8, No. 2.

24. Rio-Branco to Brazilian Legation, Jan. 31, 1905, AHI, Despachos 235/2/5.

25. Rio-Branco to Assis Brasil, Jan. 23, 1906, AHI, Despachos 217/4/9.

26. Rio-Branco to Olynto de Magalhães, Jan. 23, 1906, ABR-BI; Delgado de Carvalho, *História Diplomática,* p. 206; Perkins, *Hands Off,* pp. 186–87.

27. Rio-Branco to Brazilian Legation, Washington, March 4, 1904, AHI, Teleg. Exp. 235/3/15.

28. Gomes Ferreira to Rio-Branco, March 30, 1904, AHI, Ofícios 234/1/2.

29. Rio-Branco to Brazilian Embassy, Washington, Dec. 8, 1905, AHI, Teleg. Exp. 235/3/15.

30. Nabuco Diary, Dec. 12, 1905.

31. " 'Chronic wrongdoing, or an impotence which results in a general loosening of the ties of civilized society, may in America, as elsewhere, ultimately require intervention by some civilized nation, and in the Western Hemisphere the adherence of the United States to the Monroe Doctrine may force the United States, however reluctantly, in flagrant cases of such wrongdoing or impotence, to the exercise of an international police power.' " Dwight Lowell Dumond, *America in Our Time* (New York, 1947), p. 135.

32. Perkins, *Hands Off*, p. 246; Washington, *A Study of Causes: Brazil*, p. 18.

33. March 17, 1905, p. 1.

34. Dec. 28–29, 1904, p. 2.

35. Dec. 6, 1905, p. 1.

36. Jan. 4, 1905, p. 1.

37. That paper was the *Jornal do Brasil*. Rio-Branco to Brazilian Legation, Washington, Jan. 31, 1905, AHI, Despachos 235/2/5.

38. Abranches, *Rio Branco*, II, 40; Chilean Minister, Rio de Janeiro to Minister of Foreign Relations, Santiago, Dec. 26, 1904, ARE, Ch, Oficios received from the Chilean Legation in Brazil, No. 6.

39. Rio-Branco to Brazilian Legation, Washington, Jan. 31, 1905, AHI, Despachos 235/2/5.

40. *La Nación* (Buenos Aires), July 26, 1906, p. 8.

41. *Obras,* IX, 102.

42. Hilton, "Joaquim Nabuco e os Estados Unidos," *Revista do Instituto Brasil–Estados Unidos,* VII (July–Dec., 1949), p. 36; Chicago *Tribune,* July 10, 1905, p. 17.

43. Rio-Branco to Brazilian Legation, Buenos Aires, Nov. 22, 1904, AHI, Despachos 207/4/8.

44. Rio-Branco to Gomes Ferreira, Nov. 24, 1905, quoted in Gomes Ferreira to Rio-Branco, Nov. 30, 1904, AHI, Ofícios 234/1/2.

45. Rio-Branco to Nabuco, Dec. 22, 1906, AHI, Despachos 235/2/6.

46. Chilean Minister, Rio de Janeiro to Minister of Foreign Relations, Santiago, March 30, 1906, ARE, Ch, Oficios received from Chilean Legation in Brazil.

47. Rio-Branco to Brazilian Legation, Buenos Aires, Nov. 22, 1904, AHI, Despachos 207/4/8.

48. *La Prensa* (Buenos Aires), Aug. 18, 1904, p. 5.

49. Washington, *A Study of Causes: Brazil,* p. 18.

50. Dudley to Secretary of State, March 17, 1911, NA, Brazilian Dispatches, 812.00/1462.

51. *Jornal do Commercio* (Rio de Janeiro), March 15, 1911, p. 2.

52. Rio-Branco to Brazilian Embassy, Washington, Oct. 2, 1905, AHI, Teleg. Exp. 235/3/15.

53. "The preliminary step for the formation of the American conscience is that the Latin Republics look to the part the United States had and has to play in guarding the Monroe Doctrine as in no way offensive to the pride and the dignity of any of them, but, on the contrary, as a privilege which they ought to support, at least with their sympathy and their loyal acknowledgment of the service rendered to all. That will no doubt be the ultimate result of the Pan American Conference." Joaquim Nabuco, "The American Conscience and American Public Opinion," *Supplement to the Annals of the American Academy of Political and Social Science,* May, 1906, p. 14.

54. Nabuco to Rio-Branco, March 10, 1909, AHI, Teleg. Receb. 235/3/3; Dudley to Knox, April 3, 1909, NA, Brazilian Dispatches, 2761/32.

55. Nabuco to Rio-Branco, July 31, 1909, enclosed in Nabuco to Rio-Branco, Sept. 11, 1909, AHI, Ofícios 234/1/9.

56. Rio-Branco to Nabuco, Sept. 3, 1909, enclosed in Nabuco to Rio-Branco, Sept. 11, 1909, AHI, Ofícios 234/1/9.

57. Ganzert, "The Baron," pp. 401–2; Samuel Guy Inman discusses the evolution and treatment of that resolution in detail in *Problems in Pan Americanism,* pp. 207–9.

58. Lugo, *La Cuarta Conferencia Internacional Americana,* p. 40.

59. New York *Herald,* July 23, 1910, p. 11.

60. João Pandiá Calógeras, "Discurso sobre o orçamento do exterior," *Anais da Câmara dos Deputados,* Anais V, Vol. VI, p. 784; Ganzert, "The Baron," p. 403; Alvarez, *The Monroe Doctrine,* p. 195; Perkins, *Hands Off,* p. 319; New York *Herald,* Sept. 4, 1910, 3d Section, p. 3.

61. Alvarez, *The Monroe Doctrine,* p. 195.

62. Rippy, *Latin America in World Politics,* p. 250.

63. Inter-American Conference, Buenos Aires, *Fourth International Conference of American States,* 61st Congress, 3d Session, Senate Doc. No. 744, p. 46; Truda, *O Brasil e a Doutrina de Monroe,* pp. 86–87.

64. Inter-American Conference, Buenos Aires, *Fourth American International Conference, Daily Account of Sessions,* I, 531.

65. *Obras,* IX, 97.

66. Rio-Branco to Domício da Gama, Sept. 28, 1911, AHI, Despachos 235/2/8.

67. *Obras,* IX, 98.

68. *La Nación* (Buenos Aires), Nov. 5, 1906, p. 6.

69. P. 64.

70. Alvarez, *The Monroe Doctrine,* p. 293.

71. Root to Nabuco, Nov. 25, 1908, AJN.

72. Rio-Branco to Nabuco, March 31, 1905, AHI, Despachos 235/2/6.

73. Reid, "Barão do Rio-Branco—Lawyer, Historian, Statesman," *Brazilian-American Survey,* XII (1960), 31.

74. Lobo, *O Pan-Americanismo e o Brasil,* p. 69.

75. Dávila, "El Barón de Rio Branco," p. 23.

76. Ganzert, "José Maria da Silva Paranhos, Baron do Rio Branco," *Bulletin of the Pan American Union* (Washington), March, 1937, p. 237. Oliveira Lima held a similar view. Alvarez, *The Monroe Doctrine,* pp. 292–93.

Chapter VII. THE REASONS WHY

1. Rio-Branco to Nabuco, July 23, 1902, ABR-BI.

2. Rio-Branco to Brazilian Minister, Washington, Jan. 5, 1903, AHI, Teleg. Exp. 235/3/15.

3. Rio-Branco to American Legation, Feb. 20, 1903, AHI, Represent. Americanas, Notas, EUA 280/3/16.

4. Rio-Branco to Brazilian Minister, Santiago, Nov. 24, 1909, AHI, Teleg. Exp. 231/4/15.

5. Rio-Branco to Gomes Ferreira, Sept. 30, 1904, AHI, Despachos 235/2/5.

6. Chilean Minister, Rio de Janeiro, to Minister of Foreign Relations, Santiago, April 26, 1903, ARE, Ch, Oficios received from Chilean Legation in Brazil, No. 4.

7. Chilean Minister, Rio de Janeiro, to Minister of Foreign Relations, Santiago, Oct. 16, 1907, ARE, Ch, Oficios received from Chilean Legation in Brazil, 1904–8, No. 6.

8. Caroline Nabuco, *The Life,* p. 305. Some four years earlier, Nabuco already had observed in his diary: "The legation here in London is of minor importance politically, but of greater importance financially. The political significance of the Washington post is greater

than all of those in Europe, and the American post is steadily becoming more important financially." *Ibid.,* p. 308.

9. Nabuco was always bitterly disappointed by the award. *Ibid.,* p. 299. Rio-Branco, while not expressing any comment on the subject, never again resorted to arbitration. All Brazilian diplomatic histories regard the decision as unfair. Even today Brazilians commonly explain the decision as English bribery of, or diplomatic pressure on, the Italian king.

10. March 16, 1905, p. 1.

11. Jorge, *Introdução,* p. 228; Calógeras, *Rio-Branco,* p. 58.

12. Rio-Branco to Nabuco, July 23, 1902, ABR-BI.

13. Jan. 8, 1905, p. 1.

14. *O Paiz* (Rio de Janeiro), March 17, 1905, p. 1.

15. March 17, 1905, p. 1.

16. Nabuco to Rio-Branco, Nov. 16, 1905, AHI, Ofícios 234/1/3. There was even some sound historical basis for those conjectures. As far back as 1820, Thomas Jefferson had spoken of a unity of purpose between the two countries in which he "would rejoice to see the fleets of Brazil and the United States riding together as brethren of the same family, and pursuing the same object." To William Short, Monticello, Aug. 4, 1820. A. A. Liscomb and A. E. Bergh, eds., *The Writings of Thomas Jefferson* (Washington, 1905), XV, 262–64.

17. Nabuco to Rio-Branco, Oct. 27, 1905, AHI, Teleg. Receb. 235/2/14.

18. Nabuco to Rio-Branco, Nov. 14, 1905, AHI, Teleg. Receb. 235/2/14. Roosevelt spoke in a similar manner when he visited Brazil some years later. Abranches, *Rio Branco,* II, 41.

19. Root to Nabuco, Nov. 28, 1905, AJN.

20. Nabuco to Rio-Branco, Dec. 2, 1905, AHI, Ofícios 234/1/3.

21. Nabuco Diary, Dec. 12, 1905.

22. Nabuco to Rio-Branco, Jan. 3, 1906, AHI, Ofícios 234/1/4.

23. March 23, 1906, p. 14. Nabuco called the article "interesting" and immediately forwarded it to Rio. Nabuco to Rio-Branco, March 26, 1906, AHI, Ofícios 234/1/4.

24. Root, *Speeches,* p. 61.

25. Chilean Minister, Rio de Janeiro, to Minister of Foreign Relations, Santiago, Sept. 16, 1907, ARE, Ch, Oficios received from the Chilean Legation in Brazil, No. 6.

26. Rio-Branco to Brazilian Embassy, Washington, Dec. 7, 1908, AHI, Teleg. Exp. 235/4/1.

27. *A Imprensa* (Rio de Janeiro), Jan. 20, 1908, p. 1. *Diário de Notícias* (Rio de Janeiro), Jan. 21, 1908, p. 1. Both of these articles were forwarded to the State Department. Dudley to Root, Jan. 27, 1908, NA, Brazilian Dispatches, 8258/164–184.

28. Octavio, *Rasgos de la Política Internacional del Brasil en América,* p. 11.

29. Abranches, *Rio Branco,* II, 96.

30. *Jornal do Commercio* (Rio de Janeiro), April 20, 1910, p. 2; Sensabaugh, Unpublished Ms, p. 112.

31. For statements of leading Brazilian policy makers on this subject see: Rodrigues Alves in the *Evening Post* (New York), May 4, 1906, p. 3; Rio-Branco in Root, *Speeches,* p. 36; Abranches, *Brazil and the Monroe Doctrine,* p. 7. Later historians have agreed with the traditional friendship reason for the approximation. For a sampling of their views see: Afonso de Carvalho, *Rio-Branco,* p. 215; João Frank da Costa, "Rio Branco, Nabuco e o americanismo," *Jornal do Commercio,* Feb. 18, 1962, 2° caderno, p. 5; Ganzert, "The Baron," p. 385; Botelho, *Le Brésil,* p. 160; Hilderbrando Accioly, "Uma Amizade Sólida e Duradoura," ed. by *Diário de Notícias* (Rio de Janeiro), *Brasil–Estados Unidos,* p. 26.

32. *Bulletin of the International Bureau of the American Republics* (Washington), June, 1905, p. 630.

33. Department of Commerce, *Daily Consular and Trade Reports,* Dec. 13, 1912, p. 1329.

34. Root, *Speeches,* p. 84.

35. Pires do Rio, "Motivos de Pan Americanismo," *Diário de Notícias, Brasil–Estados Unidos,* p. 42.

36. João Cruz Costa, *Esbozo,* p. 89.

37. Arthur Guimarães, *Actualidades,* pp. 47–52.

38. Rio-Branco to Brazilian Legation, Washington, Jan. 31, 1905, AHI, Despachos 235/2/5.

39. *La Nación* (Buenos Aires), July 26, 1906, p. 8.

40. Chilean Minister, Rio de Janeiro, to Minister of Foreign Relations, Santiago, Feb. 29, 1909, ARE, Ch, Oficios received from the Chilean Legation in Brazil, 1909, No. 2.

41. Nabuco to Knox, March 22, 1909, NA, 18643/1; Lima, *The*

Relations of Brazil with the United States, pp. 9, 13; Manoel de Oliveira Lima, lecture series entitled "Modern Brazil in Its Political, Economic, and Social Aspects" delivered at the Institute of Politics of Williams College, Lecture III, "Brazil's Foreign Policy with Special Reference to Her Relations with the United States" (Aug. 19, 1922), pp. 13–14, OL Lib.

42. *O Paiz* (Rio de Janeiro), Jan. 8, 1905, p. 1; *Gazeta de Notícias* (Rio de Janeiro), March 17, 1905, p. 1; *Correiro da Manhã* (Rio de Janeiro), Feb. 1, 1911, p. 1.

43. Joaquim Nabuco, *The Spirit,* p. 8.

44. Root, *Speeches,* p. 49.

45. *Ibid.,* 49–50.

46. Hawes, "The New Constitution of Brazil," *Overland Monthly,* XIX (Feb., 1892), 161, 164, 167; Chamberlain, "A Letter from Brazil," *Atlantic Monthly,* XC (Dec., 1902), 825; Denis, *Brazil,* p. 118; Abranches, *Brazil and the Monroe Doctrine,* p. 5; João Cruz Costa, *Esbozo,* p. 83; Bryce, *South America,* p. 411; Freyre, *Ordem e Progresso,* I, 34.

47. João Cruz Costa, *Esbozo,* p. 62; Sensabaugh, "The Coffee-Trust Question in United States–Brazilian Relations: 1912–13," *Hispanic American Historical Review,* XXVI (Nov., 1946), 480; Hill, *Diplomatic Relations,* p. 282; Edwin Borchard, "Relações Diplomáticas Brasil–Estados Unidos," *Diário de Notícias, Brasil–Estados Unidos,* p. 31.

48. Thompson to Gresham, April 15, 1895, NA, Brazilian Diplomatic Dispatches; Root, *Speeches,* pp. 49–50.

49. Root, *Speeches,* pp. 49–50.

50. *Obras,* IX, 236.

51. For an excellent résumé of the beginnings of the rivalry between Brazil and her Spanish American neighbors see Burr, *The Stillborn Panama Congress,* pp. 7–14, 29.

52. Rio-Branco to Nabuco, Jan. 5, 1908, AHI, Teleg. Exp. 235/4/1.

53. Rio-Branco to Brazilian Minister, Asunción, Jan. 25, 1912, quoted in Luiz Viana Filho, "A Morte do Barão," *Jornal do Commercio* (Rio de Janeiro), Feb. 18, 1962, 2° caderno, p. 1.

54. Rio-Branco to Nabuco, March 26, 1906, AHI, Despachos 235/2/6.

55. Dudley to Root, Aug. 26, 1907, NA, Brazilian Dispatches, 40/476.

56. Thompson to Hay, Jan. 15 and March 8, 1905, NA, Brazilian Dispatches, 71/252 and 71/9. Lorillard to Root, Feb. 4, 1907, NA, Brazilian

Dispatches, 836/65; Sherill to Knox, Aug. 2, 1909, NA, Argentine Dispatches, 534/99; Chilean Minister, Rio de Janeiro, to Minister of Foreign Relations, Santiago, Oct. 16 and Dec. 10, 1907, ARE, Ch. Oficios received from the Chilean Legation in Brazil, Nos. 6 and 69.

57. Thompson to Hay, Jan. 15, 1905, NA, Brazilian Dispatches, 71/ 252.

58. Dudley to Secretary of State, Sept. 6, 1907, NA, Brazilian Dispatches, 40/444.

59. Rio-Branco to da Gama, Dec. 15, 1908, ABR-BI.

60. Nineteenth-century Brazilian-Chilean diplomatic relations are treated in Alfredo Valladão, *Brasil e Chile na Epoca do Império* (Rio de Janeiro, 1959).

61. Dudley to Root, Sept. 11, 1907, NA, Brazilian Dispatches, 40/ 539.

62. Washington, *A Study of Causes: Brazil,* p. 31; Abranches, *Brazil and the Monroe Doctrine,* p. 10; Ganzert, "The Baron," p. 379; Lins, *Rio-Branco,* II, 493; Afonso de Carvalho, *Rio-Branco,* p. 214.

63. Rio-Branco to Nabuco, Nov. 23, 1909, AHI, Teleg. Exp. 235/4/1; Dudley to Root, Sept. 11, 1907, NA, Brazilian Dispatches, 40/539; Rio-Branco to Rui Barbosa, Aug. 27, 1907, Casa, Telegrama No. 455.

64. Rio-Branco to Nabuco, Jan. 5, 1908, quoted in Nabuco to Rio-Branco, Jan. 15, 1908, AHI, Ofícios 234/1/7.

65. Rodrigues, "The Foundations of Brazil's Foreign Policy," *International Affair,* XXXVIII (July, 1962), 331.

66. Abranches, *Rio Branco,* II, 95.

67. In his correspondence with Rui Barbosa during The Hague conference, Rio-Branco was constantly preoccupied with Brazil's prestige, as may be seen in his many telegrams to Rui Barbosa preserved in the Casa Rui Barbosa. In a later letter to da Gama, Rio-Branco made repeated references to Brazil's prestige and the fact that it must be maintained. Rio-Branco to da Gama, Dec. 15, 1908, ABR-BI. Freyre treats some interesting aspects of Rio-Branco's concern for Brazilian prestige. *Ordem e Progresso,* I, cxlvi, cxlix, cl.

68. *Obras,* IX, 76.

69. Nabuco to Rio-Branco, Aug. 1, 1907, AHI, Ofícios 234/1/7.

70. Fernandes Levi Carneiro, *Discursos,* p. 70.

71. Chilean Minister, Rio de Janeiro, to Minister of Foreign Relations, Santiago, July 5, 1907, ANCh, Chilean Legation in Brazil, 1907,

No. 41; Argentine Legation in Brazil to Minister of Foreign Relations, Buenos Aires, Sept. 10, 1908, ARE, Arg, Caja No. 1115, No. 216/908; *La Nación* (Buenos Aires), Jan. 10, 1910, p. 4; Gorostiaga, "Rio Branco," *El Economista Argentino,* XXII (May 31, 1913), 2.

72. Of the very many examples in the Brazilian press, these are typical: *Journal do Commercio* (Rio de Janeiro), Dec. 11, 1905, p. 2; *Gazeta de Notícias* (Rio de Janeiro), March 17, 1905, p. 1; *O Paiz* (Rio de Janeiro), Jan. 8, 1905, p. 1.

73. Joaquim Nabuco, *The Spirit,* p. 9; Ganzert, "The Boundary Controversy," *Hispanic American Historical Review,* XIV (Nov., 1934), 437; Argeu Guimarães, *Diccionário Bio-Bibliográphico,* p. 406; Calógeras, *Rio Branco,* pp. 17, 32, 37, and 67; Jorge, *Introdução,* p. 210; Paulo Filho, *Ensaios,* p. 175; Amado, *Rio-Branco,* p. 5.

74. Nabuco to Graça Aranha, quoted in Caroline Nabuco, *The Life,* p. 307.

75. Nabuco to Rio-Branco, Jan. 18, 1908, ABR-BI.

76. "[Rio-Branco] spoke . . . of the firm plan of Brazil to maintain close relations with the United States because it is *a strong country."* Chilean Minister, Rio de Janeiro, to Minister of Foreign Relations, Santiago, Nov. 8, 1908, ARE, Ch, Oficios received from the Chilean Legation in Brazil, 1904–8. No. 13.

77. Rio-Branco to Magalhães, Dec. 6, 1902, ABR-BI; *La Nación* (Buenos Aires), July 26, 1906, p. 1; Rio-Branco to Brazilian Legation, Washington, Jan. 31, 1905, AHI, Despachos 235/2/5; Calmon, *História do Brasil,* V, 238–39.

78. Lins, *Rio-Branco,* II, 491; Carlos Sussekind de Mendonça, *Salvador de Mendonça,* p. 263; Gutiérrez, *Hombres,* p. 180.

79. Rio-Branco to Nabuco, Jan. 5, 1908, AHI, Teleg. Exp. 235/4/1.

80. Thompson to Hay, Jan. 15, 1905, NA, Brazilian Dispatches, 71/252; Calmon, *Brasil e América,* p. 87.

81. *A Notícia* (Rio de Janeiro), March 16, 1905, p. 1. Alcides Gentil discusses the Baron's ability to use the power and prestige of the United States to Brazil's advantage. *O Brasil e o Internacionalismo,* pp. 40–41.

82. Rio-Branco to Nabuco, March 26, 1906, AJN.

83. Amaral, "Política Internacional," *Jornal do Commercio* (Rio de Janeiro), Jan. 13, 1910, p. 2. The British vice-consul in Rio at the end of the Rio-Branco ministry noted that it was the Baron's "ambition to

make Brazil the dominant South American nation." Hambloch, *British Consul,* p. 133.

84. Rio-Branco to Nabuco, Jan. 5, 1908, quoted in Nabuco to Rio-Branco, Jan. 15, 1908, AHI, Ofícios 234/1/7; Laet, "Rio Branco," *Revista Americana,* IV (April, 1913), 20.

85. Sargento Albuquerque, *A Cilada Argentina,* p. 14.

86. March, 17, 1905, p. 1.

87. Jan. 20, 1908, p. 1.

88. March 16, 1905, p. 1.

89. Jan. 18, 1908, p. 1.

90. Jan. 26, 1905, p. 1. The American minister sent the article to Washington and commented as follows on the author of the unsigned piece: "Astonishing as it may seem, I am compelled to say that there is no doubt that this article was inspired by Baron Rio Branco, Foreign Minister, as on the day on which it appeared he called my special attention to it, asking that I read it without fail, and his actions seemed to clearly indicate his previous knowledge of its being written." Thompson to Hay, Feb. 1, 1905, NA, Brazilian Dispatches, 71/263.

91. Nabuco to Rio-Branco, Dec. 18, 1908, AHI, Teleg. Receb. 235/3/2.

92. Chilean Minister, Rio de Janeiro, to Minister of Foreign Relations, Santiago, Dec. 30, 1905, and March 30, 1906, ARE, Ch, Oficios received from the Chilean Legation in Brazil, 1904–8, Nos. 8 and 2.

93. Dec. 14, 1902, 2nd Section, p. 5.

94. Botelho, *Le Brésil,* pp. 168–69.

95. Jan. 16, 1908, p. 8; June 26, 1908, p. 6.

96. Napoleão, *Rio Branco,* p. 179; Heitor Lyra, *História Diplomática,* p. 194.

97. *O Paiz* (Rio de Janeiro), Jan. 8, 1905, p. 1.

98. Thompson to Hay, Jan. 15, 1905, NA, Brazilian Dispatches, 71/252.

99. João Frank da Costa, "Rio Branco e o americanismo," *Jornal do Commercio,* Feb. 18, 1962, 2º caderno, p. 5.

100. Rodrigues, "The Foundations of Brazil's Foreign Policy," *International Affairs,* XXXVIII (July, 1962), 333.

101. Chilean Minister, Rio de Janeiro, to Minister of Foreign Relations, Santiago, March 30, 1906, ARE, Ch, Oficios received from the Chilean Legation in Brazil, 1904–8, No. 2.

102. Dudley to Root, May 5, 1908, NA, Brazilian Dispatches, 6047/9; Rio-Branco to Nabuco, Nov. 23, 1908, AJN.

103. Chilean Minister, Rio de Janeiro, to Minister of Foreign Relations, Santiago, April 25, 1908, ARE, Ch, Oficios received from the Chilean Legation in Brazil, No. 3.

104. Griscom to Root, July 16, 1906, NA, Brazilian Dispatches, 1113/2.

105. Jessup, *Root,* I, 412.

106. Root, *Speeches,* p. 24.

107. *Ibid.,* p. 27.

108. Jessup, *Root,* I, 474.

109. *Ibid.*

110. *Brazilian Review* (Rio de Janeiro), Aug. 27, 1907, p. 1000.

111. *Through the Brazilian Wilderness.* In speaking with his famous guide in Brazil, Cândido Rondón, Roosevelt was lavish in his praise of the Brazilians and their country. Freyre, *Ordem e Progresso,* I, clxi–clxii.

112. Rio-Branco to Magalhães, Dec. 6, 1902, ABR-BI; Rio-Branco to Gomes Ferreira, Oct. 29, 1904, AHI, Despachos 235/2/5.

113. Rio-Branco to Gomes Ferreira, Feb. 9, 1905, AHI, Despachos 235/2/5.

114. João Frank da Costa, "Rio Branco Nabuco e o americanismo," *Jornal do Commercio,* Feb. 18, 1962, 2° caderno, p. 5.

115. Rio-Branco to Brazilian Embassy, Washington, Nov. 22, 1909, AHI, Teleg. Exp. 235/4/1; Da Gama to Rio-Branco, Jan. 31, 1912, AHI, Ofícios 234/1/3.

116. Rio-Branco to Brazilian Embassy, Washington, Jan. 22, 1909, AHI, Teleg. Exp. 235/4/1.

117. Rio-Branco to Brazilian Legation, Washington, Jan. 31, 1905, AHI, Despachos 235/2/5; Rio-Branco to Brazilian Legation, Santiago, June 19, 1908, AHI, Teleg. Exp. 231/4/15.

118. Ganzert, "The Baron," p. 56.

119. Gomes Ferreira to Rio-Branco, May 5, 1905, AHI, Ofícios 234/1/3; Nabuco Diary, June 8, 1908.

120. Nabuco Diary, June 11, 1905.

Chapter VIII. FOREIGN REACTIONS TO
THE ALLIANCE

1. Washington, *A Study of Causes: Argentina,* p. 92; Burr, *The Still-born Panama Congress,* pp. 7–14, 24–29.

2. Aug. 14, 1906, p. 4; another statistical comparison of the period whose purpose was to extol Argentine superiority in South America was: Ministerio de Agricultura, *Le Commerce Argentin International, No. 6.* Freyre refers to the period 1870–1910 in Brazilian-Argentine relations as the era of the war of statistics because each of the nations was attempting to prove its superiority over the other by the use of comparative statistics. *Ordem e Progresso,* I, cxxxv.

3. Sargento Albuquerque, *A Cilada Argentina,* p. 22.

4. Rio-Branco to Homen de Melo, Sept. 5, 1882, ADC.

5. Rio-Branco to Joaquim Nabuco, Aug. 29, 1882, AJN.

6. New York *Sun,* March 4, 1903, p. 3; *La Nación* (Buenos Aires), May 18, 1904, March 3, 1905, p. 5; *La Prensa* (Buenos Aires), May 31, 1904, pp. 3–4; Thompson to Hay, June 1, 1904, NA, Brazilian Dispatches, 70/171.

7. Rio-Branco to Brazilian Minister, Buenos Aires, Nov. 21, 1904, AHI, Despachos 207/4/9.

8. Rio-Branco to C. de Azevedo, Feb. 22, 1905, AHI, Despachos 207/4/9.

9. Dudley to Root, May 5, 1908, NA, Brazilian Dispatches, 6047/9.

10. Rio-Branco to Rui Barbosa, Aug. 28, 1907, Casa, Telegram No. 447.

11. Dudley to Root, May 5, 1908, NA, Brazilian Dispatches, 6047/9; *Diário de Notícias* (Rio de Janeiro), April 8, 1908, p. 1.

12. Lascano, *Argentine Foreign Policy in America,* "University of Miami, Hispanic-American Studies," No. 2, p. 30.

13. Eddy to Root, Sept. 24, 1908, NA, Argentine Dispatches, 15865/6–7.

14. Rio-Branco to Nabuco, Dec. 12, 1906, quoted in Nabuco to Rio-Branco, Jan. 3, 1907, AHI, Ofícios 234/1/6; Rio-Branco to Nabuco, Dec. 7, 1908, AHI, Teleg. Exp. 235/4/1.

15. Wilson to Root, Aug. 11, 1908, NA, Argentine Dispatches, 6047/15.

16. Melo, *Textos,* pp. 205–9.

17. Wilson to Root, June 25, 1908, NA, Argentine Dispatches, 4519/37.

18. Viana Filho, *A Vida do Barão do Rio Branco,* p. 390.

19. Dudley to Secretary of State, Aug. 27, 1910, NA, Brazilian Dispatches, 732.35/20.

20. "Argentina–Brazil–Chile," *El Diario* (Buenos Aires), Jan. 8, 1910, p. 8.

21. *La Nación* (Buenos Aires), Jan. 10, 1910, p. 4; Argentine Legation, Rio de Janeiro, to Minister of Foreign Relations, Buenos Aires, March 28, 1910, ARE, Arg, Caja No. 1154, Carpeta No. 51g.

22. Argentine Legation, Rio de Janeiro, to Minister of Foreign Relations, Buenos Aires, May 26, 1912, ARE, Arg, Caja No. 1292, Carpeta No. 93b, No. 142.

23. Argentina decreed a day of mourning with flags at half-mast for the death of Rio-Branco. Information on Rio-Branco's death is contained in ARE, Arg. Caja No. 1290, Carpeta No. 41. *La Prensa* (Buenos Aires), Feb. 11, 1912, p. 11; *La Nación* (Buenos Aires), Feb. 11, 1912, p. 10; Centro Cívico Sete de Setembro, *À Memória,* p. 119.

24. Beaupré to Root, Aug. 19, 1907, NA, Argentine Dispatches, 6047/2.

25. *La Prensa* (Buenos Aires), Jan. 14, 1904, p. 4.

26. "Rio-Branco," *El Economista Argentino* (Buenos Aires), May 31, 1913, p. 2.

27. *La Nación* (Buenos Aires), Jan. 19, 1905, p. 5.

28. Beaupré to Root, Aug. 19, 1907, NA, Argentine Dispatches, 6047/2.

29. *La Nación* (Buenos Aires), May 10, 1906, p. 6; White to Root, May 10, 1906, NA, Argentine Dispatches, 47/353; Buenos Aires *Herald,* Aug. 14, 1906, p. 1; Beaupré to Root, Aug. 24, 1907, NA, Argentine Dispatches, 6047/1; Wilson to Root, July 31, 1908, NA, Argentine Dispatches, 15504; Eddy to Root, Sept. 16, 1908, NA, Argentine Dispatches, 15865/1; Sherrill to Secretary of State, Jan. 6, 1910, NA, Argentine Dispatches, 1113/13; Argentine Legation, Rio de Janeiro, to Minister of Foreign Relations, Buenos Aires, April 30, 1911, ARE, Arg, Caja No. 1222, Carpeta No. 120, No. 161.

30. Argentine Legation, Rio de Janeiro, to Minister of Foreign Relations, Buenos Aires, Feb. 10, 1910, ARE, Arg, Caja No. 1154, Carpeta No. 41f, No. 139.

31. Assis Brasil to Rio-Branco, Nov. 15, 1906, AHI, Ofícios 206/2/1.

32. *La Nación* (Buenos Aires), Jan. 14, 1904, p. 3.

33. Beaupré to Root, Aug. 19, 1907, NA, Argentine Dispatches, 6047/2; *Brazilian Review* (Rio de Janeiro), Aug. 20, 1907, p. 974.

34. McGann, *Argentina,* p. 237; Washington, *A Study of Causes: Argentina,* pp. 29–30.

35. Jan. 19, 1905, p. 5.

36. José do Patrocínio, "A Embaixada," *O Paiz* (Rio de Janeiro), Jan. 26, 1905, p. 1.

37. Beaupré to Root, Aug. 19, 1907, NA, Argentine Dispatches, 6047/2.

38. Gurgel do Amaral to Rio-Branco, Oct. 9, 1906, AHI, Teleg. Receb. 235/3/1A.

39. Richardson to Root, Dec. 1, 1905, NA, Argentine Dispatches, 72/113.

40. Beaupré to Root, Dec. 4, 1905, NA, Argentine Dispatches, 46/263.

41. Nabuco to Rio-Branco, March 1, 1906, AHI, Ofícios 234/1/4.

42. *El Diario* (Buenos Aires), April 6, 1906, p. 3.

43. *La Nación* (Buenos Aires), Aug. 14, 1906, p. 7.

44. Teffé von Hoonholtz to Rio-Branco, Aug. 17, 1906, AHI, Ofícios 206/2/1.

45. Wilson to Root, Jan. 22, 1908, NA, Argentine Dispatches, 8258/163.

46. Chilean Minister, Washington, to Minister of Foreign Relations, Santiago, Nov. 27, 1909, ANCh, Chilean Legation in the USA, 1909, 2⁰ S.

47. Sherrill to Secretary of State, Dec. 4, 1909, NA, Argentine Dispatches, 1154/236.

48. McGann, *Argentina,* p. 261.

49. *La Prensa* (Buenos Aires), April 21, 1904, p. 7. Brazil took more than four fifths of Argentine flour exports during this decade. In 1911, for example, 83 percent of Argentine flour exports went to Brazil. Ministerio de Agricultura, Argentine Republic, *Le Commerce Argentin International, No. 6,* p. 35.

50. *Le Prensa* (Buenos Aires), July 8, 1906, p. 5.

51. *Ibid.,* April 20, 1904, p. 7; *La Nación* (Buenos Aires), April 22,

1904, p. 5; *A Notícia* (Rio de Janeiro), April 22–23, 1904, p. 1; C. de Azevedo to Rio-Branco, April 26, 1904, AHI, Ofícios 206/1/13.

52. Dudley to Secretary of State, Jan. 31, 1911, NA, Brazilian Dispatches, 611.3231/191; *Correio da Manhã* (Rio de Janeiro), Feb. 1, 1911, p. 1.

53. *La Nación* (Buenos Aires), Aug. 22, 1904, p. 6.

54. *El Diario* (Buenos Aires), Dec. 1, 1905, p. 3.

55. Dudley to Root, June 24, 1908, NA, Brazilian Dispatches, 836/118; *Jornal do Commercio* (Rio de Janeiro), Sept. 15, 1908, p. 2.

56. Nabuco to Rui Barbosa, June 13, 1907, Casa, Pasta J. Nabuco.

57. Rio-Branco to Gomes Ferreira, Jan. 21, 1905, AHI, Despachos 235/2/5.

58. Gomes Ferreira to Rio-Branco, July 12, 1904, AHI, Ofícios 234/1/2; Gomes Ferreira to Rio-Branco, Sept. 30, 1904, AHI, Ofícios 234/1/2.

59. Chilean Minister, Rio de Janeiro, to Minister of Foreign Relations, Santiago, Dec. 8, 1906, ANCh, Chilean Legation in Brazil, 1906–7.

60. *El Mercurio* (Santiago), Feb. 12, p. 9; Feb. 13, p. 11; and Feb. 14, 1912, p. 1.

61. The references in the ANCh and the ARE, Ch are innumerable. Two examples would be: Chilean Minister, Rio de Janeiro, to Minister of Foreign Relations, Santiago, June 13, 1903, ANCh, Chilean Legation in Brazil, 1902–3; Chilean Minister, Rio de Janeiro, to Minister of Foreign Relations, Santiago, Aug. 31, 1905, ANCh, Chilean Legation in Brazil, 1904–5.

62. For an interesting essay on Chile's isolation in South America see Moraga, *El Aislamiento.*

63. *Ibid.,* p. 87.

64. For an intriguing essay on the importance of the balance of power in intra-South American relations see Burr, "The Balance of Power in Nineteenth-Century South America: An Exploratory Essay," *Hispanic American Historical Review,* XXXV (Feb., 1955), 37–60.

65. Chilean Minister, Rio de Janeiro, to Minister of Foreign Relations, Santiago, Jan. 7, 1905, ARE, Ch, Oficios from the Chilean Legation in Brazil, 1904–5.

66. Chilean Minister, Rio de Janeiro, to Minister of Foreign Relations, Santiago, ANCh, Chilean Legation in Brazil, 1904–5 (found with

miscellaneous, undated papers in that volume, seemingly misfiled); *El Mercurio* (Santiago), April 25, 1909, p. 3.

67. Chilean Minister, Rio de Janeiro, to Minister of Foreign Relations, Santiago, June 1, 1907, ARE, Ch, Oficios from the Chilean Legation in Brazil, 1904–8.

68. Chilean Minister, Rio de Janeiro, to Minister of Foreign Relations, Santiago, June 1, 1907, ARE, Ch, Oficios from the Chilean Legation in Brazil, 1904–8.

69. Chilean Minister, Rio de Janeiro, to Minister of Foreign Relations, Santiago, Sept. 16, 1907, ARE, Ch, Oficios from the Chilean Legation in Brazil, 1904–8.

70. *El Mercurio* (Santiago), April 25, 1909, p. 3.

71. Moraga, *El Aislamiento,* pp. 87–104.

72. *Bulletin of the International Bureau of American States* (Washington), June, 1905, p. 609.

73. *Gazeta de Notícias* (Rio de Janeiro), March 17, 1905, p. 1.

74. In his book, *British Preeminence in Brazil,* Alan K. Manchester carefully details the nineteenth-century relations between the two countries. He emphasizes British economic dominance over Brazil.

75. *Ibid.,* p. 321.

76. *Ibid.,* pp. 334–35.

77. *Diario da Bahia* (Salvador, Bahia), Aug. 31, 1907, p. 1.

78. *The Times* (London), Jan. 12, 1905, p. 5.

79. Jan. 16, 1905, p. 9.

80. Hambloch, *British Consul,* p. 95.

81. *Ibid.*

82. *Ibid.*

83. *The South American Journal* (London), Nov. 26, 1904, p. 568.

84. *Ibid.,* June 10, 1905, p. 629.

85. *Ibid.,* March 18, p. 293; March 25, pp. 318, 321; April 15, p. 401; and April 29, 1905, p. 458.

86. *Ibid.,* Nov. 19, 1904, p. 556.

87. Koebel, *British Exploits in South America,* pp. 529–530, 532; *The Times* (London), Aug. 31, 1903, p. 4.

88. *Brazil in 1909; Brazil in 1911; Brazil in 1913; Brazil, Past, Present and Future.*

89. *British Consul; Forty Years in Brazil; The United States of Brazil.*

90. *British Consul,* p. 133.

91. *Ibid.*
92. *South America,* pp. 366–421.
93. *Le Progrès Brésilien,* p. 41.
94. *Denis, Brazil,* p. 122.
95. *South America Today,* p. 329.

A BIBLIOGRAPHICAL ESSAY
ON RIO-BRANCO

T HOUGH I consulted many works and manuscripts in the preparation of this study, the following bibliography includes only those materials which were of direct use. Because these sources vary greatly in quality and significance, this bibliographical essay is designed to facilitate their use.

While the history of the republican period receives increasing attention, there is still a lack of good, solid, analytical histories of the period. A standard history of the republic, and probably the best, is José Maria Bello's *História da República* (publication data for the works mentioned in this essay can be found in the bibliography), which covers the Rio-Branco era in some detail. Volume V of Pedro Calmon's *História do Brasil* also treats the period rather thoroughly. Although repetitive, Gilberto Freyre's *Ordem e Progresso* is essential for an understanding of the first decades of the republic. Following the pattern of his previous works, this is a sociological history full of penetrating insights and ideas. Harry Bernstein in *Modern and Contemporary Latin America* gives the best account in English of this period in Brazilian history.

Unlike some other Latin Americans, Brazilians have given considerable attention to chronicling their diplomatic history. I purposely use the verb "chronicle" rather than "study" because as yet there have been few analytical or critical studies, while the chronicles in article, monograph, and book form are many. Two diplomatic histories merit special attention: *História Diplomática do Brasil,* by the historian Hélio Vianna, and *História Diplomática do Brasil,* by the diplomat Delgado de Carvalho. Both cover the sweep of four hundred and fifty years of Luso-Brazilian diplomacy well. Perhaps the Carvalho work is the more analytical of the two. He also adds to each of his chapters readings from documents or commentators germane to the topic discussed. It is interesting to note that, in diplomatic histories covering the period from 1493 to the present, both authors devote approximately one quarter of the entire text to the ten-year ministry of Rio-Branco. José Honório Rodrigues has admirably synthesized Brazilian diplomatic history in an interpretive essay entitled "The Foundations of Brazil's Foreign Policy," in which he pays homage to the outstanding role of Rio-Branco.

Despite the importance of Rio-Branco in Brazilian diplomatic history, no full-length biography of the Baron appeared during his lifetime and not until two decades after his death did a few sketchy biographies reach print. The most important of these were *Rio-Branco,* by Max Fleiuss (1931), *O Barão,* by João Lyra Filho (1936), *Duas Histórias em Três Vidas,* by David Carneiro (1939), *O Segundo Rio-Branco,* by Aluízio Napoleão (1940), and *História do Grande Chanceler,* by Deoclécio de Paranhos Antunes (1942). Those biographies uncritically lionized their hero.

The focus of attention on Rio-Branco on the occasion of the centennial celebration of his birth in 1945 animated historians and dilettantes to begin to study their eminent countryman. In the same year, Alvaro Lins published his *Rio-Branco,* the first significant biography of the chancellor and until today one of the two first-rate biographies of him. Lins's book marked the initial attempt of a biographer of Rio-Branco to study and use primary sources, to interpret the facts, to give meaning and significance to events, and to temper praise with reason. In another long biography appearing at the same time, Afonso de Carvalho brought together many of the anecdotes (and they were many) concerning the Baron. The book is amusing reading—and the style is excellent—but dangerous because fact and fancy mix freely. The undocumented did-you-hear-this-one augments the already voluminous mythology which surrounds the Baron's life and obscures historical truth. Two other biographies of considerably lesser importance appeared during the centenary: *Pequena Biografia do Barão do Rio-Branco,* by Demósthenes de Oliveira Dias, and *Perfil de um Estadista da República: Ensaio Biográfico do Barão do Rio Branco,* by Antônio Carlos Vilaça.

Adding its voice to the paeans of praise during the centenary, the

Instituto Histórico e Geográfico Brasileiro devoted most of the April-June, 1945, edition of its *Revista* to Rio-Branco. The best article of the edition was "O Barão do Rio Branco e a Diplomacia Brasileira," by A. Teixeira Soares, published in book form the following year in Porto Alegre. That essay is an effort, although not entirely successful, to interpret the significance of the ten-year ministry of Rio-Branco. Without doubt the most important work in the *Revista* was "Contribuição para o Estudo de Rio Branco," by Cláudio Ganns, the first and only bibliographical guide to the study of Rio-Branco. Containing omissions and errors and now outdated, the sixty-page guide is still the starting point for anyone who wants to investigate the life of Rio-Branco, his career, his accomplishments, or his ministry. The "Contribuição" is particularly valuable in indicating pertinent newspaper articles.

The years following the centennial celebration witnessed the publication of more biographies, the most important of which were Gilberto Amado, *Rio-Branco* (1947), Mário de Barros e Vasconcellos, *O Barão do Rio-Branco* (1954), and Alfredo Balthazar da Silveira, *Barão do Rio Branco* (1956). These were regurgitations of what had already been said ad infinitum and showed scant effort toward or interest in presenting either new source material or new interpretations.

Happily, 1959 marked the beginning of a new period in the study of Rio-Branco. In that year the José Olympio Editôra in Rio de Janeiro published *A Vida do Barão de Rio Branco,* by Luiz Viana Filho, who had already established a solid reputation as a biographer with *A Vida do Rui Barbosa* and *A Vida do Joaquim Nabuco.* The genuine scholarship, based entirely upon primary sources, the significant interpretations, the excellent prose, make the work a biographical masterpiece. Viana Filho concentrated on Rio-Branco the man, and without resorting to the empty rhetoric of adulation told a moving story of one of Brazil's greatest statesmen. His Rio-Branco is not the demigod; he is a human being. Because of that realistic treatment, he emerges as a greater figure in Brazilian history than all the bombastic barrage of sycophantic praise heaped upon him by former dilettante biographers (Lins excepted) could hope to make him. It is an outstanding biography, *the* biography of Rio-Branco. Along with Cláudio Gann's bibliography, this book is essential for the study of Rio-Branco.

Over the years, there have been six studies made of the ministry of Rio-Branco. None of them approaches being the definitive study but each contributes toward a fuller understanding of the events during the Rio-Branco decade. Five of those studies were written by contemporaries of Rio-Branco. Dunshee de Abranches, a federal deputy and close friend of the Baron, wrote the two-volume *Rio Branco e a Política Exterior do Brazil,* which factually is the most important of the five studies. That work contains, among many other things, his well-known speech in the Chamber of Deputies in defense of Rio-Branco's policies, "Discurso sôbre o orçamento do exterior." João Pandiá Calógeras, another deputy and friend of Rio-Branco, was the author of *Rio-Branco e a Política Exterior,* a long essay on the Baron's diplomacy. Rio-Branco's protégé and young secretary, A. G. de Araujo Jorge, years after his mentor's death, set down many of his recollections and impressions in the *Introdução às Obras do Barão do Rio-Branco.* To balance the picture, it is necessary to peruse a curious and informative book by Salvador de Mendonça, one of the Baron's enemies, *A Situação Internacional do Brasil.* Although hostile to and critical of one another, the chancellor and the former minister to the United States and Portugal often displayed a surprising similarity in their foreign policy ideas.

Special mention should be made of Alcides Gentil's book, *O Brasil e o Internacionalismo.* To commemorate the first anniversary of Rio-Branco's death, this twenty-year-old student wrote a critical study of the Baron's diplomacy. His abilities to analyze, to use sources, and to make excellent citations are superior to those of older, more experienced, and recognized writers and scholars. The terse and informative work is favorable to the Baron but not in the customary unbalanced fashion. While paying tribute to the accomplishments of Rio-Branco, the author also criticizes him for being too friendly to the United States, for failing to solidify closer relations with Spanish America, and for opposing the Drago Doctrine. Gentil's handling of accusations of Brazilian imperialism, recognized but rationalized, follows traditional patterns both past and present.

Frederic William Ganzert is the only foreigner and noncontemporary to make a study of Rio-Branco's ministry. His doctoral dissertation at the University of California in 1933 was entitled "The Baron do Rio-Branco and Brazilian Foreign Relations." Despite the fact that Ganzert did not have access to many primary sources, the important Historical Archives of Itamaraty, for example, his work clarifies many hitherto vague aspects of the ministry and is especially strong in the diplomacy of the boundary settlements. It is a pity that the dissertation was never published as a whole. However, in three separate articles, Ganzert re-made some of the principal contributions of his dissertation: "The Boundary Controversy in the Upper Amazon between Brazil, Bolivia, and Peru, 1903–1909" simplifies and explains the complications of the Acre controversy; "José Maria da Silva Paranhos, Baron do Rio Branco" is a general biographical essay; and "The Baron do Rio Branco, Joaquim Nabuco, and the Growth of Brazilian-American Friendship, 1900–1910" discusses the rapprochement between Brazil and the United States under Rio-Branco's guidance.

The diplomatic relations of Brazil with the United States during the Rio-Branco ministry have been treated in several books and articles, although none of them have made full use of diplomatic archives. Certainly the best is Caroline Nabuco's *The Life of Joaquim Nabuco,* which treats in detail the five years her father served as Rio-Branco's ambassador in Washington. She used Nabuco's diaries and letters to present an intimate picture of the vital years in Brazilian-American relations. A penetrating article of great value is João Frank de Costa's brief "Rio Branco, Nabuco e o americanismo," which discusses Brazilian-American friendship. Two other important articles on the same topic are "Joaquim Nabuco nos Estados Unidos," by Raul d'Eça, and "Joaquim Nabuco e os Estados Unidos," by Ronald Hilton. Aluízio Napoleão's *Rio-Branco e as Relações entre o Brazil e os Estados Unidos* does not live up to the expectations its title arouses because it is too incomplete and uncritical. Differences over the Bolivian Syndicate and at The Hague are minimized in order to emphasize harmony. Two short essays deserve attention: "As Relações entre os Estados Unidos e o Brasil," by Hélio Lobo, and "Relações Políticas e Econômicas entre o Brasil e os Estados Unidos," by Armando Vidal.

Within general historical résumés of diplomatic relations between the two countries, four authors treat, at least briefly, the Rio-Branco ministry: Manoel de Oliveira Lima, *The Relations of Brazil with the United States;* Lawrence F. Hill, *Diplomatic Relations Between the United States and Brazil;* Pedro Calmon, *Brasil e América;* and A. Curtis Wilgus, *A Brief Survey of the Political Relations Between Brazil and the United States.* These works are most notable for their omissions, but as general surveys for the layman they are adequate.

Although Rio-Branco's policy toward the United States has received the most attention, there have been brief studies made of his relations with other countries. Lidia Besouchet's *Rio-Branco e as Relações entre o Brasil e a República Argentina* is misleading in its attempts to emphasize only the positive side. The reader is not told that between 1905 and 1910 the two nations engaged in a dangerous arms race and that at one point were on the verge of breaking diplomatic relations and declaring war. It is more a history of how Brazil might have wished the relations had been than a history of how they actually were. Hildebrando Accioly has analyzed Brazil's role at the Hague Peace Conference in 1907, an important landmark in Brazilian diplomatic history, in "O Barão do Rio Branco e a 2ª Conferência da Haia" and in "Rui Barbosa na Segunda Conferência da Haia." I analyzed briefly Rio-Branco's relations with the new Republic of Panama in "Rio-Branco e o Reconhecimento do Panamá."

A number of authors have discussed Rio-Branco's relations with other eminent Brazilians of the period. The most important of those studies are: Rodrigo M. F. de Andrade, *Rio-Branco e Gastão da Cunha;* Américo Jacobina Lacombe, *Rio-Branco e Rui Barbosa;* M. Paulo Filho, an essay entitled "Rio Branco e Nabuco" in his book *Ensaios e Estudos;* and Francisco Venâncio Filho, *Rio Branco e Euclides da Cunha.*

The memoirs of the period which touch upon or mention Rio-Branco fall into two categories. The first are those written by Brazilians who knew Rio-Branco. Their memoirs tend to be more laudatory than objective. The most valuable of these, the memoir which definitely sets the stage and creates the atmosphere for the Rio-Branco ministry, is *O Meu Velho Itamarati,* by Luís Gurgel do Amaral, who began his diplomatic career under the Baron's guidance and looks back with misty eyes to the "good old days" at the foreign ministry. João do Rio gives a limited but amusing insight into Rio-Branco in his "A Minha Primeira Entrevista e o Meu Primeiro Pedido." *Reminiscências do Barão do Rio-Branco* contains many observations made by Raul do Rio-Branco concerning his father. Turning his mind back half a century, Carlos Martins Pereira de Souza wrote an informative acount of "O Barão que Eu Conheci."

The second category of memoirs consists of works written by foreigners. Often these are more akin to journalistic reporting than memoirs but the result is the same. Many distinguished foreigners visited Brazil during the Rio-Branco ministry. The affable Baron entertained and charmed them. Those foreigners, Europeans as well as Americans, left accounts of their visits which speak highly of the foreign minister. In contrast to those of the Brazilians, their accounts tend to be more objective. Four Spanish American diplomats who served their countries in Rio de Janeiro later wrote about Rio-Branco. The Paraguayan minister, Juansilvano Godoi, set down his favorable impressions in *El Barón de Río Branco*. A section on the chancellor can be found in *Hombres y Cosas de Ayer*, by the Bolivian Alberto Gutiérrez, and the former Argentine minister to Brazil, Manuel Gorostiaga, left his impressions in two articles entitled "Rio-Branco." Another Argentine diplomat whose memoirs deserve consideration for their remarks on the Brazilian foreign minister is Vicente G. Quesada, author of *Mis Memorias Diplomáticas*. The Uruguayan journalist Manuel Bernárdez made an extensive visit to Brazil in 1908 and was captivated by the Baron, to whom he devoted a chapter in *Le Brésil*.

A relatively large number of Europeans visited Brazil at the turn of the century and published their impressions. Georges Clemenceau, in his newspaper article on Brazil for the New York *Times,* spoke highly of Rio-Branco and James Bryce did likewise in *South America: Observations and Impressions*. Undoubtedly one of the most candid and critical, although unbalanced, insights by a European is the amusing *British Consul: Memories of Thirty Years' Service in Europe and Brazil,* by Ernest Hambloch.

North Americans also added their views of Rio-Branco. Probably the closest North American friend of the Baron was John Bassett Moore, the eminent jurist of Columbia University. Moore related his impressions of his colleague in "Rio-Branco." William Jennings Bryan visited Brazil and left his favorable opinions of Rio-Branco in "My Visit to Brazil, the Giant of South America." For a digest of American opinion about Rio-Branco see my "Rio-Branco Visto pelos seus Contemporáneos Norteamericanos."

A source of an interesting and novel perspective of the Baron and his diplomacy is the dispatches of foreign diplomats sent from Rio de Janeiro to their respective foreign ministers. Those of the United States, Argentina, and Chile are excellent examples. Their pointed (but nevertheless laudatory) remarks and observations provide a wealth of information on Rio-Branco, the men who surrounded him, and Brazilian public opinion concerning him. Frequently those dispatches contain quotations of the Baron unavailable from any other sources.

Primary sources, such as those dispatches sent by foreign diplomats, will provide the basis for any serious study of Rio-Branco, regardless of the value of a few of the secondary works. Fortunately the primary sources are extensive, and, as yet, they have been practically untapped.

A few of the writings of Rio-Branco have been published. His essay, "Brazil, the United States, and the Monroe Doctrine," first published in Rio de Janeiro in 1906, then published in English in 1908 in the United States, and many times reprinted since then, expounds his view of the historic friendship between Brazil and the United States. Also indispensable for the study of Brazilian diplomacy is his *Relações Exteriores do Brasil durante a Administração do Presidente Rodrigues Alves,* published in the *Diario Official* and also separately. The presidential messages to Congress, read in May of each year and printed thereafter by the government, contain a section on foreign affairs written by Rio-Branco. During his decade in office, the Ministry of Foreign Relations published only one *Relatório* for the period of May 28, 1902, through August 31, 1903. Itamaraty has published nine volumes of the *Obras do Barão do Rio-Branco.* The final volume, his speeches, probably is the most important for the study of the statesman because it is the only one filled with his political opinions and ideas.

The outstanding source of information on and about Rio-Branco is the archives, public and private. His important letters, instructions, and memorandums contain the real key to the man and to his work. The most important archive is the Historical Archive of Itamaraty, which contains his official papers, principally the telegrams, memorandums, and instructions to the Brazilian diplomats abroad, and his private papers, notebooks, and letters. Two other archives of great value, because of the large number of Rio-Branco's letters they contain, are the archive of Joaquim Nabuco and the archive of the Casa Rui Barbosa. Smaller numbers of his letters can be found scattered through a variety of other archives: the manuscript section of the National Library, the archives of the National Museum of History, the archives of the David Carneiro Museum, the archives of Assis Brasil, etc.

I spent approximately a year exploring those Brazilian archives, which in all cases seemed unrestrictedly open to me. Access to some of the private archives depends upon the personal rapport the researcher establishes with the owner; others, such as the important Historical Archive of Itamaraty, are open at least theoretically to all scholars. However, a letter of recommendation and personal contact with the authorities greatly facilitate use of even those public archives. The Brazilian embassy in Washington, as well as influential American and Brazilian contacts, aided me greatly in gaining access to the archives. In general, the archives which I had occasion to consult were in good shape and reasonably well organized; the service was friendly and sufficient. All the public archives have at least some kind of index or catalogue. The Casa Rui Barbosa and Itamaraty have published some informative guides and catalogues to their collections.

Another valuable source of information is the Brazilian newspapers of the period. They contain an almost daily account of the principal diplomatic events and, of course, of the Baron's role in them. Since Rio-Branco never abandoned his avocation for journalism, he was a frequent contributor to the *Jornal do Commercio* and at times to *O Paiz*. A serious analysis of some of the editorials in those two papers will probably result in the discovery of some valuable foreign policy pronouncements and opinions of Rio-Branco.

A review of the bibliographical material for the study of the Brazilian-American approximation and Rio-Branco's role in it leads to the following four conclusions. First, two indispensable aids for the study of the topic have been published: Cláudio Gann's "Contribuição" and Luiz Viana Filho's *A Vida do Barão do Rio Branco*. They are the starting point for any study of Rio-Branco. Second, the archives in Brazil, as well as in other countries, contain rich and almost unused source material on Rio-Branco. The Brazilian archives are becoming increasingly better organized and more accustomed to their role to facilitate scholarly research. No serious study of Rio-Branco is possible without consulting at least the Historical Archive of Itamaraty. Third, there is a surprising dearth of worthy studies of Rio-Branco and his diplomacy because the majority of the authors undertook their work to praise blindly rather than to analyze and to study. The traditional historical institutes throughout Brazil encouraged those eulogies rather than penetrating studies of Rio-Branco. The universities, which only in the past few decades have added history to their curriculums, and the historical profession, which they now are encouraging, have not as yet given the emphasis to the study of Rio-Branco merited by his role in modern Brazilian history. Fourth, there is a need for academically solid monographic studies, interpreting other aspects of the diplomacy of the Baron of Rio-Branco and his times.

A SELECTED BIBLIOGRAPHY
WITH ANNOTATION

I. ARCHIVAL SOURCES

For those archives from which material has been quoted, the abbreviation used in the footnotes follows the full and official name of the archives.

Archives of the Organization of American States, Washington, D.C.

Archivo del Ministerio de Relaciones Exteriores y Culta de la Argentina, Buenos Aires (ARE, Arg).

Archivo del Ministerio de Relaciones Exteriores de Chile, Santiago (ARE, Ch).

Archivo Nacional de Chile, Santiago (ANCh).

Archivo de la Secretaría de Relaciones Exteriores del México, Mexico City (ARE, Mex).

Archivo de la Secretaría de Relaciones Exteriores de la República del Panamá, Panama City (ARE, Pan).

Arquivo da Casa de Rui Barbosa, Rio de Janeiro (Casa).

Arquivo de Joaquim Nabuco, Rio de Janeiro (AJN).

Arquivo do Museu David Carneiro, Curitiba, Paraná (ADC).

Arquivo do Barão do Rio-Branco, Itamaraty, Rio de Janeiro (ABR-BI).

Arquivo Histórico de Itamaraty, Rio de Janeiro (AHI).

Biblioteca Nacional do Brasil, Secção de Manuscritos, Rio de Janeiro.

Instituto Histórico e Geográfico Brasileiro, Secção de Manuscritos, Rio de Janeiro.

Museu Nacional de História, Secção de Manuscritos, Rio de Janeiro.

National Archives of the United States of America, General Records of the Department of State, Washington, D.C. (NA).

Oliveira Lima Library, Catholic University of America, Washington, D.C. (OL Lib).

II. PUBLISHED DOCUMENTS

A. ARGENTINA

Inter-American Conference, 1910. *Fourth American International Conference.* Vol. I: *Daily Account of Sessions.* Buenos Aires: Est. Gráfico A. de Martino, 1911.

—— *Program and Regulations for the 4th International American Conference.* Buenos Aires: Kraft, 1910.

Ministerio de Agricultura. *Le Commerce Argentin International, No. 6.* Buenos Aires: Direction Meteorologique Argentine, 1912.

An excellent statistical guide. It is a comparison with all other Latin American republics of data for the period 1900–1911, emphasizing the comparison with Brazil.

B. BRAZIL

Calógeras, João Pandiá. "Discurso sôbre o orçamento do exterior," *Anais da Câmara dos Deputados.* Anais V, Vol. VI (Rio de Janeiro, 1914), pp. 762–89.

This important and informative speech in defense of Rio-Branco is reprinted in Calógeras' book *Relações Exteriores do Brasil.*

Campos, Raul Adalberto de. *Legislação Internacional do Brazil.* 2 vols. Rio de Janeiro: Impr. Nacional, 1929.

All decrees issued by the Minister of Foreign Relations and decrees issued by other ministers germane to international relations.

—— *Relações Diplomáticas do Brazil, Contendo os Nomes dos Representantes Diplomáticos do Brazil.* Rio de Janeiro: Typ. do Jornal do Commercio, 1913.

A list of all Brazilian chiefs of mission and diplomatic posts abroad as well as of all foreign chiefs of mission in Rio de Janeiro from 1808 to 1912 with miscellaneous commentaries on diplomatic events of importance.

Conselho Nacional de Estatística. *Contribuições para o Estudo da Demografia do Brasil.* Rio de Janeiro: Servico Gráfico do IBGE, 1961.

An excellent analysis of population trends and composition throughout Brazilian history with emphasis on the modern period.

Departmento Nacional de Indústria e Comércio. *Brasil-Argentina, Um*

Século de Paz, de Amizade, e de Comércio. Rio de Janeiro: Tip. Mercantil, 1940.

Estado de Amazonas. *Leis, Decretos e Regulamentos, Tomo XI, 1910.* Manaus, 1911.

—— *Relatório da Directoria do Banco Amazonese.* Manaus, 1911.

Inter-American Conference, 1906. *Memoria de la Delegación de la República Argentina.* Rio de Janeiro: Impr. Nacional, 1906.

—— *Minutes, Resolutions, Documents.* Rio de Janeiro: Impr. Nacional, 1907.

Medeiros, Fernando Saboia de. *Precedentes Diplomáticos de 1889 a 1932.* Rio de Janeiro: Impr. Nacional, 1940.

An index to the annual *Relatório* of the Ministry of Foreign Relations.

Mensagens Presidenciais Apresentadas ao Congresso Nacional, 1903–1913. Rio de Janeiro: Impr. Nacional, 1903–13.

These messages were read every May and printed thereafter. The summary of foreign affairs for the year was made by Rio-Branco. It is an excellent résumé of the diplomatic history of the period.

Ministério de Agricultura. *Annuaire Statistique du Brésil, 1ᵉʳᵉ Année 1908–1912.* Vol. I: *Territoire et Population.* Rio de Janeiro: Imprimerie de la Statistique, 1916.

An informative guide to the basic statistics of the period.

—— *O Brasil Actual.* Rio de Janeiro: Lit. Typ. Fluminense, 1929–30.

—— *Resumo de Várias Estatísticas Económico-Financeiras.* Rio de Janeiro: Typ. da Estatística, 1924.

Excellent source of statistics. Emphasis is on the 1920 census.

—— *Synopse do Recenseamento Realizado em 1 de Setembro de 1920.* Rio de Janeiro: Typ. da Estatística, 1924.

Ministério da Fazenda. *Commércio Exterior do Brazil, 1910 a 1914.* Vol. I: *Principaes Mercadorias de Exportação e Importação, por Portos e Paizes.* Paris: Société Générale d'Impression, n.d.

Excellent statistics on Brazil's foreign commerce.

—— *Foreign Trade of Brazil. 1910–1912.* Paris: Escritório de Informações do Brasil, 1912.

Ministério das Relações Exteriores. *Relatório Apresentado ao Presidente da República dos Estados Unidos do Brasil pelo Ministro de Estado das Relações Exteriores Comprehendendo o Período Decorrido de 28 de Maio de 1902 a 31 de Agosto de 1903.* Rio de Janeiro: Impr. Nacional, 1904.

This is the only *Relatório* published by Rio-Branco during his ministry. Informative for a study of the Acre problem.

—— *Relatório Apresentado ao Presidente da República dos Estados Unidos do Brasil pelo Ministro de Estado das Relações Exteriores Comprehendendo o Período Decorrido de 1 Janeiro a 30 de Abril de 1912.* Rio de Janeiro: Impr. Nacional, 1912.

—— *Relatório Apresentado ao Presidente da República dos Estados Unidos do Brasil pelo Ministro de Estado das Relações Exteriores Comprehendendo o Período Decorrido de 1 de Maio de 1912 a 17 de Maio de 1913.* Rio de Janeiro: Impr. Nacional, 1913.

This *Relatório* contains information and documents on the tariff concessions Brazil granted to the United States. Essential information for the commercial relations between the two countries.

—— *Relatório Apresentado ao Presidente da República dos Estados Unidos do Brasil pelo Ministro de Estado das Relações Exteriores Comprehendendo o Período Decorrido de 18 de Maio de 1913 a 3 de Maio de 1914.* Rio de Janeiro: Impr. Nacional, 1914.

Oliveira, José Manoel Cardoso de. *Actos Diplomáticos do Brasil.* 2 vols. Rio de Janeiro: Typ. do Jornal do Commercio, 1912.

All treaties into which Brazil entered from 1493 to 1912.

Secretaria da Agricultura, Comércio, e Obras Públicas do Estado de São Paulo. *O Café, 1919.* São Paulo: Escolas Profissionaes, 1920.

Contains statistics of the coffee trade during the Rio-Branco period.

C. CHILE

Ministerio de Relaciones Exteriores. *La Conferencia Pan Americana de Buenos Aires, Informe presentado por los Delegados Plenipotenciarios de Chile.* Santiago: Impr. Barcelona, 1911.

D. GREAT BRITAIN

Foreign Office. *British and Foreign State Papers, 1901–1912.* Vols. XCV–CV. London: His Majesty's Stationery Office, 1905–15.

E. THE UNITED STATES OF AMERICA

Department of Commerce and Labor. *Daily Consular and Trade Reports.* Washington, D.C.: Government Printing Office, July 5, 1910–Dec. 30, 1912.

—— *Special Agent Series.* Washington, D.C.: Government Printing Office.

No. 45. *Trade Development in Latin America,* by John M. Turner. 1911.

No. 81. *South America as an Export Field,* by Otto Wilson. 1914.

No. 90. *Banking and Credit in Argentina, Brazil, Chile, and Peru,* by Edward N. Hurley. 1914.

No. 106. *Banking Opportunities in South America,* by William H. Lough. 1915.

—— *United States Consular Reports, 1902–1910.* Washington, D.C.: Government Printing Office, 1902–10.

Department of State. *Foreign Relations of the United States. Diplomatic Papers. 1903–1911.* Washington, D.C.: Government Printing Office, 1904–13.

—— *Register of the Department of State, 1902-1912.* Washington, D.C.: Government Printing Office, 1902–12.

Inter-American Conference, 1906. *Report of the Delegates of the U.S. to the 3rd International Conference of the American States.* Washington, D.C.: Government Printing Office, 1907.

Inter-American Conference, 1910. *Fourth International Conference of American States, Delegation from the United States.* 61st Congress, 3d Session, Senate Doc. No. 744. Washington, D.C.: Government Printing Office, 1911.

Malloy, William M. *Treaties, Conventions, International Acts, Protocols and Agreements Between the United States of America and Other Powers, 1776–1923.* 3 vols. Washington, D.C.: Government Printing Office, 1910–23.

Root, Elihu. *Address Before the Trans-Mississippi Congress, Kansas City, Missouri, November 20, 1906.* Document No. 211. 59th Congress, 2d Session.

—— *Speeches Incident to the Visit of Secretary Root to South America.* Washington, D.C.: Government Printing Office, 1906.

III. OTHER PUBLISHED WORKS

Abranches, Dunshee de. *Brazil and the Monroe Doctrine.* Rio de Janeiro, 1915.

—— *Limites com o Perú.* Rio de Janeiro: Impr. Nacional, 1910.

—— *Rio Branco e a Política Exterior do Brazil.* 2 vols. Rio de Janeiro: Oficinas Gráficas do Jornal do Brasil, 1945.
An important study of the ministry of Rio-Branco and its accomplishments.

Accioly, Hildebrando. "O Barão do Rio-Branco e a 2ª Conferência da Haia," *Revista do Instituto Histórico e Georgráfico Brasileiro,* CLXXXVII (April–June, 1945), 61–104.
An interesting study of one of the most important events in modern Brazilian diplomatic history. The article was published the same year in separata by the Ministry of Foreign Relations.

—— "Rui Barbosa na Segunda Conferência da Haia," *Revista do Instituto Histórico e Geográfico Brasileiro,* CCXXXVII (Oct.–Dec., 1957), 164–77.
This is the companion piece to the above-mentioned article on the role of Rio-Branco at The Hague.

Alberdi, Juan Bautista. *El Brasil ante la democracia de América: Las disensiones de las repúblicas del Plata y las maquinaciones del Brasil.* Buenos Aires, 1946.

Albuquerque, Matheus de. "Rio Branco," *Jornal de Alagoas,* X (Maceió, Feb. 10, 1917), 1.

Albuquerque, Sargento. *A Cilada Argentina Contra o Brasil.* Rio de Janeiro: Editores Monitor Mercantil, 1917.
An outstanding example of the jingoist opinion of the period and Brazilian distrust of Argentina.

Alencar, Fernando Ramos de. "Some Postulates of Brazilian Foreign Policy," *Brazilian-American Survey,* XII (1960), 6–7.

Almanaque Brasileiro Garnier. Nos. 1–10. Rio de Janeiro, 1903–12.
Valuable for an insight into the period. It contains monetary conversion tables, statistics, biographies, comments on the year's most important events, photographs, etc.

Alvarez, Alejandro. *The Monroe Doctrine.* New York: Oxford University Press, 1924.

Amado, Gilberto. *Rio-Branco.* Rio de Janeiro: Impr. Nacional, 1947.

Amaral, Angelo de. "Política Internacional," *Jornal do Commercio* (Rio de Janeiro), Jan. 13, 1910.

Amaral, Luís Gurgel do. *Cousas Idas e Vividas.* Rio de Janeiro: São José, 1959.

——*O Meu Velho Itamarati.* Rio de Janeiro: Impr. Nacional, 1947.

An interesting account of a young secretary in Itamaraty during the Rio-Branco ministry. He sets the stage for the study of the Rio-Branco ministry.

"American Capital in Brazil," *Scientific American,* LXXX (Jan. 28, 1899), 53.

Andrade, Rodrigo M. F. de. *Rio-Branco e Gastão da Cunha.* Rio de Janeiro: Impr. Nacional, 1953.

Anthouard, Albert François Ildefonse d', baron. *Le Progrès Brésilien.* Paris: Plon, 1911.

Antunes, Deoclécio de Paranhos. *História do Grande Chanceler.* Vol. LIII, Biblioteca Militar. Rio de Janeiro: Gráficos Bloch, 1942.

Associação Commercial de Amazonas. *State of the Amazonas, Brazil.* New York, 1912.

A useful guide to the Amazon of the period with many statistics.

Assumpção, Roberto. "Rio-Branco e 'L'Illustration,' " *Revista do Instituto Histórico e Geográfico Brasileiro,* CLXXXVIII (July–Sept., 1945), 10–13.

Avellar, Vicente. *O Barão do Rio Branco e o Brazil.* Rio de Janeiro: Impr. Gutenberg, 1909.

Azambuja, Graciano A. de. "Biografia," *Revista do O Jornal* (Rio de Janeiro), April 22, 1945, pp. 1, 6–8.

Baldwin, Elbert F. "The Brazil of Today," *The Outlook,* XCIV (Oct. 21, 1911), 424–27.

"O Barão do Rio Branco e o 'Jornal do Commercio,' " *Jornal do Commercio* (Rio de Janeiro), April 21, 1957, p. 2.

An acknowledgment of the contributions, direct and indirect, which the Baron frequently made to the *Jornal* while he was minister.

"El Barón de Rio Branco, Figura Continental," *Toda América* (Buenos Aires, 1945).

A special edition of this magazine was dedicated to the Baron and his accomplishments.

Barreto, Carlos Xavier Paes. *Rio Branco, O Geógrafo.* Rio de Janeiro: Editora Minerva, 1947.

The influence and use of geography in the ministry of Rio-Branco.

Basdevant, J. *La Conférence de Rio-de-Janeiro de 1906 et l'union internationale des Républiques américaines.* Paris: A. Pedone, 1908.

Bastos, Humerto. *A Economia Brasileira e o Mundo Moderno.* São Paulo: Livraria Martins Editôra, 1948.

Bello, José Maria. *História da República*. São Paulo: Companhia Editôra Nacional, 1959.
Considered one of the best histories of the republic, this book places the Rio-Branco ministry in its proper context.
Bennett, Frank. *Forty Years in Brazil*. London: Mills & Boon, 1914.
The emphasis is on the commercial aspects of Brazil.
Bernárdez, Manuel. *Le Brésil: Sa Vie, Son Travail, Son Avenir*. Buenos Aires: Ortega y Radaelli, 1908.
A Spanish edition appeared at the same time. A favorable view of Brazil and Rio-Branco by a Spanish American.
Bernstein, Harry. *Modern and Contemporary Latin America*. New York: Lippincott, 1952.
The best history of the republic in English.
Besouchet, Lidia. *Rio-Branco e as Relações entre o Brasil e a República Argentina*. Rio de Janeiro: Impr. Nacional, 1949.
Written for political purposes with little regard for historical context or the whole truth. It gives a false picture of cordial relations between the two countries when the relations were tense and unpleasant most of the time.
Bevilaqua, Clovis. *Direito Público Internacional*. Rio de Janeiro: F. Alves, 1911.
Contains an interesting commentary on the Alsop case.
—— "A Educação Histórica do Barão do Rio-Branco Explica a Extensão de sua influencia na Vida Nacional do Brasil," *Revista Americana,* IV (April, 1913), 14–17.
Bingham, H. *Across South America*. Boston: Houghton Mifflin, 1911.
It provides good information on Brazilian trade of the period.
Bittencourt, Feijó. "Quem Escreveu e Como Escreveu Acerca do Barão do Rio Branco," *Revista do Instituto Histórico e Geográfico Brasileiro,* CLXXXVII (April–June, 1945), 3–60.
Contrary to what the title indicates, this is not a bibliographical essay although several books and articles are mentioned and quoted.
Bittencourt, Liberato. *Psicologia do Barão do Rio Branco*. Rio de Janeiro, 1913.
Botelho, A. Roberto de Arruda. *Le Brésil et ses Relations Extérieures*. Paris: Les Editions Mazarines, 1935.
"Brazil and the United States," *The Living Age,* 7th series, LXI (Oct. 11, 1913), 191–20.

Brazilian Society of International Law. *The Monroe Doctrine Centenary.* Rio de Janeiro: Typ. do Jornal do Commercio, 1924.

"Brazil's Quarter Century," *The Nation,* XCIX (Nov. 26, 1914), 622–23.

Bryan, William Jennings. "My Visit to Brazil, the Giant of South America," New York *World* (June 19, 1910), Magazine Section, p. 5.

Bryce, James. *South America: Observations and Impressions.* New York: Macmillan, 1912.

His views on Brazil during the Rio-Branco ministry deserve consideration.

Buley, E. C. *North Brazil.* London: Pitman & Sons, 1914.

Burns, E. Bradford. "A Bibliographical Essay on the Baron of Rio-Branco and His Ministry," *Inter-American Review of Bibliography,* XIV (Oct–Dec., 1964), 406–14.

—— "Rio-Branco e o Reconhecimento do Panamá," *Jornal do Commercio,* March 1, 1963, p. 4–5.

—— "Rio-Branco e sua política externa," *Revista da História,* XXVIII (April–June, 1964), 367–82.

—— "Rio-Branco Visto pelos seus Contemporáneos Norteamericanos," *Jornal do Commercio,* Aug. 11, 1962, p. 4.

Burr, Robert N. "The Balance of Power in Nineteenth-Century South America: An Exploratory Essay," *Hispanic American Historical Review,* XXXV (Feb., 1955), 37–60.

A valuable introduction to intra-South American diplomacy and an essential study for South American international relations.

—— *The Stillborn Panama Congress.* Berkeley: University of California Press, 1962.

The initial chapters continue the study of the balance of power in South America found in the above-mentioned article.

Calmon, Pedro, "O Barão do Rio Branco," *Ilustração Brasileira,* CII (Rio de Janeiro, Oct. 1943), 5–11.

—— *Brasil e América.* Rio de Janeiro: José Olympio, 1944.

—— *História Diplomática do Brasil.* Belo Horizonte: Livraria Ed. Paulo Bluhm, 1941.

—— *História do Brasil.* Vol. V: *A República.* São Paulo: Companhia Editôra Nacional, 1956.

Calógeras, João Pandiá. *Estudos Históricos e Políticos (res nostra . . .).* 2d ed. São Paulo: Companhia Editôra Nacional, 1936.

—— *Rio-Branco e a Política Exterior*. Rio de Janeiro: Impr. Nacional, 1916.
A valuable introduction to the Rio-Branco ministry.

Cardim, Elmano. "A Imprensa na Vida e na Obra de Rio Branco," *Revista do Instituto Histórico e Geográfico Brasileiro*, CLXXXVIII (July–Sept., 1945), 123–37.

Carneiro, David. *Duas Histórias em Três Vidas*. Curitiba, Paraná: Universal, 1939.

—— *Galeria de Ontem e de Hoje*. Curitiba, Paraná: Vanguarda, 1963.

Carneiro, Fernandes Levi. *Discursos e Conferências*. Rio de Janeiro: Editôra Sul Americana, 1954.
This book contains an excellent essay on Rio-Branco entitled "Rio-Branco e 'a sempre tão limpa e generosa Política internacional do Brasil.' "

—— "Rio-Branco e seu Espírito de Tradição," *Revista do Instituto Histórico e Geográfico Brasileiro*, CLXXXVIII (July–Sept., 1945), 113–22.

Carvalho, A. de A. Mello. "El más distinguido de los brasileños— Necrologio Político (Versión)," *Revista Americana*, IV (April, 1913), 191–96.

Carvalho, Afonso de. *Rio-Branco*. Rio de Janeiro: Editôria Biblioteca Militar, 1945.

Carvalho, Delgado de. *História Diplomática do Brasil*. São Paulo: Companhia Editôra Nacional, 1959.
The best diplomatic history of Brazil.

Centro Cívico Sete de Setembro. *À Memória do Barão do Rio Branco*. Rio de Janeiro: Impr. Nacional, 1912.

Chamberlain, George. "A Letter from Brazil," *Atlantic Monthly*, XC (Dec., 1902), 821–31.

—— "Our Neglect of South American Markets," *North American Review*, CLXXXI (July, 1905), 117–22.

Classe Acadêmica do Rio de Janeiro. *À Memória do Barão do Rio Branco*. Rio de Janeiro: Impr. Nacional, 1912.

Clemenceau, Georges. "Brazil," New York *Times* (April 23, 1911), Magazine Section, p. 5.

—— *South America Today*. New York: G. P. Putnam's Sons, 1911.

Correia, Oswaldo Moraes. "Rio Branco e a Política Exterior do Brasil," *Revista do Instituto Histórico e Geográfico Brasileiro*, CLXXXVII (April–June, 1945), 163–72.

Costa, João Cruz. *Esbozo de una Historia de las Ideas en el Brasil.* Mexico City: Fondo de Cultura Económica, 1957.
This book provides the intellectual background for the period. The original Portuguese-language edition contains more details.
Costa, João Frank da. "Rio Branco, Nabuco e o americanismo," *Jornal do Commercio,* Feb. 18, 1962, 2º Caderno, pp. 1 and 5.
One of the best brief analyses of Rio-Branco's foreign policy.
Delgado, Luiz. *Rui Barbosa.* Rio de Janeiro, 1945.
Denis, Pierre. *Brazil.* New York: Charles Scribner's Sons, 1911.
Diário de Notícias. *Brasil-Estado Unidos.* Rio de Janeiro: Diário de Notícias, 1939.
A collection of articles and essays published in 1938 in the *Diário de Notícias* about Brazilian-American relations. They vary widely in quality.
Dias, Demósthenes de Oliveira. *Pequena Biografia do Barão do Rio-Branco.* Rio de Janeiro: Editôra "A Noite," 1945.
Domville-Fife, Charles W. *The United States of Brazil.* London: Francis Griffiths, 1910.
Eça, Raul d'. "Joaquim Nabuco nos Estados Unidos," *Revista do Instituto Brasil-Estados Unidos,* VII (Rio de Janeiro, July–Dec., 1949), 43–61.
Elliott, L. E. *Brazil Today and Tomorrow.* New York: Macmillan, 1917.
Espanet, A. d'. *Barão do Rio Branco.* Rio de Janeiro: Impr. Nacional, 1911.
Fernándes, Anibal. *Nabuco, Cidadão do Recife.* Recife, 1949.
Ferreira, Manoel Rodrigues. *A Ferrovia do Diabo.* São Paulo: Edições Melhoramentos, 1959.
Ferreira Filho, Cosme. *A Borracha na Economia Amazônica.* Manaus, 1952.
Fleiuss, Max. *Rio-Branco.* Rio de Janeiro, 1931.
Franca, Antônio. *Modernismo Brasileiro.* Recife: Edições Região, 1959.
Freyre, Gilberto. *Ordem e Progresso.* 2 vols. Rio de Janeiro: José Olympio, 1959.
The best social history of the Rio-Branco period.
Ganns, Cláudio. "Contribuição para o Estudo de Rio Branco," *Revista do Instituto Histórico e Geográfico Brasileiro,* CLXXXVII (April–June, 1945), 186–246.
An indispensable bibliography.

Ganzert, Frederic W. "The Baron do Rio Branco, Joaquim Nabuco, and the Growth of Brazilian-American Friendship, 1900–1910," *Hispanic American Historical Review,* XXII (Aug., 1942), 432–51.

—— "The Boundary Controversy in the Upper Amazon Between Brazil, Bolivia, and Peru, 1903–1909," *Hispanic American Historical Review,* XIV (Nov., 1934), 427–49.

—— "José Maria da Silva Paranhos, Baron do Rio Branco," *Bulletin of the Pan American Union* (Washington, March, 1937), pp. 231–38.

Gentil, Alcides. *O Brasil e o Internacionalismo.* Rio de Janeiro: Ed. Jacintho Silva, 1913.

Godoi, Juansilvano. *El Barón de Río Branco.* Asunción, 1912.

Godoi served for three months in 1911 as Paraguayan minister to Brazil. He knew and admired Rio-Branco.

—— "El Barón de Río Branco," *Revista Americana,* IV (April, 1913), 4–13.

Gorostiaga, Manuel. "Argentina-Brazil-Chile," *El Diario* (Buenos Aires), Jan. 8, 1910, p. 8.

—— "Rio-Branco," *El Economista Argentino,* XXII (May 31, 1913), 2.

—— "Rio Branco," *Revista Americana,* IV (April, 1913), 22–26.

Gosálvez, Raúl Botelho. *Proceso del Imperialismo del Brasil.* Buenos Aires: La Compañía Impresora Argentina, 1960.

Goycochêa, Luis Felippe de Castilhos. *Assiz Brasil.* Porto Alegre: Publicações da Academia Riograndense de Letras, 1941.

The only study of one of the most important diplomats of the Old Republic.

Guimarães, Argeu. *Diccionário Bio-Bibliográphico Brasileiro de Diplomacia, Política Externa e Direito Internacional.* Rio de Janeiro, 1938.

A valuable commentary on all of the important diplomats and personalities of the Rio-Branco period.

Guimarães, Arthur. *Actualidades Brasileiras.* Porto, Portugal, 1915.

Guimarães, Mário. *Política Exterior do Brasil.* Mimeographed. San José, Costa Rica, 1956.

Gutiérrez, Alberto. *Hombres y Cosas de Ayer.* La Paz: Impr. Velarde, 1918.

Hale, Albert. *The South Americans.* Indianapolis: Bobbs-Merrill, 1907.

—— "The South American Situation," *The Reader,* VIII (Oct., 1906), 458–74.

Hambloch, Ernest. *British Consul: Memories of Thirty Years' Service in Europe and Brazil.* London: Harrap and Co., 1938.
An informative, English view of the Baron with some interesting sidelights on his personality.

Hart, Albert Bushnell. *The Monroe Doctrine: An Interpretation.* Boston: Little, Brown & Co., 1916.

Hawes, James W. "The New Constitution of Brazil," *Overland Monthly,* XIX (Feb., 1892), 161–68.

Hill, Lawrence F., ed. *Brazil.* Berkeley: University of California Press, 1947.
This book contains several chapters on diplomacy.

—— *Diplomatic Relations Between the United States and Brazil.* Durham, N.C.: Duke University Press, 1932.

Hilton, Ronald. "Joaquim Nabuco e os Estados Unidos," *Revista do Instituto Brasil-Estados Unidos,* VII (Rio de Janeiro, July–Dec., 1949), 26–43.

Holborn, Hajo. *The Political Collapse of Europe.* New York: Alfred A. Knopf, 1951.

Hull, W. I. *Two Hague Conferences and Their Contributions to International Law.* Boston: Ginn & Co., 1908.

—— *The United States and Latin America at The Hague.* International Conciliation Pamphlet No. 44, New York, 1911.

Inman, Samuel Guy. *Problems in Pan Americanism.* New York: Doran Co., 1921.

Ireland, Gordon. *Boundaries, Possessions, and Conflicts in South America.* Cambridge, Mass.: Harvard University Press, 1938.

James, Preston E. *Latin America.* 3d ed., rev. New York: Odyssey Press, 1950.

Jessup, Philip C. *Elihu Root.* 2 vols. New York: Dodd, Mead & Co., 1938.

Jorge, A. G. de Araujo. *Ensaios de História Diplomática do Brasil no Regímen Repúblicano, 1889–1902.* Rio de Janeiro: Impr. Nacional, 1912.

—— *Ensaios de História e Crítica.* Rio de Janeiro: Min. de Relações Exteriores, 1948.

—— *Introdução às Obras do Barão do Rio-Branco.* Rio de Janeiro: Impr. Nacional, 1945.

This book provides a wealth of information and some interpretation by a former secretary of Rio-Branco.

Kelsey, Vera. *Seven Keys to Brazil.* New York: Funk & Wagnalls, 1941.

Koebel, W. H. *British Exploits in South America.* New York: The Century Co., 1917.

Lacerda, Virgínia Côrtes de, and Regina Monteiro Real. *Rui Barbosa em Haia.* Rio de Janeiro: Casa de Rui Barbosa, 1957.

A bibliography of all material dealing with Brazil at the Second Hague Conference. It contains a list of correspondence between Rui Barbosa and Rio-Branco on the subject.

Lacombe, Américo Jacobina. *Rio-Branco e Rui Barbosa.* Rio de Janeiro, n.d.

Laet, Carlos de. "Rio Branco," *Revista Americana,* IV (April, 1913), 18–21.

Lascano, Víctor. *Argentine Foreign Policy in America.* "University of Miami, Hispanic American Studies," No. 2 (Jan., 1941). Coral Gables, Fla.: University of Miami Press, 1941.

Lawrence, T. J. *International Problems and Hague Conferences.* London: Dent & Co., 1908.

Leão, Múcio. *Salvador de Mendonça.* Rio de Janeiro: Tupy, 1952.

Lee, Joseph Jenkins. "Trials of an American Syndicate in South America," *Harper's Weekly,* XLVII (May 30, 1903), 919–21.

Lima, Manoel de Oliveira. *The Evolution of Brazil Compared with That of Spanish and Anglo-Saxon America.* Stanford, Calif.: Stanford University Press, 1914.

—— *The Relations of Brazil with the United States.* International Conciliation Pamphlet No. 69. New York, 1913.

Lins, Alvaro. *Rio-Branco.* 2 vols. Rio de Janeiro: José Olympio, 1945. One of the two best biographies of Rio-Branco.

Lobo, Hélio. *Brasilianos & Yankees.* Rio de Janeiro: Pimenta de Mello, 1926.

—— *Cousas Diplomáticas.* Rio de Janeiro: Leite Ribeiro & Maurillo, 1918.

—— *De Monroe a Rio-Branco.* Rio de Janeiro: Impr. Nacional, 1912.

—— *O Pan-Americanismo e o Brasil.* São Paulo, 1939.

—— *A Paso de Gigante.* Rio de Janeiro: Impr. Nacional, 1925.

—— "As Relações entre os Estados Unidos e o Brasil," *Revista Americana,* VII (Nov., 1917), 79–102.

Lugo, Américo. *La Cuarta Conferencia Internacional Americana.* Sevilla: Diaz, 1912.

Lyra, A. Tavares de. "Rio Branco e o Instituto Histórico e Geográfico Brasileiro," *Revista do Instituto Histórico e Geográfico Brasileiro,* CLXXXVI (Jan.–March, 1945), 3–38.

Lyra, Heitor. *Ensaios Diplomáticos.* São Paulo: Monteiro Lobata & Cia., 1922.

—— *História Diplomática e Política Internacional.* Rio de Janeiro, 1941.

Lyra Filho, João. *O Barão.* Rio de Janeiro: Alba, 1936.

McGann, Thomas F. *Argentina, the United States, and the Inter-American System, 1880–1914.* Cambridge, Mass.: Harvard University Press, 1957.

Maior, Souto. "O Novo Brasil e o Barão do Rio-Branco," *Jornal do Commercio,* April 20, 1910, p. 2.

Manchester, Alan K. *British Preeminence in Brazil: Its Rise and Decline.* Chapel Hill, N.C.: University of North Carolina Press, 1933.

Mangabeira, João. *Rui—O Estadista da República.* Rio de Janeiro, 1943.

Melby, John. "Rubber River: An Account of the Rise and Collapse of the Amazon Boom," *Hispanic American Historical Review,* XXII (Aug., 1942), 452–69.

Mello, Afonso de Toledo Bandeira de. *Politique Commerciale du Brésil.* Rio de Janeiro: Impr. Nacional, 1935.

Melo, Rubens Ferreira de. *Textos de Direito Internacional e de História Diplomática.* Rio de Janeiro: A. Coelho Branco, 1950.

Mendonça, Carlos Sussekind de. *Salvador de Mendonça.* Rio de Janeiro: Empr. Grafica da Revista dos Tribunais, 1960.
The best biography of the precursor of the Brazilian-American rapprochement.

Mendonça, Salvador de. *A Situação Internacional do Brazil.* Rio de Janeiro: Livraria Garnier, 1913.

Mérou, Martín García. *El Brasil Intelectual.* Buenos Aires: Félix Lajouane, Editor, 1900.
An Argentine interpretation of Brazilian cultural history.

Ministerio das Relações Exteriores. *Arquivo Histórico do Itamaraty,* Rio de Janeiro: Impr. Nacional, 1952.
An excellent general guide to what is contained in the Historical Archives of Itamaraty. An essential catalogue for consulting those archives.

—— *Bibliografia de Joaquim Nabuco*. Rio de Janeiro: Impr. Nacional, 1949.

Moog, Clodomir Viana. *Bandeirantes e Pioneiros*. Rio de Janeiro: Editôra Globo, 1957.

Moore, John Bassett. *Brazil and Peru Boundary Question*. New York: Knickerbocker Press, 1904.

—— "Rio-Branco," *Revista Americana,* IV (July–Aug., 1913), 39–41.

Moraga, Oscar Espinosa. *El Aislamiento de Chile*. Santiago: Nascimento, 1961.

Morse, Richard M. *From Community to Metropolis: A Biography of Sao Paulo, Brazil*. Gainesville, Fla.: University of Florida Press, 1958.

Motto, Rocque da. *Rio-Branco, Cincuentario de su Muerte*. Montevideo: Revista Cultural Intercambio, 1963.

Miller, Lauro. "Elógio do Barão do Rio Branco," *Revista Americana,* VI (Aug.–Sept., 1917), 11–35.

Nabuco, Caroline. *The Life of Joaquim Nabuco*. Stanford: Stanford University Press, 1950.

Nabuco, Joaquim. "The American Conscience and American Public Opinion," *Supplement to the Annals of the American Academy of Social Science* (May, 1906), pp. 14–16.

—— *The Approach of the Two Americas*. International Conciliation Pamphlet No. 10. New York, 1908.

—— *Lessons and Prophecies of the Third Pan-American Conference*. 1907.

—— *Lincoln's World Influence*. 1906.

—— *Minha Formação*. Rio de Janeiro: José Olympio, 1957.

—— *The Spirit of Nationality in the History of Brazil*. New Haven, Conn.: Yale University Press, 1908.

Nabuco, Maurício. *Algumas Reflexões Sôbre Diplomacia*. Rio de Janeiro: Pongetti, 1945.

Napoleão, Aluízio. *Os Arquivos Particulares do Itamaratí*. Rio de Janeiro: Impr. Nacional, 1940.

A guide to the private archives contained in Itamaraty.

—— *Rio Branco e as Relações entre o Brasil e os Estados Unidos*. Rio de Janeiro: Impr. Nacional, 1945.

Expository rather than interpretive. Although it is incomplete, the book should be consulted for a study of the diplomatic relations between the two countries.

—— *O Segundo Rio-Branco.* Rio de Janeiro, 1940.

—— "A Tribute to Barão do Rio Branco," *Brazil* (July, 1945), pp. 8–9.

Nunes, Reginaldo. *As Duas Conferências de Haia.* Rio de Janeiro: Forense, 1958.

Oakenfall, J. C. *Brazil in 1909.* Paris, 1909.

The emphasis is on the commercial aspects; statistics and prices are given.

—— *Brazil in 1911.* Frome, England, 1912.

—— *Brazil in 1913.* Frome, England, 1914.

—— *Brazil, Past, Present, and Future.* London, 1919.

Contains a wealth of statistical and commercial data.

Octavio, Rodrigo. *Rasgos de la Política Internacional del Brasil en América.* Havana: El Siglo XX, 1925.

O.N.B. [Otávio Nascimento Brito]. *Brasil e Estados Unidos da America.* Rio de Janeiro, 1930.

The first part contains the article "O Brasil, Os Estados Unidos e O Monroismo," by Rio-Branco, with notations by O.N.B. The second part is a commentary entitled "De Rio Branco aos Nossas Dias."

Orlando, Arthur. *Pan-Americanismo.* Rio de Janeiro: Typ. do Jornal do Commercio, 1906.

Ortega, A. Nuñez. *Memorias sobre las Relaciones Diplomáticas de México con los Estados Libres y Sobernos de la America del Sur.* Mexico City: Imprenta del Gobierno, 1878.

Paulo Filho, M. *Ensaios e Estudos.* Rio de Janeiro: Livraria Freitas Bastos, 1961.

It contains a valuable essay entitled "Rio Branco e Nabuco" which discusses the relations between the foreign minister and his ambassador.

Pereira, Baptista. *Directrizes de Ruy Barbosa.* Sao Paulo, 1938.

—— *Ruy Barbosa, Catálogo das suas Obras.* Rio de Janeiro, 1929.

Perkins, Dexter. *Hands Off: A History of the Monroe Doctrine.* Boston: Little, Brown & Co., 1948.

—— *The Monroe Doctrine, 1823–1826.* Cambridge, Mass.: Harvard University Press, 1932.

Pires, Homero. *Anglo-American Political Influences on Rui Barbosa.* Rio de Janeiro: Gráfica Olímpica, 1949.

Piza, Gabriel de Toledo. *Incident Piza-Rio Branco, Grave Situation Politique au Brésil.* Paris, 1912.

Quesada, Vicente G. *Mís Memorias Diplomáticas.* 2 vols. Buenos Aires: Impr. de Coni Hermano, 1907.

Reid, Douglas. "Barão do Rio Branco—Lawyer, Historian, Statesman," *Brazilian-American Survey,* XII (1960), 31–32.

Reinsch, Paul S. "The Third International Conference of American States," *American Political Science Review,* I (Feb., 1907), 187–99.

Ribeiro, Adalberto Mário. *O Centenário do Barão do Rio Branco.* Rio de Janeiro: Impr. Nacional, 1945.

Rio, João do. "A Minha Primeira Entrevista e o Meu Primeiro Pedido," *Revista Americana,* Vol. IV (April, 1913).

A young man's first favorable impressions of the Baron.

Rio-Branco, José Maria da Silva Paranhos, barão do. *Brazil, the United States, and the Monroe Doctrine.* Rio de Janeiro: Jornal do Commercio, Jan. 20, 1908.

The English translation of the 1906 article by Rio-Branco emphasizing the historically friendly relations between the United States and Brazil.

—— *Obras do Barão do Rio-Branco.* 9 vols. Rio de Janeiro: Impr. Nacional, 1945–48.

Volume IX is the most important. It contains all the speeches made by the Baron, including some foreign policy statements.

—— *Relações Exteriores do Brasil durante a Administração do Presidente Rodrigues Alves.* Rio de Janeiro: Typ. do Jornal do Commercio, 1906.

The same as "O Dr. Rodrigues Alves, O Seu Governo, 1902–1906—III—Exterior—Politica Internacional," *Diário Oficial,* XLV (Nov. 15, 1906), 6157–72. It is Rio-Branco's account of the diplomatic highlights of the four-year administration of Rodrigues Alves.

Rio-Branco, Paul do. *Reminiscências do Barão do Rio-Branco.* Rio de Janeiro: José Olympio, 1942.

Rippy, J. Fred. *Latin America and the Industrial Age.* 2d ed. New York: G. P. Putnam's, 1947.

—— *Latin America in World Politics.* 3d ed. New York: F. S. Crofts & Co., 1938.

Rivas, Angel César. "El Barón de Rio-Branco," *Revista Americana,* Vol. IV (July–Aug., 1913).

Rocha, Júlio. *O Acre.* Lisbon: Minerva Lusitânia, 1903.

Rocha, Pinto da. "O Barão do Rio-Branco e o Direito Internacional," *Revista Americana,* IV (April, 1913), 27–34.

Rodó, José Enrique. "Rio-Branco," *Revista Americana,* IV (April, 1913), 181–83.

Rodrigues, José Honório. "The Foundations of Brazil's Foreign Policy," *International Affairs,* XXXVIII (London, July, 1962), 324–38. An important general introduction to the historical aims of Brazil's foreign policy.

—— *Teoria da História do Brasil.* São Paulo: Inst. Progresso Editorial, 1949.

Prado, Víctor N. Romero del. *Argentina y Brasil en la Obra Panamericanista.* Córdoba, Argentina: Imprenta de la Universidad, 1939.

Roosevelt, Theodore. *Through the Brazilian Wilderness.* London: J. Murray, 1914.

Sandberg, Harry O. "Mission of Dr. Lauro S. Muller to the United States," *Bulletin of the Pan American Union,* XXXVII (July, 1913), 1–31.

Sanz, Luís Santiago. *La Cuestión de Misiones.* Buenos Aires: Ed. Ciencias Económicas, 1957. The Argentine side of the Missions dispute told from a very fair point of view.

Scott, James Brown. *The Hague Peace Conferences of 1899 and 1907.* Vol. I. Baltimore: Johns Hopkins Press, 1909.

—— *The Proceedings of the Hague Peace Conferences: The Conference of 1907.* New York: Oxford University Press, 1920.

Sensabaugh, Leon F. "The Coffee-Trust Question in United States-Brazilian Relations: 1912–13" *Hispanic American Historical Review,* XXVI (Nov., 1946), 480–96.

Serpa, Phocion. "O Apóstolo da Paz," *Revista Iberoamericana,* X (March, 1946), 407–11.

"Sessão Solene Comemorativa do Primeiro Centenário do Nascimento do Barão do Rio-Branco. Discursos e Palestras," *Revista do Instituto Histórico e Geográfico de Minas Gerais,* II (1945), 3–24.

Shepherd, William R. "The Pan-American Conference at Buenos Ayres," *Columbia University Quarterly,* XIII (June, 1911), 299–308.

Silveira, Alfredo Balthazar da. *Barão do Rio Branco.* Rio de Janeiro: Impr. Nacional, 1956.

Soares, A. Teixeira. "O Barão do Rio Branco e a Diplomacia Brasileira," *Revista do Instituto Histórico e Geográfico Brasileiro,* CLXXXVII (April–June, 1945), 175–85.
Published in expanded form the following year in Porto Alegre. It is a reasonably good essay, more expository than interpretive, on the diplomacy of Rio-Branco.

Soares, José Carlos de Macedo. *Discursos Rumos da Diplomacia Brasileira.* Rio de Janeiro: José Olympio, 1937.

Souza, Carlos Martins Pereira de. "O Barão que Eu Conheci," *Jornal do Commercio,* Feb. 18, 1962, 2° caderno, pp. 1–2.

Souza, J. P. Coelho de. *O Pensamento Político de Assis Brasil.* Rio de Janeiro: José Olympio, 1958.

Stanford University. *Stanford Conference on Brazil, May 28–30, 1950, Conference Report.* Stanford: Stanford University Press, 1950.

The Statistician and Economist, 1903–04. San Francisco: L. P. McCarty, 1903–4.

Stead, William T. *O Brazil em Haya.* Rio de Janeiro: M. Piedade & Cia, 1908.

Stuart, Graham H. *Latin America and the United States.* 5th ed. New York: Appleton-Century Crofts, Inc., 1955.

Thomas, David Y. *One Hundred Years of the Monroe Doctrine, 1823–1923.* New York: Macmillan Company, 1923.

Tinoco, Brígido. *A Vida de Nilo Peçanha.* Rio de Janeiro: José Olympio, 1962.

Tocantins, Leandro. *Acre, Rio Branco e Espírito Luso.* Rio de Janeiro: SPVEA, 1962.

—— *Formação Histórica do Acre.* 3 vols. Rio de Janeiro: Conquista, 1961. A well-written, solid, and definitive history of Acre.

Travassos, Mário. *Projeção Continental do Brasil.* São Paulo, 1935.

Truda, P. de Leonardo. *O Brasil e a Doutrina de Monroe.* São Paulo: Monteiro Lobato, 1924.

Trueblood, Benjamin F. *The Two Hague Conferences and Their Results.* Washington, D.C.: American Peace Society, 1914.

Turner, Charles William. *Ruy Barbosa, Brazilian Crusader for the Essential Freedoms.* New York: Abingdon-Cokesbury Press, 1945.

Vasconcellos, Mário de. *O Itamaraty e o Barão.* Rio de Janeiro: Impr. Nacional, 1943.

—— *Motivos de História Diplomática do Brasil.* Rio de Janeiro: Impr. Nacional, 1930.

Vasconcellos, Mário de Barros e. *O Barão do Rio-Branco.* Rio de Janeiro, 1954.

Vega, M. C. Blanch González de la. *Brasil en el Corazón de los Argentinos.* Buenos Aires: Impr. Lopez, 1937.

Venáncio Filho, Francisco. *Rio Branco e Euclides da Cunha.* Rio de Janeiro: Impr. Nacional, 1946.

Verrill, A. Hyatt. *South and Central American Trade Conditions of To-day.* New York: Dodd, Mead & Co., 1914.

Viana Filho, Luiz. "A Morte do Barão," *Jornal do Commercio,* Feb. 18, 1962, 2° caderno, 1.

—— *Rui e Nabuco.* Rio de Janeiro, 1949.

—— *A Vida do Barão do Rio Branco.* Rio de Janeiro: José Olympio, 1959.

The best biography of Rio-Branco. It is well written and based entirely on primary sources. The biography provides a wealth of information on Rio-Branco, his contemporaries, and Brazil.

—— *A Vida de Joaquim Nabuco.* São Paulo: Companhia Editôra Nacional, 1952.

—— *A Vida de Rui Barbosa.* São Paulo: Companhia Editôra Nacional, 1960.

Vianna, Hélio. *História Diplomática do Brasil.* São Paulo: Edições Melhoramentos, n.d.

—— *História das Fronteiras do Brasil.* Rio de Janeiro: Gráfica Laemmert, 1949.

Vidal, Armando. "Relações Políticas e Econômicas Entre o Brasil e os Estados Unidos," *Revista do Instituto Brasil-Estados Unidos,* Vol. I (Rio de Janeiro, May, 1943).

Vidal, Barros. "Getúlio Vargas e Rio Branco," *Jornal do Commercio,* Feb. 18, 1962, 2° caderno, p. 5.

Vilaça, Antônio Carlos. *Perfil de um Estadista da República: Ensaio Biográfico do Barão do Rio Branco.* Rio de Janeiro: Est. Gráficos Muniz, 1945.

Wagley, Charles. "Brazil," in *Most of the World,* ed. Ralph Linton. New York: Columbia University Press, 1949.

Washington, S. Walter. *A Study of the Causes of Hostility Toward the*

United States in Latin America: Argentina. Department of State External Research Paper No. 126.2. Washington: Government Printing Office, 1957.

—— *A Study of the Causes of Hostility Toward the United States in Latin America: Brazil.* Department of State External Research Paper No. 126. Washington: Government Printing Office, 1956.

Wilgus, A. Curtis. *A Brief Survey of the Political Relations Between Brazil and the United States.* Latin American Economic Institute Publication No. 2. Boston, n.d.

—— "The Third International Conference at Rio de Janeiro, 1906," *Hispanic American Historical Review,* XII (Nov., 1932), 420–56.

Wythe, George, Royce A. Wight, and Harold M. Midkiff. *Brazil: An Expanding Economy.* New York: Twentieth Century Fund, 1949.

Zeballos, E. S. *Conferencias Internacionales Americanas.* Valencia, Spain: Editorial Prometeo, n.d.

IV. UNPUBLISHED MATERIAL

Aragão, José Joaquim Moniz de. Personal interview on December 13, 1962, in Rio de Janeiro.

Dávila, Raul Bazán. "El Barón de Rio Branco." Manuscript copy of a speech given by Dávila when he was Chilean ambassador to Brazil, in the possession of the author.

Ganzert, Frederic William. "The Baron do Rio-Branco and Brazilian Foreign Relations." Unpublished Ph.D. dissertation, University of California, Berkeley, 1933.

Jorge, A. G. de Araujo. Personal interview on December 14, 1962, in Rio de Janeiro.

Lima, Manoel de Oliveira. I. "Modern Brazil in Its Political, Economic, and Social Aspects." II. "Brazil's Foreign Policy with Special Reference to the Neighboring Latin-American Republics." Aug. 3, 1922. III. "Brazil's Foreign Policy with Special Reference to Her Relations with the United States." Aug. 1 [*sic*], 1922. V. "Brazil's Economic and Financial Problems." Aug. 19, 1922. Lectures delivered at the Institute of Politics of Williams College during August, 1922. Manuscript copies found in the Oliveira Lima Library, The Catholic University of America, Washington, D.C.

McCarthy, Catherine Anna. "Latin American Attitudes Toward the

Monroe Doctrine as Shown by Argentina, Brazil, and Chile." Unpublished Master's essay, Columbia University, 1929.

Nabuco, Maurício. Personal interviews in November, December, 1962, and in January, February, 1963, in Rio de Janeiro.

Reis, Artur Cesar Ferreira. "Discurso Pronunciado sôbre o Barão do Rio-Branco, sua vida e obra." Speech given at Itamaraty on Feb. 14, 1962. Copy of the speech on file in the Historical Archives of Itamaraty.

Sensabaugh, Leon F. Unpublished manuscript on Brazil. In the process of being expanded and revised.

Stauffer, David Hall. "The Origin and Establishment of Brazil's Indian Service: 1889–1910." Unpublished Ph.D. dissertation, University of Texas, 1955.

A Portuguese translation of this dissertation, *Origim e Fundação do Serviço de Proteção dos Indios,* appeared in serialized form in the *Revista de História* (São Paulo) beginning with the Jan.–March, 1959, issue.

INDEX

Abranches, Dunshee de, 53, 148, 164, 176
Acre, 42–47, 93–95, 201, 219; dispute with Bolivia, 76–86 *passim,* 90, 114, 171, 183
Agadir Incident, 103
Alberdi, Juan Batista, 94
Albuquerque, Joaquim Arcoverde de, 50
Alcorta, José Figueroa, 184
Aldrich, Nelson Wilmarth, 66
Alexander III, Czar of Russia, 28
Alsop Company, 136–39 *passim,* 140, 179, 189
Alves, Constâncio, 32, 68, 69
Amapá, 32, 33, 85
Amazonas, 11–12
Amazon River, 11, 45, 80, 82, 83
American Chamber of Commerce for Brazil, 74
American Illusion, The (Prado), 61
Andrade, Baron Aguiar de, 30
Andrade, Neves, 25
Anthonard, Baron d', 197
Aragão, Moniz de, 53
Aramayo, Félix, 76
Aranha, José Pereira da Graça, 19, 98, 102–3, 176
Argentina, 1, 16, 22, 30, 33, 42, 50, 52, 55, 85, 88–90, 108, 120–22, 143, 144, 151, 153, 154, 155, 169, 181–87, 188, 190, 198, 208, 209
Arquivo do Barão do Rio-Branco, 27

Assis, Machado de, 19
Assis Brasil, J. F., 44, 51, 53, 77–79, 82, 83, 84, 90–97, 157
Asunción, 158, 175
Azambuja, Graciano de, 31

Bahia, 7, 15, 16, 22
Baltimore *Sun,* 104
Barbosa, Rui, 15, 54, 133, 141, 168, 239, 242, 255; and Hague Conference, 116–31 *passim,* 172
Barreto, Lima, 19
Barreto, Mena, 18
Belgium, 127
Bennett, Frank, 196
Berlin, 103–4
Bernárdez, Manuel, 56
Bernhardt, Sarah, 52
Beviláqua, Clovis, 148
Bezzi, Guido, 27
Bilac, Olavo, 19
Blaine, James G., 108, 156
Bogotá, 50
Bolivar, Simon de, 183
Bolivia, 42–46, 48, 76–86 *passim,* 108, 136, 171, 191, 204
Bolivian Syndicate, 76–78, 81–83, 95, 132, 136, 150
Braga, João Evangelista, 19
Brazil and Bolivia Boundary Settlement, 84
Brazil and Peru Boundary Question (Moore), 94

Brazilian Geographical and Historical Institute, 25, 28
British Guiana, 47, 48, 85, 161
Bryan, Charles Page, 78–79
Bryan, William Jennings, 52, 141, 142, 174, 176
Bryce, James, 56, 196, 197
Buchanan, William I., 77, 173, 239
Buenos Aires, 50, 89, 141, 154, 155, 184, 185, 188–89
Bulgaria, 143
Bunau-Varilla, Philippe, 88
Bureau of the American States, 110

Cabo Frio, Viscount of, 38
Caixa de Conversão, *see* Conversion Office
Calderón, Alvarez, 91
Calógeras, João Pandiá, 53, 54, 147, 161
Campista, David, 39
Campos, Bernardino, 9
Campos Salles, Manuel Ferraz de, 4, 5, 62, 183
Canaan (Aranha), 19
Caracas, 108, 142
Castro, Plácido de, 43
Caxias, Duque de, 25
Chávez, Bruno Gonçálvez, 50
Chicago *Tribune,* 104, 148
Chile, 1, 40, 52, 88–90, 108, 121–22, 135–39, 141, 143, 151, 153–55, 169, 175, 179, 181, 185, 189, 191–93, 198, 205
Choate, Joseph H., 118–20, 123, 125, 126–27, 129–30, 179
Cisplatine War, 25
Clemenceau, Georges, 52, 56, 197, 198
Cleveland, Grover, 30–32, 61, 85, 135
Cocoa, 63, 166
Coffee, 2–4, 10, 28, 53, 60, 62–67, 69, 166; and Brazilian politics, 4, 5, 7

Colombia, 48, 50, 86, 111
Congress of Americanists, 28
Constitution of 1891, 168
Convention of Taubaté, 8–10, 14, 64
Conversion Office, 13
Correia, Raymundo, 19
Correia, Rivadávia, 18
Correio de Manhã (Rio de Janeiro), 71, 87, 147, 149, 151
Costa Rica, 50, 89, 108
Court of Arbitration, 121
Cruz, Dr. Oswaldo, 6, 136
Cuba, 6, 50, 89, 152–53
Cunha, Euclides da, 19, 39, 53, 56
Cunha, Gastão da, 53, 122

Darío, Rubén, 113
Denis, Pierre, 197
Detroit *Free Press,* 31
Dewey, George, 177
Dingley Tariff, 61, 63
Dominican Republic, 50, 155
Domville-Fife, Charles W., 56, 196
Drago, Luís María, 120, 121
Drago Doctrine, 120, 128, 152
Dudley, Irving Bedell, 122, 129, 134, 137, 139, 141, 169
Du Pont, Henry Algernon, 66

Ecuador, 48, 50, 86, 144
Edward VII, King of England, 138
Efemerides Brasileiras (Rio-Branco), 29
Egypt, 51
Elkins, Stephen Benton, 66, 223
El Salvador, 50
Evans, Robley D., 132
Exposition of St. Petersburg, 28

Faria, Tersa de Figueiredo, 22
Federalist Papers, 58
Fernández, Julio, 184

Ferrero, Guglielmo, 52
First Commercial, Industrial, and Agricultural Congress of the Amazon, 67
First International Peace Conference, 116, 121
First Pan American Conference, 108–9, 156
Fonseca, Hermes da, 15–18, 29, 141, 186
Fonseca, Manuel Deodoro da, 15
Fourth Pan American Conference, 51, 154–55, 159
France, Anatole, 52
France, 32, 33, 198
French Guiana, 32, 42, 199

Gálvez, Luís, 43
Gama, Domício da, 51, 53, 62, 74, 141, 157, 255
Gazeta de Notícias (Rio de Janeiro), 69, 99, 162, 172
Germany, 16, 17, 73, 103–4, 121, 166
Gomes Ferreira, Alfredo, 51, 89, 91, 93, 99, 137
Gómez, Juan Vincente, 142–43
Gonçalvez, Barbosa, 18
Gorostiaga, Manuel, 186–87
Grande Encyclopédie, 28
Great Britain, 60, 62, 73, 76, 121–22, 126, 127, 161, 166, 168, 187, 194, 196, 198, 205
Greece, 51
Guatemala, 50, 86, 89
Guayaquil, 86
Gurgel do Amaral, Luís, 118, 120, 148

Haggard, Sir William, 195–96
Hague Conference, *see* Second International Peace Conference
Hague Permanent Tribunal, 144

Haiti, 50, 237
Hambloch, Ernest, 195–96
Hay, John, 78–79, 82, 88, 90–91, 102, 116, 169, 173, 219
History of the War of the Triple Alliance (Schneider), 27–28
Honduras, 50
Hopkins, E., 31
Huet de Cacellar, Duarte, 115

Iguaçú River, 186
Illustration, L' (Paris), 24
Immigration Service of Brazil (Paris), 29
Imprensa, A (Rio de Janeiro), 172
Inconfidência, 58
Indian Service, 14
International Court of Justice, 121–22, 126, 128, 130, 202
International Prize Court, 126, 128
Irigoyen, Hipólito, 187
Isle of Cobras, 18
Itajaí, Santa Catarina, 103–4
Itamaraty, 27, 37–40, 53–55, 64, 71, 87, 91–92, 95, 106, 118, 129, 131, 137, 142–44, 160–61, 188, 191, 197, 207; Map Library, 27, 39

Jamestown Exhibition, 52
Jefferson, Thomas, 58
João VI, Emperor, 21, 58
Jorge, Araujo, 53, 161
Jornal do Brasil (Rio de Janeiro), 29, 100
Jornal do Commercio (Rio de Janeiro), 91, 92, 101, 125, 151, 153, 161, 173
Juca, *see* Rio-Branco, Baron of

Knox, Philander C., 66, 36, 138, 140, 179, 203

Lamont, Daniel, 31
La Paz, 45, 46, 78
La Plata, 152
Lima, Barbosa, 54
Lima, Manoel de Oliveira, 55, 148, 157, 167, 236
Lima, 51, 91–93, 144
Lisbon, 62
Loomis, Francis B., 81, 88, 99
Lorena Ferreira, Luís Rodriguez de, 142
Lorillard, G. L., 4

Machado, Pinheiro, 9, 16, 18
Madeira River, 46
Madeiro-Mamoré Railway, 14
Magalhães, Olynto de, 44, 82
Maia, José Joaquim, 58
Manaus, 11, 67, 214
Martínez, Walker, 135
Martin García Island, 184
Martins, Enéas, 53, 71
Mato Grosso, 26
Mauá Bank, 23
Mendonça, Salvador de, 31, 55, 60–62, 64, 176
Mercurio, El (Santiago), 139
Mexico, 51–52, 86, 89, 102, 108, 116, 163, 190
Mexico City, 109
Military History of Brazil (Rio-Branco), 28
Minas Gerais, 2–4, 8–10, 15–16, 58
Minas Gerais (ship), 17
Mirim, Lake, 48
Monroe, James, 61, 146
Monroe Doctrine, 58, 62, 81, 98, 107, 146–59 *passim,* 163, 171, 173, 201, 207–8, 250; Roosevelt Corollary, 151–53, 174
Montevideo, 23
Montez, Ismael, 45

Montt, Pedro, 139
Moore, John Bassett, 31, 56, 81, 93–94
Morais Barros, Prudente de, 4–5, 168
Morning Post (London), 195
Mota, José Pereira da Costa, 103, 106
Müller, Lauro, 135
Murtinho, Joaquim, 5

Nabuco, Joaquim, 34–35, 40, 47–48, 53, 54, 62, 65–66, 97–100, 102, 134, 140–43, 167, 170, 175–78, 180, 195, 201, 203, 220, 223, 233, 251–52; and *Panther* affair, 103–8 *passim;* and Root's visit, 109–15 *passim,* 163; and Hague Conference, 116–31 *passim;* and Alsop case, 135–39 *passim,* 189; and Monroe Doctrine, 147–48, 152, 154–55, 162–63, 171
Nación, La (Buenos Aires), 108, 188
National City Bank of New York City, 73–74
Netherlands, 48, 116
New York *Daily Tribune,* 174
New York *Herald,* 98, 173
New York *Times,* 104, 148, 174
Nicaragua, 50, 89, 113
Noronha, Júlio de, 16
Norway, 51
Notícia, A (Rio de Janeiro), 151
Nova Friburgo, 25

Oakenfall, J. C., 196
Orlando, Arthur, 157

Paiz, O (Rio de Janeiro), 151, 162, 173
Panama, 6, 50, 86–90 *passim,* 114, 142, 153, 231, 241
Panama City, 87, 89, 231
Pan Americanism, 146–59 *passim*
Pan-Americanismo (Orlando), 157

Pan American Union, 179
Pando, Juan Manuel, 43, 45
Pan Latinism, 157
Pan Saxonism, 157
Panther affair, 16, 103–8 *passim,* 114, 150, 201
Paraguay, 22, 42, 121, 152, 173, 184, 204
Paraná, Viscount of, 22
Paraná River, 181
Paranhos, José Maria da Silva, Sr., *see* Rio-Branco, Viscount of
Paranhos, José Maria da Silva, Jr., *see* Rio-Branco, Baron of
Pardo, José, 89
Payne, Sereno E., 65
Payne-Aldrich Tariff, 71
Peçanha, Nilo, 4, 10, 14, 141
Pedro II, Emperor, 1–2, 10, 23, 27–28, 59, 117, 165
Pedro II College, 24–25
Pena, Afonso Augusto Moreira, 4, 9, 10–15, 133, 135, 148
Penã, Roque Saenz, 52, 186
Pereira, Luiz Barroso, 24
Pereira Passos, Francisco, 6
Pernambuco, 3, 4, 213
Persia, 51
Peru, 1, 42, 46–48, 81, 89, 90–95 *passim,* 108, 144, 171, 175, 184, 199
Philippines, 65
Pius X, Pope, 50
Piza, Gabriel de, 54
Plaza, Victoriano de la, 186
Port-au-Prince, 50
Porter, Horace, 121
Porter Resolution, 120–21
Portugal, 21, 40, 127, 143–44, 160, 199
Prado, Eduardo, 61
Praia Vermelha, 7
Prensa, La (Buenos Aires), 182
Puerto Rico, 65, 78

Quintana, Manuel, 184
Quito, 50, 194

Raguet, Condy, 59
Rayner, Isidor, 74
Rebellion in the Backlands (Cunha), 19, 39
Recife, 213; Law Faculty at, 24
Richthofen, Baron Oswald von, 106
Rio-Branco, Baron of: appointed Minister of Foreign Relations, 20–21, 68; ancestry and early life, 21–24; as war correspondent, 24–25; tours Europe, 25; begins diplomatic career, 25; consul at Liverpool, 26–29, 196; writings, 27–29; named Counselor of the Empire, 28; named Baron of Rio-Branco, 28; appointed director of Immigration Service of Brazil (Paris), 29; appointed to head mission to Washington, D.C., 30–32, 85, 182; made chief of mission to Swiss Council, 32–33; and Brazil's border disputes, 32–49 *passim;* minister to Germany, 33; and first South American cardinal, 49–50; and Latin American diplomatic ties, 50–51; and Old World diplomatic ties, 51; and international conferences, 51–52; and visiting celebrities, 52; and treaties of arbitration, 52–53; assistants to, 53–54; criticism of, 54–56; death, 57, 67; concern with commerce, 63–75 *passim,* 166–67; cements relations with United States, 76–114 *passim;* and Acre dispute, 76–86 *passim;* and recognition of Panama, 86–90 *passim;* and Peruvian-Brazilian controversy, 90–95 *passim;* and elevation of legations to embassies, 95–102 *passim,*

Rio-Branco, Baron of (*Continued*)
192, 196; and *Panther* affair, 103–
8 *passim,* 150; and Root's visit,
108–14 *passim,* 163; and Hague
Conference, 116–31 *passim,* 164,
172, 179; and fleet visit, 132–35
passim; and Alsop case, 135–39
passim, 179, 189; and Monroe Doctrine, 146–56 *passim,* 165, 171, 174,
207–8; and Pan Americanism, 156–
59 *passim,* 169, 208; and *Sarmiento*
affair, 190
Rio-Branco, Viscount of, 22–23, 25–
27, 35, 44
Rio-Branco Law (1871), 23
Rio de Janeiro, 18, 21, 23, 26, 33–
34, 58, 61, 67, 70, 74–75, 79, 82, 84,
89, 92, 95, 98–100, 104, 107, 108–9,
132, 135, 137, 139, 151, 161–62, 164,
171–72, 176–77, 179, 184, 188–89,
191–95
Río de la Plata, 22–26, 181–82, 184
Rio Grande do Sul, 9, 15–16, 18, 215
Roca, Julio A., 52, 183
Rodriguez, José Carlos, 176
Rodriguez Alves, Francisco de Paula,
4–9, 19–20, 33–34, 86, 88, 99–100,
102, 132, 176
Romero, Lino, 45–46
Roosevelt, Alice, 97
Roosevelt, Theodore, 95–97, 99–100,
109, 112–13, 115, 120, 129, 133–34,
136, 139, 148–53, 163, 170, 173, 177–
79, 190, 195
Roosevelt, W. E., 78
Roosevelt Corollary, 151–53, 174
Root, Elihu, 52, 56, 66, 70–71, 105,
107, 108–14 *passim,* 115–20, 125,
129, 131, 134–36, 138, 139, 141–42,
148, 158, 162–64, 171–72, 175–78,
188, 201–3, 236
Rosas, Juan Manuel, 23

Rubber, 2, 11–12, 45–46, 60, 63, 67–
68, 90, 166
Rubber Defense Law, 12
Rumania, 127
Russia, 28, 116

St. Louis Exhibition, 52, 97, 112, 177
Santiago, 50, 89, 137, 185
Santo Domingo, 50
Santos, 3–4
São Paulo, 2–5, 8, 10, 13, 15–16, 112,
213
Sarmiento (ship), 190
Schneider, L., 27–28
Second International Peace Confer-
ence, 54, 109, 112, 116–31 *passim,*
132–34, 141, 145, 163, 172, 179, 188,
202–3, 208, 255
Slechta, J. J., 72
South American Journal, The (Lon-
don), 195–96
Spanish-American War, 61
Sternberg, Speck von, 105–6
Sugar, 2–3
Surinam, 48
Swiss Council, 32
Switzerland, 32

Taft, William A., 66, 140–41
Telegram Number Nine, 143, 185
Texas, 78
Texeira, Pedro, 204
Third International Conference of the
American States, 109–13
Third Pan American Congress, 52,
124–25, 141, 156, 175, 188, 202
Thompson, David E., 70, 84, 87–90,
92–93, 99–100, 169, 219
Times, The (London), 195
Toledo Herrarte, Luís, 155
Torres, Alberto, 148
Tosta, Ignácio, 70

Trans-Mississippi Congress, 148
Travassos, General, 7
Travassos revolt, 16
Treaty of La Paz de Ayacucho, 42–43
Treaty of Madrid, 40, 44
Treaty of Petrópolis, 46, 83, 91
Treaty of San Ildefonso, 40, 44
Treaty of Tordesillas, 40
Treutler, Karl von, 104
Triple Alliance, 42
Turkey, 127, 144, 172

Uhl, Edwin F., 31
Uruguay, 22–24, 42, 48–49, 121, 152, 173, 184, 186, 199, 204
U.S. House of Representatives, Tariff Committee, 66
U.S. Senate, Tariff Committee, 66
U.S.S. *Iowa*, 132

Vatican, 50
Veiga, Francisco, 53
Velarde, Hernán, 47, 90, 92–93

Venezuela, 42, 48, 52, 85, 89, 108, 142–43, 194, 237
Victor Emmanuel III, King of Italy, 47–48, 161

War of the Triple Alliance, 23–25, 42
Washington, D.C., 30, 50, 54, 59, 61, 77–78, 91–92, 95, 98, 100, 102, 105, 108, 115, 117–18, 134–35, 137, 160–62, 163, 168, 170–71, 174, 176, 179, 195, 202, 206
Washington *Post*, 104
Washington *Star*, 163–64
Webb, James Watson, 59
White, Andrew D., 104
Whitridge, Frederick Willingford, 76, 82, 83
Wilhelm II, Kaiser of Germany, 33
Wise, Henry A., 59
World's Columbian Exposition, 31
World War I, 13–14, 19, 74, 115, 181, 194
World War II, 159

Zeballos, Estanislau, 184–85